Further Praise for *The Girlfriends' Guide to Surviving the First Year of Motherhood*:

"Invaluable . . . [a] funny, honest new volume."—*L.A. Parent*

"If humor is the best medicine, Vicki Iovine has all the tonic a new mother should need. Her information comes from experience and her humor from the heart. An invaluable dialogue with a girlfriend who's been there, and got the most from her adventure."—*Rocky Mountain News*

Praise for *The Girlfriends' Guide to Pregnancy*:

"A chatty, candid, laugh-out-loud primer for unseasoned moms-to-be."
—*People*

"Iovine and her gaggle of Girlfriends are ready with reassuring and frequently irreverent advice."—*Newsweek*

ALSO BY VICKI IOVINE

The Girlfriends' Guide to Pregnancy
The Girlfriends' Guide to Pregnancy Daily Diary
The Girlfriends' Guide to Surviving the First Year of Motherhood
The Girlfriends' Guide to Getting Your Groove Back

Most Perigee Books are available at special quantity discounts for bulk purchases for sales promotions, premiums, fund-raising or educational use. Special books, or book excerpts, can also be created to fit specific needs.

For details, write: Special Markets, The Berkley Publishing Group, 375 Hudson Street, New York, New York 10014.

The Girlfriends' Guide to Toddlers

A survival manual to the "terrible twos" (and ones and threes) from the first step, the first potty and the first word ("no") to the last blankie

VICKI IOVINE

A Perigee Book

A Perigee Book
Published by The Berkley Publishing Group
A division of Penguin Putnam Inc.
375 Hudson Street
New York, New York 10014

*Some of the Girlfriends' names have been changed to protect their privacy . . .
but, Girlfriends, you know who you are.*

First edition: February 1999

Published simultaneously in Canada.

The Penguin Putnam Inc. World Wide Web site address is
http://www.penguinputnam.com

Library of Congress Cataloging-in-Publication Data

Iovine, Vicki.
    The girlfriends' guide to toddlers : a survival manual to the
"terrible twos" (and ones and threes) from the first step, the first
potty and the first word ("no") to the last blankie / Vicki Iovine.
        p.   cm.
    ISBN 0-399-52438-X
    1. Toddlers—Care—Popular works.   2. Child rearing—Popular
works.   3. Motherhood—Popular works.   4. Mother and infant—Popular
works.   I. Title.
RJ61.I67   1999
649'.1—dc21   98-45260
                                                          CIP

Printed in the United States of America

15 14 13 12 11 10 9 8

My dad died this year. So did Dr. Benjamin Spock. From my point of view, the world lost two exceptional men, each with his own brand of uncommon wisdom about children. I don't know if it was just coincidence that there was always a copy of *Baby and Child Care* in our house while I was growing up, or if my own father learned his coolheaded parenting style from Dr. Spock's classic. Either way, my dad seemed to have an innate faith that if he showed up and loved us and set a few unwavering rules, we kids would turn out pretty much all right. He started with the belief that most of what we children did was "normal" kid behavior, nothing more exotic or troublesome than that. (Now that you are a parent yourself, you can see the value of that kind of calm and steady-in-the-saddle attitude.) Then he decided which normal kid behavior would be nipped in the bud by identifying what was a nuisance to him, my mother or other adults. I can't recall a time when he wavered in his conviction that parents knew more than kids and therefore were the bosses. But he still treated my brother and me as though we were his intellectual equals. Even when I was a teenager and clearly deranged on that cocktail of adolescent hormones, he would talk to me as if I were a healthy, intelligent quasi-adult. Somehow he trusted that this "normal" behavior, too, would pass and that his real daughter would return to him. Not only did I return, I clung to him like glue.

Now that I am a mother several times over, I can really appreciate how helpful it was to have someone tell me, often several times a day, that I was not only up to the job, but might actually be pretty good at it. My dad was the king of "Don't worry, he'll grow out of it." He had tremendous faith in Mother Nature's plan of allowing young and inexperienced people to be entrusted with the care of infants. The divine plan provided for both parents and children to grow up and learn together, in the unique way that suited their particular family. It's no mistake that we parents are so clueless; it's just Nature's way of making sure we customize our brand of parenting for each individual child.

I wept the first time I read Dr. Spock's line "You probably already know more about being a parent than you think you do," I was so desperate to believe him and to prove him right. I, along with millions of other bleary-eyed, overworked and under-rested new mommies just gave it up to Dr. Spock. If he said that everything was going to be fine, then it was. There are many times in your parenting life where you work yourself into a dither because you've consulted so many "authorities" about some problem like potty training or thumb sucking that you are paralyzed by your competing options and the overriding fear that you'll pick the wrong thing. This is the time for you to kneel and be knighted by the spirit of Dr. Spock and arise as The Mother. You are the one who knows your baby, you are the one who is taking responsibility for your baby's life and you are the one who will smite herself with her own sword if you fail in your loving duty to your baby. It is YOU, the Mother, who will choose the correct path and will prevail!

Dr. Spock, on behalf of the baby boomers and our own babies, thank you for your wisdom. Dad, on behalf of your own kids and your kids' kids, thank you for always believing and always loving. I miss you every single day of my life.

The Girlfriends' Guide to Toddlers

C o n t e n t s

Contents

A Word of Thanks

*C*hris Pepe, it's a good thing you're Catholic, because I'm thinking of trying to get you considered for sainthood (or at least beatified). I am gigantically grateful for your patience and guidance throughout what must have seemed the slowest year of your life. I am even more grateful for your darling Eva, who so graciously went through toddlerhood just when we needed her inspiration.

Jodes, how in the world would our lives have stayed on track without your loving and conscientious shepherding? Thank you for keeping the balls in the air for me, and always doing so with a smile.

My children, Jamie, Jessica, Jeremy and Jade, I thank you for your rich and wonderful toddlerhoods—please don't tell your therapists on me when you grow up. I *wub wu,* and I thank you for giving my life such dimension and significance, not to mention JOY.

Jimmy, the maestro of husbands and daddies, I thank you for your love, your outrageous humor and your partnership on this family journey; you're the keeper of the compass and you force us to keep our aim true. I'm crazy about you.

Why I Wrote This Book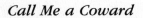

Call Me a Coward

Frankly, toddlers frighten me. I know, I know, I'm supposed to be this brave veteran of the mommy wars. After all, I've run this particular gauntlet four times with hardly a moment to regain my sanity between each foray. I should be full of wisdom, funny stories and reassurance, and I will be, I promise, just as soon as I calm down. Revisiting this territory does make me edgy and a little paranoid; I'm still stunned by the dynamic good ol' Mother Nature created when she paired babies longing to be free with mommies longing for control.

It was so much simpler when you could put the baby down in one general area and expect him to pretty much stay there safe and sound. Sure, you had to allow for the occasional rollover, and then there was that way-too-brief period when he crawled on all fours, but there was no movement so significant that it made blinking your eyes or turning your head an invitation to disaster. Now he's streaking from one peril-fraught room to another like a lunatic with a death wish and you would give anything for him just to be still. I'm beginning to find the humor in the situation now, but there were times when I felt like a fool trying to put a collar on a bumblebee.

Humans in Toddler Disguise

I know what it is that is so scary about those little people between the ages of one and four—they are raw and uncensored examples of our human nature. They are the urges, frustrations, desires and fears that all of us feel, but they have absolutely no veneer of civilization to make them more palatable to their fellow human beings. It's as if your most egotistical friend mated with your worst date in high school and their baby shared DNA with Evel Knievel. Maturity is really just a matter of learning clever ways to cover up the lively toddler in all of us. I still don't like to sit still in my chair, eat my vegetables, share my toys or wait my turn to do absolutely anything; I'm just a lot better now at pretending all those things come naturally to me. Being around toddlers is too much like reading *Lord of the Flies*—the more you know about them, the closer you feel to absolute anarchy.

Well, They Are Cute . . .

Before you become convinced that I have completely failed to grasp the charm of toddlerhood, let me reassure you that, in spite of my jumpiness, I am absolutely crazy for those little creatures. First of all, I like their bodies. One of my favorite things is how their little feet look like pork chops with toenails; a close second favorite is the way their tummies peek out from under all but their longest shirts and above all but the tightest diapers. In fact, while we're on the subject of diapers, have you ever noticed that a toddler's diapered backside makes her look like a rear view of Donald Duck? Especially when the toddler waddle is added to the mix?

I also love the impetuousness of toddlers. I envy their freedom to hurl their spinach at the kitchen wall and to loudly point out every unusual person they see in the grocery store, whether they be fat, bald, old or large-breasted. I love how they kiss you wetly on the mouth and how they love their stuffed animals or blankies. Their curiosity inspires me and their spontaneity delights me. My heart still aches when I remember how mine would whirl like dervishes until they were exhausted, then let me hold them in my arms and rock them like an infant while they gazed into my nostalgic eyes. I could cry right now. . . .

I Don't Want to Get Too Personal But . . .

Before I go out and seduce my husband into another pregnancy, let me remind us both about the fears I had that I was the worst toddler mother on the planet. I was certain that my kids would never be potty trained. I spent hours making desperate conciliatory calls to the parents of the children my kids had punched or bitten. My husband and I argued bitterly over whether spanking was acceptable for the most heinous crimes, like dashing into a parking lot. I had a toddler who was afraid of all laughter and used to rush out of movie theaters, sporting events or even the dinner table if there was any unanimous chuckling going on. I had a child who was so anal retentive that I slipped mineral oil into *its* (see, gender unspecific so nobody can claim I humiliated him or her later) bottle just to keep things moving smoothly. I even let one of my kids, and not even my first, when I wasn't expected to know better, drink juice out of a bottle so long that *it* needed a root canal and caps on *its* baby teeth. Is toddlerhood something I'd like to relive? Yeah, right after I reexperience my own trip through puberty.

The Holy Grail

Perhaps the most astonishing revelation I have to share with you now that I have crossed over to the other side for my fourth and final time (my youngest babe officially outgrew toddlerhood six months ago when she simultaneously turned four and started dancing the Macarena) is simply this:

In hindsight, toddlerhood wasn't such a big deal.

Calm down there, Girlfriend! I'm not saying that what you experience every day as the mother of a toddler isn't either terrifying, mystifying or stupefying. It is, and often all at the same time! Trust me when I tell you that I, too, watched every morning show and read every news magazine when they recently *discovered* how critical a child's first three years (maybe four) are to his development as a healthy and intelligent member of society. My Girlfriends and I have spent several frantic hours on the phone (on company time, of course) wondering whether we were wrong to go back to work outside the home when our little prince or princess was in that home that very minute, bonding with someone who wasn't even a distant relative.

What I'm trying to tell you is that toddlerhood is hell, while you're going through it. But once you've survived the journey, you realize that maybe you didn't need to get so worked up about the pottying on the houseplants; that maybe a four-year-old *could* still sleep in a crib and not suffer structural or emotional damage; and even though you would swear on a Bible that your little one ate not one organic particle for two years, look at him now, so tall and strong. Every day I thank Mother Nature for being so much smarter than the rest of us mothers. She actually devised a system in which we parents could make one mistake after another and our kids would not only survive us but turn out pretty much how they would have if we'd done our jobs perfectly.

"Somebody Get Me Dr. Spock!"

That said, I certainly don't expect you to agree with one word of my little epiphany, at least not yet. You are up to your eyeballs in one toddler crisis after another. Go ahead and freak out; that's the appropriate response while you're standing knee-deep in the Toddler Pool. It's only later, after the three years of brain erosion that parenting a toddler imposes combines with experience to make you see things more calmly. It just occurred to me that senility is the mommies' party favor for attending one too many birthday parties; her own child's.

Is this the first and only book ever to be written about these amazing little creatures? Of course not. But it is unique in this sense: It is a handbook designed to quickly and efficiently deal with many of the issues and concerns that you will have over the next couple of years. We don't go in any sort of chronological or developmental order, but rather from hot topic to hot topic. Think of the Guide as a sort of fire extinguisher. When sparks flare up, break glass and grab Guide. We know very well that you don't have one minute to spare, so we give it to you straight, fast and funny. Go to the part that deals with your crisis (since the very essence of toddlerhood is crisis), read long enough to get the reassurance, advice and laughter you need to cope (or until Junior has stopped playing quietly on the floor and begun climbing onto your TV by using the VCR as a step stool), then go back to your job as Toddler Traffic Controller. We'll be there waiting for you when you need us again, AND YOU WILL. . . .

Top Ten Toddler Myths

10. The smarter the baby, the earlier she learns to walk.

9. If they can talk, they can be reasoned with.

8. Toddlers can't wait to sleep in their own beds, especially if the sheets have race cars or Barbies on them.

7. Biters are the product of miserable parenting.

6. Boys and girls will play exactly alike if never exposed to gender specific toys like dolls and weapons.

5. Nature will ensure that toddlers are attracted to the food their growing bodies need.

4. Toddlers love newborns (especially new baby brothers or sisters) and can be counted on to treat them kindly.

3. Toddlers love animals (especially strange dogs roaming the streets) and can be counted on to treat them kindly.

2. The difference between toddlers and babies is that toddlers are better at expressing their emotions.

1. Your mother really did have you fully potty trained at eighteen months.

Who Are These People, Anyway?

Mother Nature really is so damned smart to give you your child in infant form first: There might not have been quite so many takers if she were handing out toddlers. Not that toddlers aren't adorable and captivating; it's just that it's hard to imagine devoting your life to a person who breaks your things, eats with her hands and hurls herself onto the floor if she doesn't get her way if you aren't already hopelessly devoted to the little tyrant. It was awfully nice planning on somebody's part to give you about a year to get to know your baby in a somewhat calm and orderly fashion. As an infant, she may have wreaked havoc with your sleep patterns, she may have nursed till you thought your breasts would fall off, and she may have left you with ten pounds you have no use for, but she probably cooperated most of the time. You dressed her how and when you wanted. You put her in her bouncy chair or on a blanket on the floor. You fed her what you felt was best for her and she generally accepted it graciously. But did you get down on your knees and thank your lucky stars every day that you had such a gift? Oh, no. You, like all the rest of us, just wouldn't keep the lid on Pandora's box.

The Race to Walk

You were probably getting so confident about your mothering abilities around the ninth or tenth month that you started hungering for bigger challenges. All your little one had to do was push to a stand one day while you held her in your lap, and ZOOM, you were off to the toddler races. Her walking not only seemed like an exciting new developmental stage for your child, it became *your* personal goal, too. Admit it, Girlfriend! You may not have pressured her; you may not have let her know in any overt way that the exhilarating feeling of achievement her first two steps gave you rivaled that of any climber to reach Everest. You and your mate may have tried not to squeal and slap high fives every time she bravely let go of the coffee table to tumble toward the middle of the living room; none-theless, she got the message she was doing something that rang your chimes. Think about it; isn't your lower back out of whack to this day from all the mileage you put in walking bent over behind your toddler and holding her upright hands while she swayed about on pigeon-toed feet? You may have taken the consumer's digest advice against baby walk-ers, but I bet you bought at least one push-along toy that helped her stay balanced while moving upright (you know the ones, shaped like mini shopping carts—like babies have so much marketing to do).

Walking Separates the Toddlers from the Babies

Sure, the other baby milestones were fun, especially if sleeping through the night was one of them, but really, how many of us sent telegrams when our kids rolled over for the first time? Walking, however, is the lollapalooza of baby achievements. Even if you didn't know that when you first signed up for this parenting job, you learned it soon enough; every parent of a baby over ten months of age is asked, "So, how's the baby? Is he walking yet?" As the mother of four kids who preferred sitting to walking for at least a year each, I felt a stab every time I was asked that question. With the first two kids, I lied and told anyone not likely to visually verify my statement, that they were ready to take off "any minute now." I guess I felt that my baby's failure to walk early was an indication that the mothering I was giving him wasn't nearly as enriching and, well, *good*, as I thought it should be. By the time the other two came along, however, the older toddlers had robbed me of my innocence about the beauty of walking. If anyone asked me then if my babies were walking yet, I was just as likely to snarl, "They would be if I ever took them out of their blanket sleepers...." But I'm getting ahead of myself here.

When your baby did finally master two-footed locomotion, either in spite of or because of your encouragement, it was a transcendent event. Angels were heard to sing on high, grandparents were called (as were a couple of the other mommies in your baby group; okay, maybe you gloated a little), videos and photos were shot! Your little darling had achieved his destiny and fulfilled your wishes and dreams for him—he crossed over from the world of baby to the world of toddler, ON HIS OWN TWO FEET! What on earth were you thinking?

Which Years Are the Toddler Years?

Child development authorities differ greatly on what exactly constitutes a toddler. This is understandable because a one-year-old waddling around in a diaper doesn't appear to have much in common with a lightning-fast three-year-old preschooler (even if he, too, is still wearing a diaper). Keep in mind that at the beginning of this little life era known as toddlerhood, your child won't yet be able to talk, but by the time he is ready for preschool, he will probably be fluent enough to share all of the most intimate details of your home life with all the kids at preschool. At the beginning of toddlerhood, he will probably walk with his arms held out to the side or up in the air for balance, as if all walking surfaces were tightrope wires, and by the end he will be a perpetual motion machine, running, unlocking, opening and closing, jumping and falling until he passes out. If you end up with a three-year-old like my Girlfriend Shelly's son, Bentley, you won't only be chugging after a runner, you'll be calling the fire department to get your climber down from the top of the pergola at the community center.

The Girlfriends' Definition of Toddlers

For the purposes of *The Girlfriends' Guide to Toddlers*, we will focus on those little people whose abilities range from just learning to walk unassisted (about one year old) to those who are negotiating the challenges of preschool (three-year-olds in all their glory). In other words, most of our anecdotes and advice will focus on those fascinating creatures between the ages of one and one day shy of their fourth birthday. Pediatricians and other authorities will certainly have more exacting criteria, but my Girlfriends and I have noticed that even a one-year-old who is barely toddling can exhibit those charming particular personality quirks of toddlerhood, and some of our most cherished three-and-a-half-year-olds are still reluctant to let go of such toddler souvenirs as binkies, bankies and Pull-Ups.

After years of watching all our babies enter toddlerhood and come out on the other side, the Girlfriends and I have identified what we think are the behaviors and concerns that make toddlers toddlers:

1. The struggle for independence is the hallmark of this entire age group. Walking is the first step in that direction (yeah, pun) because it manifests the child's very real ability to leave its mommy or other symbol of safety and security. Your little one spends much of his toddlerhood experimenting with leaving you. Don't cry, Mommy; they almost always come back! Whether they have just toddled into another part of the house where you can't see them or they have just waved goodbye to you for their first unchaperoned day of preschool, they are learning to separate. We Girlfriends will remind you now and several more times in the Guide that the goal is to raise a child who can eventually enter the world *without* you in tow—that's why they invented Miami—the all-American reward for a parenting job well done.

The universal toddler declaration of independence is the phrase "I do myself!" You can be late for the most important appointment of your life (like getting your tubes tied), and your usually compliant toddler will pick that moment to demonstrate his ability to squeeze toothpaste onto his toothbrush and clean his teeth ALL BY HIMSELF. This desire for mastery, terrific though it may be in concept, can be counted on to add a good five to ten minutes to the task of getting out of your driveway. This, too, is part of that independence business, and it is sure to affect your life in several ways (like migraines and chronic tardiness, in my case).

2. The most dramatic bursts of development you and your child will experience occur during these three years. Think of it this way: Like a flower, an infant grows and blossoms in a sort of slow, constant progression. Its muscular development is greater with every day. Its hair gradually thickens and grows longer. Even the acts of rolling over and sitting up tend to be progressive and predictable to us eagle-eyed mommies. (But that doesn't mean you are guaranteed a divine prediction of when that first roll will be, so for you moms of toddlers-to-be who are reading ahead, NEVER leave your baby unattended on the bed or changing table.)

On the other hand, a toddler can best be compared to a box of fireworks with a spark loose inside. One minute the two of you can be quietly reading a picture book about animals together, and the next a Roman candle seems to go off in his head and he becomes a kind of animal himself, one that scratches and bites. For six straight days he will spend all his play hours with the Little Tykes kitchen you bought him, then, on the seventh day, he will move the entire kitchen across the room and place it directly under the cuckoo clock your grandmother gave you, and you will walk in to find him balanced on one foot on top of the plastic microwave with his fat little hand around the poor cuckoo's throat.

Cause and effect, at least as we overtired and overwrought mothers know them, have little relevance in the toddler world. Their minds seem to jump around so quickly, usually dragging their moods with them, that their little brains should smoke from all the short-circuiting going on in them. When it all gets to be too mind-bending for even your toddler to tolerate, she will blow a gasket altogether and flip out with one of those tantrums that her generation is so famous for.

This is also the age when a toddler, like Cro-Magnon Man, learns to use tools. Don't hold your breath waiting for him to build you a new deck or kitchen cabinets, but be prepared for your VCR to be "repaired" several times, for all bureau drawers to be liberated from their tracks and for your car keys to end up in the sandbox, where they were employed for digging tunnels for your automatic garage door opener to drive through. Whether you are the mother of a younger toddler, who would stick a fork in a light socket on sheer whim given half a chance, or of an older toddler, who is able to hit a ball with a bat or connect all the flowers in your wallpaper with a box of push pins, you will find that "tools" are a defining aspect of toddlerhood. And, if you'll excuse this bit of gender bias, if you have a boy toddler, he may find that his most favorite tools are those that can be used as weapons, which includes nearly everything.

3. Children in this age group are "changelings." Stop by any parent-tot gathering, and you will be sure to hear a mother declare that her toddler has more personalities than Congress. Are they babies? Are they children? Are they human? Well, the answers to these questions are yes and no. What they really are are creatures petitioning to become children, but who haven't given up their membership in the baby world.

First of all, just look at them to see how truly in-between they are. Their feet are almost perfect rectangles and their toes look like decorative fringe rather than functional balancing appendages. They often use their hands as if they were brooms or shovels, swiping and grasping things like a bear going through a picnic basket. It's only toward the end of toddlerhood that most kids can control their fingers accurately enough to pinch their baby sister's cheek or use scissors to give themselves a haircut. And speaking of hair, at the beginning of toddlerhood, many of these little tykes still have that wispy growth that sentimental mothers hate to cut, but by preschool most of them actually have enough "human" hair to snarl, tangle and be the final resting place for cookie crumbs and finger paints.

With really young toddlers, this period of being neither fish nor fowl is usually only moderately confusing because you can be pretty safe treating them like big babies most of the time. But by around eighteen months, your luck generally has run out. By then, they are such an amalgam of curiosity, energy, frustration, boldness and insecurity that they don't know whether to spit or wind their watch, as my father used to say. (Or something like that.) And there you stand, just dying to help in some way, and not knowing how to get in. Is a hug the answer? Is a firm "no" the answer? Or should you just turn and run the other way? The Girlfriends and I maintain that this critical period is second only to pregnancy in the amount of brain damage a mother sustains. It's a constant source of wonder to me that you don't see more mothers lying on the floor of Costco, kicking and screaming right alongside their toddlers, since their frustration levels must surely be just as high.

Simplistic as it sounds, the time of day can be a big factor in whether your toddler is a child or a baby. In my household, toddlers were all grown up and full of fun and "I do myseff" when they were well rested, like in the morning or after a nap. Then, as the day dragged on and the frustrations mounted, my toddlers would start disintegrating right before my eyes. That often results in the one-two punch that takes all mothers out at the knees: the needs of a cranky baby colliding with Mom's need to make dinner. Even though I'm not raising toddlers these days, I still feel my shoulders tighten as the sun goes down and the local news comes on TV. It can only mean that the dinner-bath-story-drink-of-water-back-patting-stay-in-your-bed obstacle course has begun.

4. *These little people need to be guided into society (euphemism for discipline).* For the first several months of life, a baby isn't faced with the burden of making decisions. She is pretty much a creature of cause (e.g., hunger) and effect (e.g., crying till somebody gives her something to eat). Walking, along with the bigger brain that comes with being a person who can do it, creates a whole new set of circumstances that can all be lumped under the heading of Choices. This is why discipline was invented by the cavewoman, to make sure that most of the choices made were acceptable to the mother. Parents of toddlers are constantly torn between being gloomy control freaks and being completely bulldozed by their child. We want them to be free-spirited, but not near the deep end of a pool. We want them to be creative, but not to blame the pet bunny for writing with Sharpies on their shirt. We want them to delight

in discovering the magic of the universe, but we want them up, pottied, dressed and breakfasted before we have to leave for work.

How does one accomplish this? Well, to be completely candid, with very mixed results, especially when this is our first run through the toddler gauntlet. Toddlers are so impetuous and unpredictable that we mothers are usually found reacting to one crisis after another rather than methodically training them to understand and adhere to a planned behavioral code. If sports analogies help you, think of yourself as playing defense against a mini Michael Jordan; it's all *reaction,* not action. If you occasionally feel that your best-laid plans for reasoning with your little person and helping him to cultivate a sense of freedom within a context of respect have collided head-on with a reality in which you yelp before you leap, don't take it too hard. That's usually how it goes for all of us who mother in the toddlerhood trenches.

5. During these three years, little people learn to join the community of big people. By the time a child turns four, she is officially no longer a baby. (Even though, as all mothers recite to our children, they will *always* be *our* babies.) Most of these little darlings have an active social life, leave the house for several hours a day to do fun stuff without parents, have decided that they are going to marry Daddy and know precisely why there is a day in honor of Dr. Martin Luther King, Jr. Heck, put a briefcase under a four-year-old's arm and put him on the subway, and he'll blend in as just another, albeit much shorter, commuter.

Toddlers are not yet there. In order to reach that kind of competence, they have to master certain behaviors like sleeping in a bed, using the potty, and, hey, knowing how to use a fork and spoon wouldn't hurt. In the combined experience of my Girlfriends and myself, none of these milestones is achieved in a day. Not only that, once they are achieved, they can be forgotten entirely and have to be taught again, and again and, well, you get the picture.

6. During these three years, your child gets a social life. No longer just adorable little koala bearlike appendages hanging on the mama marsupial, toddlers are literally thrusting their way into the world. It's as if there is some irresistible force pulling them away from all that is known and safe, and toward everything that vigilant mothers try to protect them against. There is something achingly symbolic about a baby's learning to walk because with that first step, they are free to walk to whomever they choose. Up until that time, we parents get to make all decisions regarding where they go and who they will meet when they get there.

Particularly compelling to toddlers are other people, especially other *very small* people, and this is the source of great fun for us parents. For some reason, we moms are drunkenly enthusiastic about our babies' interest in socializing. Like manic campaign managers of miniature politicians, we become strategists for these barely verbal socialites—spending hours finding playmates for them, scheduling playdates (when in the world did that word come into vogue?), wooing the parents of potential playmates, and getting positively giddy over the giving and attending of the countless birthday, Halloween, Valentine and Groundhog Day parties that are the toddler traditions.

As attractive as being "one of the gang" might be, learning to coexist with other little heathens can be tough for toddlers. Some kids are as gregarious as game-show hosts, and others have to be pulled screaming from their mothers and pushed into interacting. Some are naturally patient and placid, and others simply can't resist pounding on any kid within reach. Most disconcerting of all, toddlers can morph from being one kind of kid to the exact opposite, so you never know whether it's Dr. Jekyll or Mr. Hyde you'll be letting loose on the playground.

Helping your toddler adjust to civilization may be the hardest task you will face as a parent. It's just all so personal; love me, love my child. If our child is rejected in any way, we are usually the ones who feel the pain. If our child is the one who is careless about the feelings of others, we are the ones who feel we've failed to teach them any sense of morality. Take it from me, it's particularly difficult with your first toddler because you are so easily shocked by the assaults the world can throw in your darling's path, usually in the form of someone else's little darling. My Girlfriend Karen once called me from her car as she was speeding away from a two-year-olds' gymnastics class. One of the other gymnasts had bitten her little girl *right on the face,* and Karen didn't know what to do first: call the police or rush for a rabies shot. The bite alone was not what made her mental (although it would have been an acceptable defense for homicide in any mommy court in the land); it was the remark she overheard the biter's mother tell the gym teacher, "She's just overreacting because it's her only child and she doesn't know any better." The implication was clear that a more seasoned mom would take this episode in stride, apply antibiotic cream and ice and get over it. In a way, the other mother had a point, but I didn't think that our car phone conversation was the appropriate time to tell Karen. Instead, I encouraged her outrage and judged the obvious lack of parental supervision of the little heathen. It's only right that we Girlfriends should tell you; the first cut really *is* the deepest.

7. *Kids this age believe in magic.* Reality is a very amorphous concept for a little person who is stepping out into the world for the first time. For example, few things are more wondrous to a toddler than bubbles. They really see these soapy spheres as much more fantastic creations than most adults do, and bubbles never fail to elicit screaming and laughing in a gaggle of two-year-olds. They also think blimps are creations of some wizard, as is whistling or the fact that red and blue paint mixed together makes purple.

Not coincidentally, this is also the age when we parents start weaving our mythologies about everything from Santa to the Easter Bunny to Mommy the Monster Killer. Getting to participate in making magic is one of the greatest satisfactions of being the parent of a toddler because it wakes up and dusts off our old innocence as true believers. I'm pretty crazy about keeping up the myths, but my husband's even more obsessed than I. He actually goes outside on Christmas morning to bring in snow to sprinkle in front of the fireplace to show Santa's footprints. Normally, you couldn't get him outside in freezing predawn weather even if the house were on fire. He also tells our kids that the jelly beans on the floor on Easter morning are Easter Bunny poops. You gotta love a guy like that.

Since the true nature of things is still largely unknown to toddlers, even ordinary phenomena like vacuum cleaners, escalators and toilets can look like big scary monsters. You only have to spend a few hours introducing your child to the toilet to be introduced to all sorts of toddler concerns, from a fear that flushing sucks children in to a worry that their beloved poo poos will drown in there and ultimately disappear. This is also the time when struggling actors dressed up as Big Bird or Barney at a toddler birthday party can send some kids running for their therapists. My daughter used to repeat like a mantra the words "It's only peetend, it's only peetend" just to endure the time all seven of Snow White's dwarfs followed her around Disneyland.

Another aspect of this belief in magic is that toddlers affix special, feel-good powers to otherwise ordinary things, hence the devotion to the blankie or other lovey. Only a mother of a toddler can know panic in its most urgent form: when we have arrived home after a day of at least a thousand errands with toddler in tow, only to discover that the precious magic item has disappeared somewhere along the line. I have literally ripped apart the Yellow Pages in my frenzy to call everyone from the dry cleaner to the beauty supply store to the pediatrician's office to find the missing blankie before bedtime.

**By the way, take this veteran's advice and try to have doubles of any items your toddler has invested with magical powers. It can save your little darling a lot of distress and keep you from going totally gray in an afternoon.

8. Parents of these little changelings are constantly bewildered. The stakes of rearing a human being are enormous and overwhelming for any thinking person. We frantic mothers can't help but worry that every little decision we make concerning our toddlers will cement their fate as either the next Bill Gates or the next Unabomber. There are so many bizarre child-rearing philosophies floating around that we live in abject terror that we will fail to nip thumb sucking in the bud in time to protect our baby from a future of antisocial behavior.

Here's the news: **Toddlers will learn to accomplish nearly all of the milestones that signify a successful passage through this stage all by themselves.** (I know we've told you that already, but we will again, so either sigh a breath of relief or just ignore us.) You can demonstrate the function of a spoon for weeks or you can keep all spoons hidden in the drawer, and when his personal DNA says he's ready for a spoon, he'll quickly figure out how to use a spoon. Really try to hear me when I tell you that you need not teach your child to walk, to climb stairs or to drink out of a cup. There is a force of nature that compels a healthy and stimulated toddler to figure this stuff out on his own. It's that box of fireworks concept again.

Does that mean you're not needed? Of course not. But your job is not so task-oriented as you might believe. Think of yourself as a sort of cruise director, like that bouncy woman from *The Love Boat*. Your job is to provide an attractive array of activities or experiences for your toddler. Taking the analogy further, you can show him where the shuffleboard is played and where the sticks are kept, but it's not up to you to repeatedly teach the proper flick of the wrist in making the shot. In fact, if your little cruiser decides to use the shuffleboard pucks as cymbals instead, that's his business. What's needed here is your applause, your encouragement and your best efforts to ensure that the voyage is as safe and loving as possible.

Please don't think I'm suggesting that toddlers aren't paying attention to you. They are watching you with such intensity it's a wonder you don't catch fire. And here's a little parenting secret for you: they not only watch you, they WORSHIP you. This will not always be the case, so now's your window of opportunity to imprint on your little one's mind all your best habits and behaviors. They'll pick up on all that and much more. Just wait until you catch a glimpse of your toddler pretending to be you in an imaginary phone conversation—it's a hoot! But you do your best toddler teaching through being present, loving and as consistent as possible. This is something quite different from playing "Hooked on Phonics" tapes every time the two of you are in the car (as I confess I did with my oldest).

Even if your toddler isn't delivering *bon mots* with the timing of Oscar Wilde, or even stringing two words together, it's time for you to learn the age-old lesson: "Little pitchers have big ears." I may not fully understand the meaning of that cliché, but I can vouch for its truth, which is: Your little one might not be talking, but she sure as heck is listening, and understanding a lot more than you know. In the big picture, it means your toddler is sponging up your "gestalt," the way you feel about her, your level of respect for your mate, the way you address tasks and your disposition. So if your darling's first complete sentence is "You're an ass!" and she says it to her father, don't spend too much time wondering where she learned such trashy talk.

Later in toddlerhood, your little big-eared pitcher will freely march into preschool and announce that Mommy is just like Luke Skywalker because she is going to the doctor to get her face lasered. The teachers and other moms just love inside scoops like that. I, by the way, have made a pact with my children's teachers not to believe what my kids tell me about them if they promise not to believe what my kids tell them about ME.

Kids may listen and actually understand many of the words used, but that doesn't mean they pick up the correct nuance or significance. For that reason, you have to be careful not to speak of potentially alarming topics in front of any toddler, even those who can't yet talk. Once, when my oldest was a toddler, my husband and I decided to rent the old surf movie *Endless Summer*. What a disaster that little trip down memory lane proved to be. Since we live near the beach, I had to spend the next month promising that no big waves were coming to get us.

Perpetual Motion Machines

Until you have a toddler of your own, other people's stories about how traumatic it was chasing their little wobblers around sound just a tad hysterical. I mean really, how hard can it be to keep up with a tiny person whom any grown-up can outrun in a race? It's when you become the warden of a toddler yourself that you realize speed isn't the issue, it's the length of the race and the unpredictability of the terrain.

The parents of toddlers are creatures of reaction. When the toddler is in their care, meaning not with a sitter, the grandparents or some very tolerant boarding school, the parents can do little more than run a defensive line around her; after all, she is completely capable of killing the pets, you and herself if left to her own devices. Sure, we all know the delicious moments when they cuddle in our laps to read a picture book or when they learn to sing their first song. But on any given day, most parents of toddlers will agree that a disproportionate amount of time is spent averting a disaster or cleaning up after one. This is called "spontaneity" by people who are so old that they don't really remember their own children as toddlers, but to those of us living it, it's called psychological warfare.

Born to Be Wild

As someone who would almost always prefer sitting to standing and lying down to sitting, I'm astonished at how compelling the urge to move is in a person who has only recently learned to walk. Once they have felt the wind on their faces and the road beneath their feet, these little scramblers have two speeds, fast asleep or moving quickly. They may sit occasionally, perhaps to eat or to pull everything out of the bottom drawers in your bedroom, but even then their hands are in motion and their eyes are scanning the terrain to see where the next thrill lies.

My husband and I are still recovering from the L.A.–New York flights we made with little people who were obsessed with walking. Traveling with babies seemed like a day at the beach by comparison. How in the world do you explain about consideration for your fellow travelers or about sudden turbulence to a child who views sitting still on a par with illegal imprisonment? Up and down the aisles we'd walk, constantly apologizing indiscriminately to everyone we met along the way. Even during those few precious moments when we succeeded in getting them to sit in a chair, they would tap their little Stride Rites against the seat back in front of them like a podiatric form of water torture. How we yearned for a child who did nothing more distressing than cry for five straight hours.

They Pick Their Poison

Not too long into this adventure called toddlerhood, an observant mommy may discern in her young adventurer a specific preference for a kind of danger. Some kids, for example, love bathrooms and anything that involves water. Others are little climbers, while still others want to open cabinets all the livelong day. The fascination won't last long enough for you to be able to rely on it in any scientific way, but it will be interesting and can help you to anticipate some problems.

Actually, we were lucky in that all four of our kids were rather calm, at least as far as toddlers go. We didn't have one head-first kid in the bunch, but boy oh boy did a couple of my Girlfriends get a run for their money. Shelly's son, Bentley, could climb a tree before he could take two steps. Whenever we brought the kids together to play and lost sight of Bentley, all the mommy Girlfriends knew instinctively to look *up* to find him. He was certain to be on the roof of a playhouse, at the top of a staircase or hanging from a light fixture. Shelly was amazing. She never panicked and often she didn't even intervene. The way she saw it, Bentley could survive just about any fall that didn't require an orthopedist, so she was willing to let him spread his wings, even if they failed him several times. As a first-time mom at the time, I chalked up Shelly's nerve to some sort of delusional behavior, but now that I've made four trips down this road myself, I understand her calm was the direct result of Bentley having been her third child.

My Girlfriend Sonia's daughter was just as daring, but in a less acrobatic way. She could escape from any restraint, from high chair to car seat, so easily that Sonia settled for confining her to a room rather than some small part of it. The entire living room of their charming cottage was like a giant playpen. The floor was covered in toys and the coffee table was devoid of anything that wasn't plastic or rubber. Still, she was not always successful in keeping her little Kelly corralled. I recall one day we got so involved in chatting that Kelly completely disappeared. We found her *outside* the living room window, preparing to rappel down the slope into the backyard.

Do you ever see those mothers on the street or in the mall, walking with their toddlers in a harness? I used to see those poor women and immediately snap something sensitive and understanding like "I would never put my child on a leash! She clearly just doesn't have any control over the little thing." As in all issues of parenting, the Walk a Mile in My

Moccasins rule applied here. While I never got around to purchasing the harness, I still discovered four separate times that even the most vigilant of parents will be tripped up by toddlers.

My most terrifying experience as the mother of a toddler was when I walked into a shopping mall with my two-year-old son and infant daughter and immediately lost my son. I remembered some television parenting expert saying that the first thing to do when you lose your child in a crowded place is to run through it yelling "Lost child! Lost child! Two years old, brown hair! Lost child!" You know, I did just that, and I eventually found him sitting under some barstools in a café just fifty feet away. If I hadn't already been coloring my hair for ten years by then, I would have sworn I'd gone gray in those few moments. By the way, that parenting expert was right. People really perk up when you are specific in your screaming. Let them all know what your problem is and they will pay attention. It distinguishes you from all the other harried mothers around you who are just yelling out of habit.

Babyproofing

If this is your first child, you, like my Girlfriends and I, probably began babyproofing your home before the baby was even born. Who could resist the fun of preparing your home in every single way? It was kind of like decorating the nursery or washing the layette with Dreft. By the time the baby was about seven months old, however, you might have broken a few of the cabinet locks in the kitchen or even removed the clasp on the toilet lid after too many times nearly wetting yourself before you got it up.

It turns out that babyproofing is a never-ending process. Some things just break from overuse, and other things the toddler outsmarts and infiltrates, like the slide-and-turn covers on electrical sockets or the rubber sleeves with animal faces that we put on the bathtub spouts. Thank heavens the babyproofing industry recognizes this evolutionary process and responds to our needs with new products on a regular basis. For example, when my first toddler was toddling, no one had even heard of a VCR protector. The outcry from mothers who had discovered that toddlers love sliding anything from toast to TV remotes into that enticing opening inspired a great addition to the toddler defensive artillery.

The lesson to be learned here is that you must never get too complacent about your child's safety because he is developing so quickly. I wish I had a dollar for every mother whose child locked her out of the car by pushing that little button down in the moment between when she fastened him into his car seat and tried to open the door for herself. One minute they seem content to play patty-cake with their hands and the next they are using a spoon as a tool to open up the back of your clock radio. This is where recognizing your own toddler's particular tastes can give you a bit of an edge. If, like Sonia, you have a water lover, make it a house rule that no one ever leaves the bathroom door open, whether in use or not. If you have a cabinet/drawer fetishist, double up on your safety by both installing babyproofing latches *and* removing anything that would harm her if she should figure out how to open that latch (and you know she will).

In most cities large enough to warrant their own airport, you will find several professional babyproofing companies listed in those giveaway parenting magazines or the Yellow Pages. While the pros are more expensive than buying the stuff at your local Home Depot and installing it yourself, they do render a service beyond convenience in that they know more toddler tricks than you do. They can walk in and assess your home with a professional eye that you might not yet possess. I, for one, would never have known the value of the device that protects the stove top from little hands wanting to grab pot handles if a professional hadn't shown me. You might argue that it's overkill and that babyproofing companies are in the business to frighten you and convince you that your entire home needs to be surrounded by bubble wrap, but I'm a paranoid kind of gal and I'll buy whatever protection I can afford.

If you opt to go the do-it-yourself route with the babyproofing, start with a manual or guide from your local bookstore, library or pediatrician's office. It will provide a general inventory of the basics any toddler home should have to keep stitches and scalds to a bare minimum. Make sure you install everything properly and then test that it works by inviting a friend or mate to try to outsmart it. If an educated adult cannot lift the toilet seat without five minutes of verbal instruction, then you might be able to keep an eighteen-month-old out until his second birthday.

After all the protection is installed, don't sabotage your efforts by getting lazy. Yes, we all know that you can break a nail opening a vanity drawer equipped with a babyproof lock, but isn't your child's safety worth an extra manicure now and then? (Besides, Girlfriend, what are you doing with nice nails at a frantic time like this, anyway?) I know how busy and exhausted you are as the mother of a toddler, but this is really a time when cleaning up after yourself is critical. What good is it to have a locked cabinet for potential poisons if you forget to put your nail polish remover in that cabinet after your manicure? Always assume that the little shadow will find the most toxic or sharp or hot thing in the house if you don't throw it out, lock it up or keep it on the top of your highest shelf.

God Gives You a Free One

I don't have a shred of scientific evidence to support this claim, but my Girlfriends and I have experienced this phenomenon enough to believe in its truth. What we have experienced, and are eternally grateful for, is that when we slipped up in our vigilance as parents and disaster was a heartbeat away, Divine Intervention saved our asses, but only on the condition that we learn from that mistake and never make it again. My first experience with this was when my first toddler grabbed my full coffee mug off the table while I was on the phone. As if in agonizingly slow motion, I watched from across the room as the mug tipped and coffee washed over my little darling's head and into his face. I felt like fainting, but instead I leaped to him and grabbed him up, only to discover that the coffee was cold. See, that was a free one. I can't even bring myself to consider how badly this could have turned out if he had found that mug an hour earlier, but I can tell you this, that toddler is now ten years old, and I still won't allow myself to leave a cup of coffee on a table or counter.

Dearest Sonia's first experience of getting a free one came with her three-year-old son Jon. She went into her bathroom to find him with a pill bottle in his hand and a mouth full of pills. She simultaneously grabbed the bottle and swiped her other hand through Jon's mouth to get the pills out. Naturally, at a moment like this, her brain was spinning so fast that she was barely able to focus on the words on the pill bottle, but she finally made out the word fluoride. She had been giving her son supplements on the advice of her dentist, and he evidently had taken a liking to them. Not knowing whether fluoride was toxic in large doses, Sonia and Jon made a mad dash to the pediatrician where Jon was pronounced "just fine." But Sonia and the rest of us Girlfriends knew what forces were at work here: God had given her a free one and she never ever left tasty toothpaste out in the bathroom again until Jon was in the double digits.

Since the fundamental rule of parenting is that perfection is unattainable, there will come a time, or two, when your little tyke will get into trouble that you know you could have prevented. He will run into the street or open a bottle of window cleaner or slip his head between the fence and the side of the house and get stuck there. Your heart will seize, you will mentally take the calamity to its worst possible conclusion, which is always death, and something divine will intervene to save you. Never, ever take this intervention for granted, because it is precious and has a price. You must get right to the brink of disaster, feel the agony, and then come back from the precipice with a new resolve to pay better attention to protecting your toddler.

What About the Ones That Aren't Free?

You can never rely on the free one, and there will be times that something actually does penetrate your security and hurts your toddler. Ask any Girlfriend who has mothered a toddler, and she will have stories of fingers pinched in car doors, stitches on foreheads and above eyes, and goose eggs on the head. Toddlers are everywhere and into everything, and their bodies are often not up to the challenges their little minds set for them. It can be shocking to a mother who is new to the toddling ranks just how often her child hurts herself. In the beginning they fall every thirty seconds, usually into a coffee table or the leg of a desk. Later, they will have better balance, but they will be falling nearly as often because of the more challenging obstacle courses they've set up for themselves.

Aside from normal vigilance and babyproofing, there are two types of preventable injuries to toddlers that we Girlfriends feel you should know about. We single them out because they can be avoided entirely once you know them and because we have seen them occur so darn many times that they're almost boring in their predictability.

Our Furry Friends

The first preventable and predictable injury is a dog bite. If you read *The Girlfriends' Guide to Surviving the First Year of Motherhood*, you know how little I trust even the oldest, gentlest, most beloved family pooch where a baby or toddler is concerned. It's not that I don't love dogs; I do and I have two myself. It's just that I have seen or heard of so many otherwise trustworthy dogs taking a bite out of a toddler's face. You can't really blame the dog, since a toddler often acts just like another animal in the house. Toddlers will play with the dog's food bowl, stick pencils in its ears, pull its lips up to show his "smile" or any of a million other indignities. Who wouldn't bite back?

I think the single best explanation for all these dog bites in the face is that dogs are pack animals whose nature is to express dominance to all weaker dogs. If your toddler runs up to a dog, he is pretty sure to face it eye to eye (since they are both about two feet tall), and he will violate the dog's space. Before you can blink an eye, the dog has snapped. Teach your toddlers that they should never, ever approach a dog tied up outside Starbucks or walking down the sidewalk. This will be excruciatingly difficult for some moms because lots of toddlers find all animals irresistible, but other moms of toddlers who are afraid of dogs should find it much easier. And as for family dogs, always be prepared for them to lose their minds, too. I don't care how much you adore and trust them, don't be silly about it to the point where you leave the dog and toddler alone together, even for a moment.

I can't just leave well enough alone with dogs, either. Cats, hamsters and parakeets are also big toddler biters. Rare is the three-year-old who can cradle a rodent gently in its hands or carry a cat without dragging its hind legs on the ground, and this kind of cavalier behavior tends to bring out the worst in wildlife. Especially when the pet is in a shop or at a playdate's house and your toddler is unfamiliar with its care and handling, you're asking for trouble if your child is allowed to get to know the family pet without any close parental supervision. I may sound harsh, Girlfriend, but that's my job.

Furniture Acrobatics

The second absolutely predictable and preventable toddler injury is anything resulting from jumping on the bed. Once your toddler discovers the sensation of flying that can be attained from jumping on a good springy mattress, he will become addicted. This activity is so universal that it inspired its own nursery rhyme about two little monkeys jumping on the bed, one falling off and, well, you know the rest. But keep in mind what the doctor in the nursery rhyme prescribed: "NO MORE MONKEYS JUMPING ON THE BED!" and boy, did he know good medicine.

My Girlfriend Callie's toddler daughter Sally was jumping on her bed on the morning of her birthday. She was full of energy and anticipation because several of us moms and kids were going with her to Disneyland for her party. By the time I arrived with my brood, Callie had Sally in her lap and was inspecting the weeping little girl's wrist. You guessed it, Sally and Callie spent the morning at the orthopedist's office while I brought the waiting partygoers to my house to kill a couple of hours. The amazing thing is, Sally actually made it to Disneyland that day, and Minnie Mouse signed her cast. Gosh, toddlers are resilient little critters; I would have taken to my bed with a week's supply of some prescription painkiller.

I have another Girlfriend whose daughter took a leap too close to the edge of the bed and landed against the nightstand. That resulted in a couple of teeth nearly piercing her lip. Then there was the time my own son took a tumble off his bed and landed in such an odd way that he broke his elbow. The bottom line about jumping on the bed is that the game never ends until the jumper is in tears—you know, "It's always fun until somebody gets hurt." Toddlers would jump for days on end if it weren't for their precarious sense of balance that reliably sends them into a headboard or onto the floor within five minutes.

One way to keep jumping to a minimum is to keep the toddlers out of the bedrooms and in plain view. If you ask me, the Japanese have the right idea with those futons they put on the floor—there's a much shorter distance to fall that way. Another thing you can try is a toddler trampoline, a small jumping surface with a secure safety bar for the child to hold on to. You can buy one yourself through various kids' catalogs or enroll your jumping bean in a gym class that offers that kind of motion. Most important in the war against headlong dives is the consistency with which you stop the game whenever you see a leap about to launch. It's very hard to have rules where toddlers are concerned, and we will address that dilemma later, but this No More Monkeys Rule is a good place to start.

There's Safety in Numbers

So, what can you do when you have been playing man-to-man defense with a toddler for forty-eight straight hours and you think you're about to crack? Well, if dropping him off at Grandma's and whisking yourself away to St. Bart's isn't an option, we Girlfriends suggest you bring in another toddler! To the uninitiated, that suggestion sounds like pure insanity, I know. If one toddler is exhausting, two must be twice as tiring, right? Not necessarily. While toddlers won't really understand a lot of the give-and-take required for interactive play until their third and fourth years, they will still be attracted to each other. Ideally, the mother of the other toddler comes, too, and the two of you can commiserate with each other, drink diet Coke and help each other rein in the little ones.

If you aren't already part of some Mommy and Me–type group, now is a great time for you to join one. For you go-getters, classes like those offered at Gymboree can be a great chance to interact with your toddler. For us droopy moms who are upright only because of caffeine and determination, they give us a chance to be present in body, but to turn off our minds for a while. To the tired mother of a toddler, sitting cross-legged on the floor singing "The Wheels on the Bus" can be as relaxing as a day on St. Tropez because her little one is safe and occupied, and really, who could ask for anything more?

The Social Life of Toddlers

As soon as our little darlings take their first wobbly steps, we eager moms begin to fill their calendars with all sorts of social engagements. It's as if we think that the natural toddler progression is crawling-cruising-walking-cotillion. The fact that they stand upright makes them look much more like people than they did a few months ago, and we rush right into introducing them to our favorite people pastimes. If we love a party, anybody who walks on two legs must love a party, right? Though we might go a tad overboard, one of the most thrilling parts of parenting is rediscovering life's little pleasures through our children's eyes. Take Halloween, for example; to most nonparents it's a nonholiday. But the minute you have a child who can toddle around with the other kids dressed like pumpkins and little mermaids, Halloween ranks right up there near Christmas and the High Holy Days.

There are several ways to help our budding socialites make friends. Some of us join playgroups or take our kids to the park on days when we know suitable playmates will be there; some of us have our kids in child care outside the home where there are other kids; and the nuttiest of us all, which includes my Girlfriends and me, sign up for endless "enrichment" and "appreciation" classes for our toddlers. After accompanying four of my own children through toddlerhood, I can say I've been in everything from Mini Modern Music Masters (like a riot of tiny people who hit each other with musical instruments), to Toddler Gymnastics (where Mommy tweaks her already-stiff neck by enthusiastically demonstrating a forward roll while Child only wants the "tattoo" that the teacher hands out at the end of class), to Fun in the Water class (where Mommy has to put on a bathing suit and get all wet, even if she's got her hair and makeup done for the day and Child refuses to put her face anywhere near the water to blow bubbles). We mothers of toddlers are so overcome by the thrill of our child's blossoming social life that our hearts actually skip a beat when we open the mail to find that Junior's been invited to a Batman birthday party.

Our eager anticipation can, however, set us up for some disappointment. Learning to be part of civilization is not always easy for toddlers. They may love other kids so much that they hug them too hard. They may hate other kids because they look like they might steal their toys, or worse, their mommies. They may want to be around other kids, but only if you play, too. Or, for reasons I completely understand, they may be afraid of all toddlers across-the-board. What a letdown it can all be to the mom who believes that helping her child make friends is the greatest gift she can give her little sweetie. Plus, we can't help but take every perceived social foible of our children as direct reflections on ourselves. "Why," we whimper, "why can't he play nicely with others? His father and I are such *nice* people!" Or "Why don't all the kids like her? I'm always the life of the party, and her dad, well, he's okay, too." Don't fret, Girlfriend, if the idyllic playdates you imagined look more like free-for-alls and if you spend most of the time loping around like Mills Lane in a boxing ring keeping all punches legal and sending the pugilists to their corners when they need a time-out. We've all been there, and we have the bad lower backs to prove it.

How Toddlers Play Together (Or Don't)

First of all, toddlers don't know how to play together, at least not as we grown-ups define the phrase, until they are three or four years old. Putting a couple of two-year-olds in a playroom or yard is like watching a real-life version of Pac-Man: two little creatures moving unpredictably around the room, bouncing off obstacles and each other while gobbling up all the goodies in their paths. The concept of learning the rhythms of giving and taking, of speaking and listening and of teaching and learning from another little person who sees the world from the same physical vantage point and eats oatmeal with her hands, and therefore should "know where they're coming from," is a complete and utter myth. They may be curious about each other, they may covet something the other has, they may want to touch the shiny wet part in the other's eyes, but they don't really give a darn about establishing the groundwork for a loving and meaningful relationship. It's not that they're snobs or insensitive beings, it's just that their brains aren't properly wired for friendship yet. They have all the friends they need, thank you, in their immediate group of caregivers. They look at potential playmates as a source of amusement, unpredictability and, sometimes, tremendous frustration.

The baby books explain it by saying that young toddlers are capable of *parallel* play but not *interactive* play. That's just a fancy way of saying that they have little or no social skills and can only interact in the most primitive way. I read somewhere that up until about age two, human babies and chimpanzee babies develop almost identically. Remember this factoid because it will be strangely reassuring many times over the next couple of years.

The Loners

Some kids really don't seem to blossom in playgroups. Alone, they explore, run around and tear open bathroom cabinets with abandon, but put them in a group of other toddlers and they are often reduced to hiding in a corner and observing. In the spirit of always making the universe right for our kids, nearly every one of us moms of a retiring child has begged, bribed and cajoled the little one to pleeeeeease join in the play and HAVE FUN. That's just the point, playdates are almost never about two or three little kids eagerly coming together like a group of mah-jongg partners who've been doing this for decades. They are unpredictable, often random, couplings and triplings of largely nonverbal strangers who are as apt to bite eat other as offer a toy.

Don't let that ostensible awkwardness put you off toddler get-togethers. For our mutual survival, my Girlfriend Molly and I put our two toddlers together all the time. The kids were always happy to see each other, but I can't really say they played *together* in any identifiable fashion. Our experiences over those years were pretty typical of the boy-girl variety of gender blend: My memories are of my son, who could walk, but hadn't mastered running, sitting in the middle of the floor while Molly's daughter, who was five months older and had the natural sophistication that just seems to come with being a girl, twirled around him. She would play with something, tire of it, put it in my son's hands and then slyly take away from him whatever he'd been playing with. From my son's perspective, there must have been magic at work in the playroom: Just as he had nearly finished putting all the little plastic trucks in a line to form a sort of teamsters' train, he'd look up to see the tornado that was Molly's daughter dance into his space, and after the dust had settled he looked back only to find the trucks had disappeared and a naked Barbie with a crewcut lying in their place. Did he care? As I recall, very rarely.

Keep in mind that your toddler might not be antisocial, but just a homebody. I don't know how your life goes, but I know that my toddlers were dragged on my errands, dropped at baby-sitters or preschool and whisked all around town each day. I can see why a few quiet hours alone in his home can seem like Nirvana to an overstimulated toddler. Besides, there are some developmental skills that require 100 percent concentration to master, and there is no such luxury when other kids are around threatening to eat your Goldfish crackers or steal your Slinky. Putting puzzles together or stacking building blocks can be fun with another kid, later, but for the toddler, this is usually a more enjoyable challenge when it's overcome alone (or "by myseff!").

Social Ambivalence

The lesson that no toddler is an island is part of a wondrous and mysterious process. As mobile as they may look, most toddlers are still defining themselves in relation to Mommy and Daddy and whatever other beloved caregiver they know. They are not automatically prepared to run in packs with other short people, to have secrets, to move into the land of make-believe or to attend a sleepover. All of these desires will come with time, but not without a few stops and starts.

Think about it from the new toddler's perspective: It must be occasionally terrifying to realize you have the ability to just get up and walk away from the very people who exist on this planet to serve and protect you. For the first year of your life, you assume you and your mommy are connected physically and emotionally like spiritual Siamese twins. Then, when you stand on your own two feet, you discover that those bonds aren't as binding as you thought they were. If you can get up on your own and walk out the door, what's to guarantee that Mommy and Daddy don't try the same thing and leave you behind? Several times during toddlerhood, that sort of fear of too much freedom will strike your child, and you will find her seeking out the former comforts of babydom. Your job as a parent is to understand that two steps forward and one crawl back is the normal rhythm for most toddlers. A child who has been begging to go to his bigger cousin's to play can start out euphoric and end up postal. Usually, when a social engagement like this has taken a turn for the worse, it's time to go home and wait to try again another time. Trust me, there will be many other times. It's a wonderful but scary big world out there, and it's probably best taken in small doses.

Why Encourage Toddlers to Play Together?

In addition to the irresistible urge we have to introduce our little ones to the joys of society, there are actually some specific and compelling reasons to help them broaden their horizons besides our own secret desire to be popular for once in our lives.

• TO LEARN TO FUNCTION IN THE WORLD

Like it or not, we all have to share the planet. Whether we find that a good thing or a constant source of frustration is determined as early as toddlerhood. All the social skills, from the simplest (like learning that all previously unknown people are not monsters) to the complex (like learning to feel empathy toward other people) must be learned from actual experience. Some of these lessons develop with unerring destiny and grace. Others, however, hurt like hell, and I mean for the toddler *and* her parents.

One of my daughters used to go to a nursery school three mornings a week. I'm not really sure what the value to her was, but I was pregnant with my third child and I had an older child who wasn't in kindergarten yet and I needed a break. Her day would start on the playground, where she would pull wagons, learn to climb up and go down a slide, and where she would get punched in the face every single day by a little redheaded terror. I'm talking closed fist here. I won't bore you with how I ripped into the redhead's parents so severely they wouldn't get out of their car at drop off if they saw me or how my Sicilian husband called the soft-spoken Montessori teacher to say that if anyone ever touched his child like that again, the teacher would show up for school one day to find it burned to the ground. In the end, we saw the value of the lesson our precious little angel learned: Redheads roam this country wild, and they are not to be trusted (or something like that).

I got another painful dose of reality when I volunteered in my youngest child's preschool class and realized that three-year-olds were already establishing in-crowds and out-crowds. One day Terry and Jordan and Kyle were friends, and the next day Kyle was cast out and replaced by Benjamin. By the way, keep this little bit of wisdom in mind: *Never intentionally set up triangle playgroups.* Children from age two to as old as ten (or forty, for that matter) tend to pair up, leaving the third wheel feeling abandoned and miserable. You can butt in and insist that the kids include everyone in their play (and what parent could resist doing so?), but you probably won't be there every single moment, and there are bound to be hurt feelings that you can't prevent. Sure, learning that kids don't always play in a generous and all-inclusive way is an important lesson for your toddler to learn, but that's what school is for. While you still have some control over his universe, try to keep these rejection issues to a minimum, and encourage the other mothers in your social group to do so, too.

Perhaps the greatest challenge for the toddler entering the world of social interaction is learning to share. I know plenty of adults who aren't all that crazy about sharing, either, but they have had years to mask their distaste. Keep in mind that part of socialization involves learning to *subdue* a toddler's natural instinct not to share, not cure them of it. Our goal as parents is not to cinch the social saddle too tight by expecting them to behave as little ladies and gentlemen. Remember, they are still way too far down the evolutionary ladder to satisfy Miss Manners and should be rewarded just for *trying* to resist the most barbarian behavior.

• TO LEARN FROM WATCHING OTHER KIDS

There is a world of information to be gained by observing and imitating someone near your own age and abilities. Babies and toddlers are like puppies: They recognize each other as being of the same superior species and are very attracted to each other, even if only to take a taste of each other, then run and hide behind Mom. I'm sure you've seen it in your own child, the way she opens her eyes wider and starts to fidget with excitement when other children come into her universe.

We moms can drive ourselves to distraction trying to demonstrate how to do everything from skipping to making pee pee in the potty, with no results, only to have our children pick up those skills after a week of rubbing shoulders with toddlers who are skipping and pee-peeing all over the place. Since this copycat behavior is so powerful, I would suggest, as your Girlfriend, that you give yourself a break and search high and low for playmates who have already mastered whatever skill is giving you problems at home; perhaps a well-chosen three-year-old can do the job for you. While we're on this subject, let me take this opportunity to encourage you to include both younger and older toddlers in your social directory. I've noticed lots of moms knocking themselves out trying to find playmates who are so chronologically well matched they could be twins; not only is this unnecessary, it's also rather limiting. The rule of thumb is: A younger child will always be charmed by an older one who is reasonably nice to him, and an older child will like being the elder statesman to a younger child, at least until someone older than he is comes into the picture. If your toddler seems to relish the challenge of trying to keep up with a frenzied four-year-old, ignore the age difference and book the date. Just don't neglect to keep a careful eye on them, since big kids often encourage little kids to do things that we'll all later regret. Conversely, if your little one seems to need a little boost in self-esteem, a playdate with a younger toddler can be just what the therapist ordered. Being Big Man on Campus can be a tremendous confidence builder to kids who are not completely convinced that traditional toddler achievements are all they were cracked up to be. For example, if you have a toddler who is mastering the potty thing, he might find it motivating and reassuring to show "his aim is true" to a younger kid who still thinks a potty is something to throw hairbrushes and diaper wipes in.

Hanging out with other kids also gives your toddler a chance to practice and expand his vocabulary. If you have any doubts that children learn a significant part of their communication skills from their peers, just wander into any schoolyard: You'll hear more sophisticated and varied references to specific anatomical processes than you would at a proctologists' convention. Little kids are more demanding of each other than we parents could ever be, and they will badger each other into talking so that they can be understood when Mommy or Daddy would let baby talk pass unnoticed. One of my kids called pajamas *jamamas*. My husband and I thought it was absolutely adorable, and we secretly hoped he would never learn the correct pronunciation. Well, one playdate with his friend Brandon and he never said jamamas again. "What are jamamas, anyway?" demanded Brandon. "The other part of japapas?" Seven years later we're still mourning the loss of his little speech impediment.

• FOR FUN AND COMPANIONSHIP

Unless your sweetie is a complete misanthrope, he will most likely find playing with other kids addicting. Even the most timid and reluctant children grow to like the company of other kids so much they prefer it to time spent with Mommy and Daddy. (Don't worry, it doesn't reach crisis mode until the preteen years, and by then you might even be grateful for the break.) Toddler playdates may not always look pleasurable to the inexperienced observer, especially when there is mayhem involved, but a toddler's expectations for social interaction are far lower than ours. From the toddler's point of view, a playdate is worth the price of admission if it provides any kind of stimulation. Remember, these little people are still testing out their brain wiring, and anything that gets a zap is interesting to them. So while you might be disappointed in a two-hour get-together that involves watching the other child stick raisins up his nose as his mother frantically tries to remove them, your child probably thinks this is high society.

This is an important point to keep in mind: Don't try to steer the play of toddlers to fit some image *you* have of what's fun and educational. First of all, you'll annoy everyone involved. Second, you'll make yourself part of the equation, which is the opposite of what learning to play with others is about. And third, there's no way you'll be as creative as a gang of toddlers when it comes to thinking of fun things to do. Sit back and enjoy the show, and try to jump in only to avert an obvious crisis. Otherwise, remember: An afternoon spent taking off and putting on the caps of those Magic Markers that smell like fruit, with the occasional sweet marker up the nose, can be a halcyon memory in the making.

The Girlfriends and I are still coasting on the comfort of the friendships our kids formed with each other during baby and toddlerhood. Even though they were oblivious to it as it happened, our kids learned to make their first friendships among the kids they were used to and whom they saw regularly. Toddlers aren't like big people who seek friends from groups of like-minded people; they can enjoy the company of nearly anyone who doesn't intimidate or bore them.

If you and your toddler commit to a parent/tot group or a circle of friends of any sort, your child will make friends by the age of two-and-a-half to three based simply on their developmental readiness and the familiarity of the kids they've been getting to know over the previous months. That's not to imply that these friendships are merely stopgap measures for your little one until the broader social pickings of kindergarten. Quite the contrary, the Girlfriends' off-spring are all still as close as cousins, even though they are all in different schools, on different sports teams and have made new friends along the way. It's really quite delightful to see friendships that are based on knowing and accepting everything about another person—and we hope they can hold on to that gift for the rest of their lives.

• FOR MOM AND DAD TO GET A BREAK

Speaking of the rest of their lives, one of the most valid reasons to set up playdates for toddlers is so that parents can get some rest in theirs. While it may not make any sense mathematically, adding one child to your family equation can often make your work less by half. Isn't it better to sit nearby and supervise a game of let's play Mommy than to have to play yet again? If your child and her visitor are happy with each other, they can be satisfied just observing each other's play for an hour or two. As they become older toddlers, they will play together excluding you and only need your help to drive the car or light the matches.

Since I maintain that the mental aspect of parenting toddlers is often more exhausting than the physical, I relished the chance to just shut down during a playdate. Sure, I was quick to jump if the paint was spilling or if the blocks started to fly, but beyond that, I didn't have to answer fifty thousand "why?" or "what's dis?" questions or pretend to be the scary monster or the crying baby to keep my child satisfied. People used to think I was a saint (or an idiot) as I would go through the neighborhood collecting spare children for my kids, but that's only because they hadn't learned the unique nature of parental mathematics. In fact, the only way I can sit here writing this very minute is because I have two extra children here from a sleepover; they play with each other and they leave me alone.

While the kids are still very young, it often makes more sense for the playdates to include adult representatives from all involved parties. Assuming that the early playdates are set up with the children of people you happen to like, your toddler's playdate can also be yours. My Girlfriend Sonia and I used to meet at least three times a week at a little park near the beach. We'd buy cheese puffs from a nearby hippie health food store for the four toddlers we had in tow and tall diet Cokes or mocha coffees for ourselves, depending on the season. We'd sit at the edge of the sandy pit of the playground sipping and gossiping, and we'd take turns getting up to help someone down the slide or up the ladder. Sometimes we'd put all the kids on a swing set and stand behind them, pushing while we discussed the pressing news of the day.

Since most of my Girlfriends live near me in southern California, swimming and water play were big playdate activities. We moms, several of us pregnant again, would show up with big hats and sunscreen for everyone, and watch the little ones run around with a garden hose or in one of those little blue plastic pools. Since Callie almost always managed to look good in a bathing suit, even when pregnant, we appointed her chief lifeguard. The rest of us could recline on the grass in our muumuus while Callie leaped in and out of the water as needed. Every once in a while we'd offer her a sip of iced tea or a towel (but not too often because her lack of cellulite made her worthy of torture). Those were treasured times for the kids and for us, and there was no better example of the truth in the phrase "there is safety in numbers."

When Your Kid's Friends Are Strangers to You

After the birth of my second child, I returned to work outside my home, thinking I was finished with maternity clothes and stretch marks.

Sure enough, I got pregnant again, but this time I intended to continue working. Since I had far fewer of those days spent on lawns with blue plastic pools and my kids were at least as hungry for other kid-size friends as before, I enrolled them in a preschool that accepted children as young as two. I would drop them off, but a baby-sitter usually picked them up at noon, and I didn't have much time for sitting around getting to know the other parents. I would read their names off lists as we addressed valentines or birthday invitations, but otherwise they remained near strangers to me.

Not so to my kids, however. In no time I was getting phone calls that went something like this: "Hi, I'm little Bernie-from-preschool's mom, and I was wondering if you'd like to get the kids together next Saturday afternoon? Oh, by the way, my name is Bonnie." (It's stunning to me how instantaneously we go from being somebody to being somebody's mom.)

Yikes! Did that mean that I, in the name of being a good and selfless parent, had to spend my Saturday afternoon making small talk in the home of strangers? Yep, that's precisely what it meant. A couple of times it turned out to be as agonizing as I'd predicted, but most of the time it was fine. The most difficult parts arose simply because I didn't know the etiquette of toddler playdates like I do now. This is an area fraught with gray areas, but there are some guidelines that will spare you and your child unnecessary awkwardness. They are as follows:

Toddler Rules of Etiquette

1. When making a playdate, always stipulate the duration. For example, say something like, "Why don't you and little Lucy meet us at the merry-go-round for an hour? Then we will have to leave so that Junior can get his afternoon nap." (Note: Never brag that your child has given up his nap because it's a wonderful excuse to interrupt almost any unpleasant get-together.) By setting a finite time, the playdate doesn't feel burdensome and you don't seem rude when you leave before the second cup of coffee.

2. If you have been invited to play by someone, and assuming no blood was shed, then you must reciprocate by inviting them to play with you. As I mentioned before, toddler friendships often develop through habit and familiarity. It will help your little one tremendously if he has one or two other kids who he can count on seeing regularly. If those two kids don't happen to conveniently live next door, you may have to cast your net a bit farther and meet some new people. Remember, my two-and-a-half-year-old son brought me his friend Bentley and his mom, Shelly, and eight years later, we're all still crazy about each other.

3. Don't make a big deal about the playdate in advance. Some parenting authorities will differ with me on this, and while I understand the value of letting a toddler know what to expect of his future, I still never tell my kids that someone is coming over or that we're all going to Disneyland or any other such thrilling event because it leaves no room for canceling. Parents of children of all ages, but particularly of temperamental toddlers, should preserve their right to cancel playdates right up till the very last minute. Don't let some silly sense of social obligation, for example, urge you to wake up a napping toddler to get him to the park on time. Feel free to evaluate your child's emotional condition and conclude that he is too strung out or too clingy for a successful playdate that day and cancel it.

That means the inverse is true: If you are the mother who receives the cancelation notice, be gracious and grateful that they didn't come under social duress. It shouldn't be a big problem for you because your own little one should *not* have been sitting on the front porch counting the minutes until his buddy arrived anyway. If you opened your big mouth with this exciting news, then it's your own fault when he goes mental on you and you pay the price for the rest of the afternoon.

4. Don't sneak sick kids into playdates. Few of us would have the nerve to take our green-nosed child over to another mother's house for a little get-together, but somehow the rules seem to relax as the size of the group grows larger. That's why we moms see so many little bacteria disguised as children in preschool. Since playdates do not have mandatory attendance, you should be super-scrupulous about not sending toddlers with fevers, suspicious rashes or very itchy scalps to share the bounty with other people's kids, no matter how eager you and your toddler may be for some social interaction. Keep in mind that mothers of toddlers are often only a year more experienced than mothers of newborns, and they still have not overcome their heightened awareness of potential infection of their child. Now that I have four kids and most of the terrible diseases have been survived or vaccinated against, I will take playmates with very questionable health status because I think a sick child to amuse my own child is better than no child at all. I do, however, draw the line at head lice. Just mention those two words to me, and you'll see the moat start to fill around my house.

5. *Have two of the good stuff.* I'm sorry, but I just can't bear mothers who invite toddlers over for a playdate to see their little darling's new fire truck. Talk about a recipe for disaster! You just know the visitor will covet the fire truck and the new owner would rather die than let him so much as *touch* one of the ladders. With toddlers, nearly anything can be a toy. That's part of their charm; they don't discriminate between the high-priced stuff and some old ballpoint pen they found under the sofa cushions. If you're having a toddler over to play with yours, make sure that you plan ahead of time the activities to be offered and whether there are enough to go around. This is not the time or the place to teach lessons about scarcity in life to your children or anyone else's. This is the time to have fun, whether your investment is in two fire trucks or simply two bottles of bubbles and two wands.

6. *Err on the side of the visitor.* Think of a playdate as a sort of sporting match. If it's not played on some neutral playing field, but rather at one of the player's houses, there can be a distinct home-court advantage. This is particularly true as toddlers get old enough to be dropped off at playdates without their parent or other handler to function as their own personal advocate. If a toddler is playing with strange toys, eating unfamiliar food and using a potty he's never seen before, he can be temporarily thrown for a loop. All of this stimulation and unfamiliarity can make even

the most pleasant little toddlers hyperactive, hyperpossessive and just plain hyper. When you witness the inevitable toddler battle over a single paintbrush, even though you have thoughtfully provided six brushes, you will have to overcome your innate desire to protect your little cub and help out the visitor's cub first.

My daughter has a best friend who was afraid of dogs. My daughter, on the other hand, was born into a home with four dogs and has never known they weren't her biological relatives. When the girls were both about three, my little one decided that she was going to flex her queen-of-the-castle muscles and let the dogs into the house while her canine-phobic friend Cameron was visiting. I don't know what was louder, Cameron's screeches of terror or my daughter's indignant cries as I dragged the dogs by their collars back outside. But this was my child's first real lesson in the obligations of being a good host; sometimes you just have to suck it up and go along with what your guest wants to do.

7. No fair grading anyone's child. There is a temptation among mothers to measure and assess not only their own children, but everyone else's, too. I know the temptation, and I have succumbed to it on countless occasions, but the wiser me now knows that it rarely does any good to share any observations other than words of praise. You may think that a remark like "You, know, little Charlie might be able to sit still for more than five seconds at a time if he didn't drink a soda with his peanut butter and jelly sandwich" would be received in the kind spirit in which it was intended. This will never be the case; just trust us Girlfriends on this.

When you have had a child to your home to play without her parent present, it is equally important to use restraint in your reports. The other parent, if she knows the rules of toddler playdate etiquette, will call for your postgame wrap-up. If at all possible, stick to the high points and steer clear of mentioning the broken porcelain doll that was only for display, never to be played with, and any crying that lasted less than five minutes. Part of the duties of being a host mother is taking responsibility for the playdate's success, so it's up to you to try to keep everybody happy and out of harm's way, not to give a blow-by-blow commentary that makes the other mother squirm with embarrassment.

8. *Call to check on a playdate when you aren't there.* With many of us moms spending time at a job outside the home, there will be times when you cannot accompany your toddler on his social calls. Either you will have dropped him off, or his baby-sitter will have gone as his minder. Either way, try to give a call about an hour into the playdate to the host mother or caregiver to make sure that all acclimating has been successful and that your child is willing to stay. It's been my Girlfriends' experience that baby-sitters often feel slightly hamstrung when they have been asked to take a toddler to a playdate that later, for one reason or another, proves to be a disaster. They may feel as if they don't have the authority to end the date or that they would be held somehow responsible for a playdate's failure, and who can blame them? Ideally, you should call yourself, take a pulse, and speak briefly to your baby-sitter if she's there, too. Then you can make any executive decision that's required.

9. *A playdate host observes the guest's rites and rituals.* It's your worst nightmare: It's raining, you have two toddlers at your house, it's lunchtime and you haven't had a chance to hit the market yet. What do you do? Go to McDonald's, where they not only serve food that kids like but also include cute little toddler toys upon request? Not necessarily. You just might be hosting a darling little vegetarian who is also watching his cholesterol. It is never a good idea to unilaterally decide to be the one who gets to introduce him to his first burger. As a matter of fact, playdate protocol generally dictates that the guest mother list all dietary restrictions, allergies and whether the child is prone to anxiety attacks before she leaves her offspring behind. It's only fair to prepare the host as thoroughly as possible.

The same considerations extend to watching television, playing rough, getting dirty and eating sweets. Every household has its rules, and you should do your best to observe them, no matter how crazy you think they are. Try it from the reverse point of view; how would you like your toddler to come home from a playdate announcing that she had doughnuts and coffee for snack? Or that she watched the older brother's *South Park* video collection?

10. *Report any injuries that befall your little guest.* As painful as I know it is, the Girlfriends are agreed that you must fully reveal to the parents any boo-boos or bites or bonks that their child has sustained during your watch. No matter how careful and attentive you may be, it's just the nature of the beast that somebody's going to get hurt; if they didn't, how would they know the game was over? If you're lucky the injury will require little more than a hug and a kiss, and maybe a Spider-Man bandage. Toddlers are amazingly resilient; a good thing considering how often they tumble and crash. If the injury is not something that involves blood in general, or the face or head specifically, they can generally go right back to playing and you can tell Mom the story when she picks Junior up.

If the injury looks serious enough to warrant a call or visit to the doctor, then do your basic mommy first aid and call the other mom immediately. It's very important that you do your best not to begin that phone conversation crying and with the words, "I'm so sorry . . ." Any mother on the receiving end of that call risks suffering a sudden stroke and will be of no further assistance to you. There will be plenty of time later for you to blubber your sincere apologies, and trust me, the other mother will want to hear them when the crisis has passed. Even if it wasn't an accident you could have prevented, most mothers need to find someone in the universe to blame for their darlin's pain, and it might as well be you.

As tempting as it will be to stay mute about the header your little guest took on the hall carpet or how his fingers got pinched when your child slammed the toilet seat down on them, you must tell, especially since, by the end of the playdate, there may be little physical evidence. I could take the moral high ground here and tell you that disclosure is the *honest* thing to do, and therefore the best. But the truth here is, if you don't tell, the mother will find out anyway and she won't share her child with you any more. She might find out when she comes to pick up her laughing, playing child who, upon seeing her, has total recall of the incident and starts crying and begging to go home. You could just stay mute and shrug your shoulders, but even a child with very limited verbal skills will find a way to share the news. In the end you will seem like the responsible host mother that you are if you give her the basic facts and a description of what you did to make it all better. Once again, say you're sorry. It's not a statement of guilt so much as a general sorry that any toddler anywhere should feel pain.

Biters, Boppers and Pinchers

This is as good a time as any to bring up those horrible social encounters that lead to physical violence. For reasons too subconscious for me to fully understand, we mothers are shocked and appalled by toddler-on-toddler violence. If we could be objective for a moment, we'd see all the good reasons a toddler has for biting, pinching or bopping another kid with the nearest toy/weapon at hand: Perhaps the victim looks particularly delicious; perhaps she has done something to tick the offender off; or perhaps she is just the victim of a physics experiment the offender was conducting to see how far a Tonka truck would fly.

By far the most egregious crime against the humanity of mothers is biting. If you are the mother of a child who's been bitten, you can collect the condolences and righteous clucking of every other mom you know (except the mother of the biter, but more about her in a moment). Mothers are so worried about their children being bitten that they do each other the favor of identifying potential offenders to other mothers as a civic duty. "Hillary's a great gal," they'll say, "but her little girl is a *BITER*." Biters to moms are worse than communists to McCarthy. Talk about a good way to limit a toddler's social life . . .

But ostracizing the little vampires is rarely necessary. Unless they can't stop chomping every time they approach human flesh, they can usually be integrated into social situations if they are watched 100 percent of the time by someone who is within arm's reach (should an intervention become necessary). I have frequently noticed that the mother of the biter doesn't pay as close attention as the mother whose child is in the presence of a biter, so it's best if the defensive mother supervises the play. Besides, what mother in her right mind would send her little one to play with a biter and not tag along to keep an eye on things? Try your best not to get into a mind-set where you consistently view this little biter as a, well, as a little biter. This is almost always a passing fancy, and lurking beneath the fangs could be a terrific toddler.

There are generally two kinds of biters: those who bite often for a several-month period of toddlerhood and those who bite once and never do it again. There is no greater honor in being one or the other; you simply shouldn't flip out when you learn your child has bitten someone, first, because it may never happen again and second, because it is no indication of possession or even a mean temper. That said, once a child has bitten, it's only sensible to stay on the lookout and avoid that kind of confrontation whenever possible.

Having had a couple of biters in my own brood, I must say that it's nearly as horrifying to be the mother of a biter as it is to be the mother of the bitee. It's always astonishing, and, to make matters worse, it rarely occurs in the privacy of your own home. That means the entire day-care center or preschool usually knows about the assault before you do, and you can be sure they are talking about it! Even if it takes place out of your presence, you won't be able to dispute it happened because there is usually a mother at your door with her child in tow who has the imprint of your kid's pearly whites on his cheek, hand or shoulder. God, toddlers can bite hard! I've seen some bites that were red, purple and gray!

Kids don't usually bite other kids because they hate them. My son bit his best friend in preschool (poor Shelly and Bentley) because he was frustrated at not being able to keep up in a game of tag. In a way, it made it easier for me because the mother was my friend, and boy was she sweet about the whole thing, but it was also infinitely more upsetting because I knew and loved the victim like one of my own. The lesson to be learned from that scenario is similar to my advice about dogs; even the nicest, friendliest, most familiar toddler can bite unexpectedly.

If your child is bitten, stay calm and deal first with your child. If it happens in your presence, pick your child up and comfort her while moving toward a sink where you can wash the bitten area with antibacterial soap and water. If you feel lightheaded, sit down with your child in your arms and take a few deep breaths. Trust me, these bite episodes can really turn a mother inside out. While you're rinsing with water, check to see if the skin is broken. If your toddler has had a recent tetanus shot, an antibiotic cream like Neosporin or Polysporin will probably be all the medicine you'll need. Some ice on the bite helps, too, to keep the swelling and bruising from reaching maximum bloom. Go ahead and call your pediatrician if you think you'd like a professional opinion; they're good at calming *us* down as well as helping our kids.

If your child bites and you're in the room, say "NO!" firmly and remove him from the scene of the crime. Stay stern and repeat, "NO BITING!" a couple more times. As quickly as you can, with your toddler safely restrained in your arms, go to the other child and see if there is anything you can do to help. Apologize. Let your child see the upset he has caused. Apologize again. Then stand out of the other mother's way so she isn't tempted to bite your baby back (yes, that is a very real temptation when a mother lion has seen her cub attacked). Oh, yeah, apologize again. If you feel like crying, go ahead. Never, ever do what that woman did to my Girlfriend Karen and try to minimize it. You may want it all to go away, but I promise you it won't until the other mother has gone through the several stages of grief or some similar ritual. A nice touch would be for you to call later that day to see if the little victim is feeling better or to hear what the doctor had to say. When you see each other again, you guessed it: APOLOGIZE.

The Wall Comes A-Tumblin' Down

There comes a staggering moment in every parent's life when she realizes that her child has more in her head than what was fed to her at home. It might be something rather amusing, like a song that you've never heard, or it might be something rather foul like a particular swear word that you and your mate don't use. At that moment you will realize that Kahlil Gibran may not have been entirely full of soybeans when he said, "Your children are not your own. They belong to the universe." Getting along with other people and finding friends to join them on the journey are among the greatest gifts a child can receive. Sure it's challenging and painfully time-consuming for us moms to help them learn social skills, but what more important endeavor could we imagine?

The Comfort Zone

(Or, Binkies, Bankies, Loveys and Thumbs)

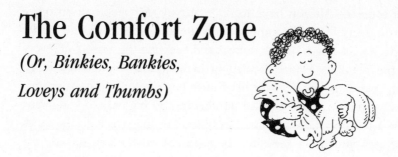

What Is the "Comfort Zone"?

The comfort zone is a blissed-out state of mind that a toddler retreats to through a particular behavior. Within this emotional grab bag, you'll find all the habits, attachments and rituals that toddlers indulge in to summon the magical powers they need to feel safe and able to cope. When these magical powers are ascribed to a particular object, professional toddler watchers call them "transitional objects," but I'm partial to Dr. Brazelton's term, "loveys." Those include such things as dolls, "bankies," stuffed pets, pieces of old clothing and pacifiers. When the magic is summoned through behavior, those same people who make careers out of watching children call it "self-soothing." This includes eye rubbing, rocking back and forth in bed, thumb sucking and the need to be tucked in "snug as a bug in a rug" before going to sleep.

While, on first glance, it may not seem that the fact that your tiny toddler can't sleep without her favorite stuffed animal has absolutely *anything* to do with your sister's little boy who loudly bangs his head against the side of the crib for at least half an hour before falling asleep, and you'd bet good money that it is in no way comparable to your best friend's toddler's incessant nose picking, I think they are more alike than different. These are, to paraphrase the old rocker Eddie Money, their "three tickets to paradise." Don't think for a moment that this behavior is the exclusive domain of toddlers. All you have to do is survey the people in an office to see nearly every kind of soothing, transitional behavior. In one corner you have Marty reading monthly reports and chewing the erasers off every pencil in the building. Hanna is digging in her purse for change to go down to the vending machines for her fourth bag of Doritos this morning. Spencer, who thinks no one can see him behind his big desk, is "adjusting himself" in a leisurely fashion, Kara has bitten her fingernails to the quick and Sheri, well you don't see Sheri because she is standing outside the nonsmoking building having a quick puff. Okay, so it's not really paradise, but it's a break from the stresses of the here and now.

Here's what the Girlfriends and I have noticed: People don't like what they can't control. Even "fun" activities, like going on a trip or taking up skiing, bring the fear of the unknown and a loss of control in all but the most evolved. Take my mother, for example. If she is going on a vacation in July, she begins her packing ritual in May. It just recently occurred to me that perhaps she is using the packing as a way to emotionally adjust to the change ahead. Either that, or she has far more wardrobe options than I ever knew. If my grown-up mommy thinks that a two-hour plane trip and a hotel stay are anxiety-producing, imagine how tough life can be for a toddler. After all, these little people are packing for a one-way trip into adulthood (with no return ticket to babyhood). Not only that, the journey can often be tormentingly turbulent, with all the changing and challenges that take place. I, for one, would give anything for a "binkie" or a "bankie" to help me get through the choppy parts.

Why Do Toddlers Do These Things, Anyway?

Here's the Girlfriends' best guess: They do them because it feels good to do them. That's the bottom line. Admit it, if you are in the privacy of your own home, or even just your car, judging from the amount of nose picking I see on our country's highways, you might still resort to some of the self-soothing habits you learned as a toddler. Several of my Girlfriends still have their bankies and beloved stuffed animals of toddlerhood, and they can only wistfully imagine that the treasured item still has the magic power to make the world seem more manageable and safe. I have watched my kids fall asleep with baby bottles in their mouths (WATER bottles, for all you members of the mommy police out there) and wished that I had something that put me in such a pleasure zone, but I don't know what it would be since no one has offered me a morphine spinal since my C-section ten years ago.

Toddlerhood is more than learning to walk and beginning to talk. It is a series of veritable developmental explosions. Little people who had no idea that they and Mommy weren't the same person a few months ago are learning that they are indeed individual and capable of moving away from the constant protection of Mommy the Monster Killer. Not only can they venture out on their own, they are often forced to do so even if they're not quite sold on the idea yet. Consider the distinct lack of joy and delight the average toddler demonstrates the first time Mom decides to leave him with a sitter or in day care.

It can be so confusing for the poor little toddlers; one minute they want to rule the house, be left to dress and feed themselves and walk alone into unknown territories, and the next they are doing their darndest to recapture their babyhood by asking to be rocked to sleep, crawling on all fours even though they've been walking for two years, or climbing into the bassinet with the new baby. And, really, who can blame them? Sure, there are some fun things about getting older, like driving a car and being able to have microwave popcorn for dinner, but a lot of it is just scary. I still don't quite understand what divine being determined that I was grown-up enough to make decisions about whether my daughter should have her adenoids removed or how old her big sister should be before she got her ears pierced. And who in their right mind would put me in charge of a seven-year-old boy who'd just fallen off the bed and broken his elbow? Yet there I was, splinting him and rushing him to the hospital, all the while wishing there were some real adult around to take care of both my son and me.

God knows I still believe in rituals, self-soothing and magic blankets. I can't face the day without a glass of fresh-squeezed orange juice, even if I'm in a hotel where such things have been known to cost upwards of ten bucks, and I can't go to sleep unless I spend an hour watching television or folding down the corners of pages in mail-order catalogs. I try not to, but I still bite my cuticles, and boy oh boy does my husband get lucky if he will just rub my back for five minutes. And four times I gave birth and each trip to the hospital I carried my own blanket and pillow from home so that labor would at least smell safe and familiar. As aware as we parents are of the helpfulness of finding our own comfort zones (particularly without the aid of any chemicals stronger than caffeine), we still get anxious when we notice our children seeming to attach what might be too much power to a thing, habit or ritual.

If It's Normal, Why Do We Care So Much?

Maybe We've Ruined Them!

Our most nagging fear as parents is that we're just not doing the job right. We have read enough pseudo-psychology to be convinced that our parenting, particularly our mothering (thank you, Dr. Freud), will make the difference between our children growing up to become healthy, contributing members of society and turning out to be guests on Jerry Springer. This responsibility is stunning in its enormity, and we secretly suspect (of course) that we are completely unprepared. I don't subscribe to Freud's children-are-but-lumps-of-clay approach to parenting (I'll take that up with him another time), but let's just stick to what's got us worried right now.

With toddlerhood comes the kinds of habits that drive us parents to compulsive behavior of our own. We don't always understand why, but our new little independent humans who can walk and are learning to talk are simultaneously taking up attachments, repetitive behavior and all sorts of obsessions that send us running for every parenting manual on the shelf. Does refusal to give up the pacifier mean that we weaned our baby too soon? And does early weaning necessarily lead to long-term personality damage like chronic overeating, nail biting or fear of intimacy? How about your little boy's newfound affection for his penis? Where in the world does that habit come from? You know one thing for sure, and that is that he certainly didn't learn it from YOU! What happens to kids who never learn to leave their privates alone? Are they predisposed to turning into an entire generation of Al Bundys or must they seek careers in professional sports when they grow up so that their behavior isn't a professional liability? As crazy-making and frustrating as this frequently off-putting behavior can be in the privacy of our own homes, it is magnified a thousand times when it occurs in public.

It's All So Embarrassing!

No matter how enlightened we parents aspire to be, none of us is above feeling the stab of humiliation that comes when our child is making a meal of his nose contents while God and everyone else are looking. We're pretty sure that nothing we've done as parents has created this little nose picker. He certainly gets plenty to eat, and there are Kleenexes in every pocket of his overalls, but we still get that sweaty, light-headed pang of shame that it is somehow a negative reflection on the entire family. Perhaps, we consider in our panic, everybody thinks the whole family does that little nose trick and Junior just picked it up from the rest of us. How can you ever clear your reputation of that?

We Girlfriends think this is a good time to remind you not to let your children's behavior in public upset you too much. If truth be told, parenting is often one long lesson in public humiliation, and it certainly doesn't pass with toddlerhood. Just wait until you have a second grader who swears every time he strikes out in baseball, then you can have a fifth grader who thinks farting on command is high art. And nothing can prepare you for the unmitigated embarrassment of having a teenager who not only thinks you are completely clueless, but won't even let you dance at parties if she's attending, too. Remember, your child is not your Secretary of Protocol. She just happens to spend your money, sleep in your house and collapse if you aren't standing in the background to prop her back up every once in a while.

For you parents of toddlers, it might help if you keep in mind that they are simply humans without the constraints of propriety, shame or manners. Every urge they have, every emotion they feel, moves from their brains directly into action without the speed bump of good judgment to slow down the traffic. Who knows, maybe their behavior drives us so batty because we secretly envy their liberation. I, for one, would love to scratch my tushy in public every once in a while.

Two additional sources of toddler parenting pressure and general *agita* come from the grandparents and child-development books. There was a time, not long ago, when children were raised according to a schedule dreamed up by the parents of what must have been a very precocious child (or, more likely, someone who had never actually raised a child himself). This mythical schedule proclaimed that all children would be sleeping through the night by three months, off the bottle by nine months, walking by a year, potty trained by two years and ready for military service by age eighteen. Rather than provide any guidance or support for us parents, these achievement deadlines have reduced most of us to puddles of inadequacy as parents. It seems that the only people who still believe in "the schedule" are our own parents.

No matter how devoted they are to our children, our parents often have a hard time restraining themselves when they see that we are raising little thumb suckers or toddlers who can't watch the *Beauty and the Beast* video unless they sit through the Pizza Hut ad in the beginning. Even if they never say a word, the tension of spending a weekend with your parents when your toddler's nose picking is at its most enthusiastic can lead you right to migraine hell. My Girlfriends and I all agree that, while visiting grandparents can be wonderful—and how about that free baby-sitting—there is still no bigger relief for the mother of a fidgety toddler than to get him or her back home where they can fidget in private.

It's a Matter of Record

Toddler habits ruin a lot of home videos. A watershed event in the history of parenting occurred when the videocamera became standard equipment in most homes. Before that time, when parents still relied primarily on snapshots, they were able to pick and choose moments that were idealistic representations of their adorable little kids. Any parent of the videocam generation, however, who has peered through the viewfinder for an entire spring sing recital or a preschool class trip to the zoo will tell you that video catches all the precious moments, plus several episodes that you could have lived the rest of your life without seeing again.

I'm still trying to forget that time when I recorded an entire inning of T-ball only to end up with indisputable evidence that my child spent the whole time playing "pocket pool" in right field. I have another home video of one of my kids' Holiday Sings (have you noticed that no one calls them Christmas Pageants, Hanukkah Shows or even Kwanza Fests anymore? We parents are getting boringly p.c., don't you think?) where I zoomed in for a close-up of my precious caroler just in time to catch my darling with her finger up her nose. Did she find what she was looking for in there and then stop? Of course not; she just picked and sang simultaneously until I was so humiliated that I considered changing schools before the end of "Winter Break" (the p.c. version of Christmas Vacation). My Girlfriend Hillary has the most adorable home video of her tiny dancer performing something to a Madonna tune. There she is, in a chorus line of miniature Rockettes, dressed in a pink tap dress with sequins on the sleeve and vogueing to perfection—with a blue plastic baby bottle in hand. Someday, I trust, these recollections will be the source of great humor and delight. Right now, however, they are what stand between our toddlers and stardom.

Perhaps someday I will buy one of those video editing machines I see on the home shopping channels and take out all the footage of my otherwise perfect children picking their noses in the Halloween parade, holding their "privates" in the outfield and sucking on a shank of hair during an entire afternoon visiting Great-aunt Eloise. Gone, too, will be any evidence of nail biting, thumb sucking, repetitive throat clearing, eye rubbing and, need I even mention the dread pacifier? All toddler archival materials will show the confident, composed and charismatic children that I so competently raised.

The Experts Say It's Wrong

I don't know what great wizard wrote the Rules of Child Development, but there does, indeed, seem to be a parenting code in the collective unconscious of parents in need of guidance (which includes nearly all of us). We all seem to have the same checklist burned into our brains, and the potty training by two is just the beginning. We're led to think thumb sucking should end by age four, or there'll be hell to pay in the dentist's chair, and that our kids should be reading before they even *start* first grade. And what about the delusional practice of sending seventeen-year-olds to college, where they'll be encouraged to choose their life's profession amid keg parties and orgies? No wonder most of us feel like we're not keeping up! Not only is it profoundly obvious that each person lives according to his or her own internal clock—and that alone should make such dicta sound like hogwash—it's also cruelly designed to guarantee that a large number of children will fail to measure up. And, as if that weren't bad enough, when our children don't follow the Rules, we parents are usually the ones held responsible. I'm sorry, but I don't want to play this game with these Rules. It's hard enough running this mothering marathon without having someone standing beside me with a stopwatch, calling out my times.

My Girlfriend Melanie took her two-year-old to the pediatrician for a checkup several years ago and mentioned that her daughter, Mariah, still drank from a bottle. Having read all the literature about the sugar in juice and milk, Mel didn't allow anything except water in the bottles, but was otherwise unconcerned. Well, let's just say she was as unconcerned as any first-time mother is when her child doesn't seem to be following the Rules, no matter how asinine those Rules are. Take it from me, if you're a truly unconcerned mother (as in barely conscious, like me), you don't even mention those things to a pediatrician unless you are prepared to deal with them. Anyway, Melanie was told that she should stop giving Mariah bottles now that she had hit the ripe old age of two. When bold Melanie asked why it was important for her darling, well-adjusted daughter to give up something she clearly loved and needed, the doctor told her that "it was time." That's all; "it was time." Talk about your lame responses. *As if* Melanie were willing to endure a temper tantrum every time she refused to give her daughter a bottle AND watch her beloved child feeling insecure and bereft, just because "it was time."

Little Mariah was quite sure that, according to her personal calendar, it was not yet time to give up the bottle. She still depended on it when she felt tired, overwhelmed or just plain bored. Melanie had the infinite wisdom to trust her toddler's instincts and let well enough alone. By her third birthday Mariah was happily bottle-free. She even created a ritual to commemorate the passing of the bottle: She and Melanie collected all the bottles and nipples in the house, put them in a bag and put them in Mel's car so that she could pass them on to "little kids" who still needed them. As I recall, Melanie discreetly dropped the bag of faded bottles and chewed nipples into a Dumpster on her way to work the next day, but Mariah felt that the circle remained unbroken.

If we Girlfriends succeed in nothing more than exposing the Rules of Child Rearing as a complete fraud, we will consider ourselves pioneers of nonneurotic motherhood. There is simply no value in a code that invalidates a huge percentage of the subscribers. Yes, I understand that mothers, especially first-timers, find tremendous reassurance in knowing what to expect and when to expect it in our unpredictable children, but that isn't a good enough reason to ascribe a timetable to the little critters. Children will achieve all those developmental milestones eventually, but not necessarily when the books say they should. That's why *The Girlfriends' Guide to Toddlers* lumps together everyone from one to four years old: We Girlfriends were sick and tired of reading books that predicted toddler development as precisely as a lunar landing. This isn't an exact science, and pretending it is just makes us all anxious when things don't proceed as promised.

My other pet peeve about deadlines and timetables for child development is that they fail to take into account setbacks and regressions. As you should have noticed by now, just because a toddler has mastered a developmental milestone, like potty training or drinking only from a cup, doesn't mean he will never again don a diaper or request a bottle. Toddlerhood is a period of flux for kids. One minute they are big kids, the next they are doing their damnedest to crawl all the way back into your uterus. Times of uncertainty or crisis can send the most "mature" toddler running for the bankie and sleeping in bed with Mommy and Daddy. We bought a new house this year, and when I shared the great news with my youngest, she took up nail biting. I'd never seen her do it before, but then, every time she had some thinking time on her hands or when we discussed the move, those nails went straight between her teeth. Clearly, our coping mechanisms are going to be pulled out of the closet on an as-needed basis.

Dumbo's Magic Feather

Remember how the flying elephant believed that he couldn't stay aloft unless he held the magic feather that his little mouse friend gave him? Then one day, in midflight, Dumbo loses his feather and it looks as if he is going to lose all confidence and come crashing to the ground. Just in time his mouse reassures him and all is saved: Dumbo goes on to become a star, and he takes his mother everywhere he goes (and really, what more could any of us want out of parenthood?).

Like Dumbo, lots of toddlers believe that there are certain magical qualities to ordinary objects. Whether they believe that baby blankets over their heads keep monsters at bay or that a superhero's cape makes pre-school a less threatening place, they cherish and depend on their "magic feathers." While this is a completely understandable dependency, it is also daunting in its power. There isn't a mother on this planet who would willingly stand between a toddler and his "feather." There is no greater feeling of parental panic than to learn that you have left "bankie" at Grandma's house (a plane ride away) or that the favorite Tweety Bird sleep shirt was inadvertently put in the washer by a housekeeper or helpful spouse, and no one remembered to dry it in time for bed.

Before going to sleep each night, my Girlfriend Alison's son, Andy, used to listen to a full-length cassette of lullaby music that his musician daddy made for him. Heaven forbid if Alison had dinner plans with the rest of us and tried to turn the tape off before the very last sleepy song was played! Andy would bolt up from what had just appeared to be a sound sleep and screech in agony that his ritual was messed with, and Alison would have to start the whole tape over from the beginning. Nine times out of ten Alison would be asleep in the chair in Andy's room by the end of the tape and the rest of us would have gone off to dinner without her. Thank heavens she had three copies of the tape, or she would have had a very cranky insomniac on her hands.

If you don't have a music- or story-dependent toddler, you could have a daughter like Julie, my Girlfriend Sharon's cherub. Julie was a remarkably calm and enchanting toddler, albeit not very conversational, as long as she had her pacifier in her mouth or at least in her hand, but if you took that "binkie" away, she would rage like a miniature Elizabeth Taylor in *Who's Afraid of Virginia Woolf?* Sharon went to such lengths to avoid losing the "binkie" and enduring a toddler incident that she carried spares in her purse, in her glove compartment and even in her earthquake kit (remember, we live in California). Eventually, and I mean before kindergarten, Julie gave up her "binkie" of her own accord. I'm not saying that Sharon didn't try several times to bribe, beg or trick her out of her plug, but, as is usually the case, she just had to stick it out until her toddler was willing to cooperate.

I think that my son had one of the weirdest toddler attachments I've ever heard of. When he was not quite two years old, he got a paper cut on his finger. Naturally, I made a big deal out of it, washed it with soap and water, applied Polysporin (one of my favorite pharmaceuticals) and then let him pick a Band-Aid with some appealing picture (at that time, it was probably Ninja Turtles or Power Rangers). I noticed at the time that the appearance of a drop of blood seemed especially disturbing to him, but I just chalked it up to his heritage: His father had to lie down for the blood test to get our marriage license. After a couple of days and several soaks in the bath, I suggested to my little sweetie that the Band-Aid was probably ready to come off, or, at the very least, to be replaced with a nice clean one. NO WAY! He not only wouldn't let me remove the Band-Aid he had, he insisted that he needed one on the opposing finger because of an imaginary scratch he had there. I resisted at first, but, wanting to have peace before we began our bedtime ritual, I finally gave in.

Within a week he started looking like Michael Jackson when he used to bind his fingers in adhesive tape. Perfectly healthy fingers were getting sick from their lack of light and abundance of moisture trapped under the bandage. One time I forced my toddler to sit in my lap while I held him with my superior strength and clipped off all the Band-Aids. His little fingers looked so shriveled and pale he nearly fainted. For the rest of the day I steadfastly refused to replace the Band-Aids, but my poor baby compensated by wrapping his fingers in his favorite bankie. He couldn't pick anything up, he couldn't feed himself, and he was absolutely shaken by his vulnerability.

Gosh, as I recount this story, I feel like slapping myself upside my head. What was the big deal? If my toddler felt better facing the world with Band-Aids over his entire body, what difference did it make? I never once stopped to consider the stress that he might have felt at that time by the birth of his little sister. I never once made allowances for his fear of potty training or moving out of his crib to free up the nursery for the new baby. No, I worried about what other people would think and whether his fingers would ultimately fall off, in that order. In hindsight, I recognize that it wasn't important whether I completely understood how Band-Aids made the world a safer place—it should have been enough that I recognized their magic and respected it. Maybe someday I'll get over this. . . .

You'd think with all the knowledge I've accumulated mothering four kids, my youngest would be an example of perfect parenting. After all, by the time she was born, I'd certainly made all my parenting mistakes and learned my lessons, right? Sorry, not the case. This little one loved her bottle so much I thought she would graduate with it, she had nighttime "accidents" for so long that her own loving sister wouldn't share a bed with her and she still can't hear the word "no" without having a system breakdown. If I learned anything raising toddlers, it was that no two children ever respond the same way to the same mothering. I guess that's Mother Nature's way of keeping us from resting on our laurels (because if we rested for a minute, we'd fall fast asleep).

Back to the feather: One compelling reason why parents of toddlers are so eager to "cure" our little ones of these intense bonds or beliefs is because we are so afraid of what will happen if the precious "lovey" is lost or the ritual is impeded in some way. The thinking is, if I, the loving mommy, can create a safe and sensitive way for my child to grow out of this dependence, he won't be caught unprepared and vulnerable in the big, scary world out there. Makes sense to me; unfortunately, I had very little personal success carrying out this smart little plan. Once again, it wasn't my lack of trying (as unenlightened as it was at times) that doomed our efforts; it was the simple fact that my toddlers needed that behavior all the way up till the time they didn't need it anymore. Their "feathers" were the very things that allowed them to enter the big scary world and bring a talisman from the nursery. If Dumbo were a real elephant, his mother would have kept a spare feather for him for all flying emergencies.

If We Can't Beat Them, Let's Join Them

The Girlfriends and I had far greater success with the old "bait and switch" method of living with magical objects or behavior than we did with convincing our toddlers that they didn't need their magic feathers. For this to work for you, you must wholeheartedly believe in your toddler's perception that certain things or rituals have powers far beyond the obvious; that they are, indeed, magical. Even the most unimaginative of us who fail to see how keeping the bedsheets from touching the floor ensures that no snakes can climb into the bed, or how a dirty piece of fabric that was once a blanket puts its user into a deep meditative state when rubbed on that soft skin under her nose, can certainly see the havoc that is wreaked when they're denied to their devotees.

The key to success in this approach lies in teaching your toddler that the magic powers are so strong that they can inhabit more than one "lovey" or routine. If, for example, your beloved has a blanket that means the world to him, BUY ONE OR TWO EXTRAS. Toddlers aren't suckers, and they won't recognize the magic in the new blankets right away, but you can help give them those special properties that make them such treasures. Here are some tricks to try:

1. Understand that one of the most enticing aspects of a "lovey" is its smell. That intoxicating combination of spilled milk, baby breath and maybe even a little pee pee makes a toddler feel right at home. Unfortunately for us moms, stores don't sell blankets and toys already imbued with toddler perfume; besides, each child has to create his own aroma. Your job here, Mommy, is to encourage your toddler to let the visiting blanket sleep and nap with him. Or, if the lovey is a doll or animal, see if your toddler can find a second favorite among his stash to invite into his bed or crib. The concept, as you must have deduced, is for the "proxy" to get broken in well before a crisis calls it into active duty.

While we're on this subject, we'd like to caution you about being too finicky about cleanliness. I recently saw a woman on *Oprah* who still has the feather pillow she had as a toddler. When Oprah asked if she'd ever had the pillow cleaned, the woman looked at Oprah as if she'd suggested burning it. If she cleaned it, it wouldn't smell like home anymore. Oprah looked a tad nauseated, but the woman looked perfectly fine in the rest of her personal hygiene and apparently had made this one exception.

2. Determine what makes a lovey so appealing to the touch. It's easy to assume that your toddler is attached to, say, a certain stuffed animal because it is so cute and even has its own video. Look again, Girlfriend, because your child may be in love with the *satin label* sewn on its behind! Perhaps that label has just the right combination of smoothness and stitching to make it delightful to rub between two fingers in those moments leading up to sleep. If kids picked loveys based on our adult standards, such as pillowlike bodies and adorable faces, then how would you explain the fact that my cousin used to sleep with a full set of toddler golf clubs and my own son's love and joy is a pancake-flat Nickelodeon creature, from which he has hung six or seven key chains and dead electronic virtual pets? Once again, the lesson here is to try to get into your toddler's mind and determine why particular objects soothe him.

3. Breed familiarity. As we suggested in the "aroma" section, it's critical to introduce the second- and third-string objects or behaviors as soon as possible, perhaps right after you finish reading this chapter. They need to acquire that magical toddler patina and familiarity well before you visit your in-laws and put your little one to bed in an unfamiliar travel crib (where the head banging doesn't make the right noise) or you mistakenly believe that, just because Pooh's head was eaten off by the family dog, it should be thrown into the trash.

If the comfort zone is induced by an object, introduce suitable alternatives and help "break them in." If the zone is achieved by some ritual or environment, try to cozy up to your true believer and figure out the essence that makes it so special. The next time you see your toddler putting himself to sleep by rocking vigorously back and forth, go in and lie down quietly nearby. Try reciting a repetitive nursery rhyme or singing "Ninety-nine Bottles of Beer on the Wall" to see if the repetition works the magic. If it appears that the motion is the magic, see if you can help him achieve a similar comfort by punching a pillow, tapping his feet or, if you're really desperate, from you patting him on the back.

4. Don't get embarrassed. Face it, one of the biggest incentives for us parents to encourage our toddlers to overcome their "comfort zone" behavior is so that we are not walking advertisements for bad parenting. So many of our worst parenting ideas stem from our desire not to be publicly humiliated by our children. First of all, let me wish you good luck, and then I'd like to say that if you are not deeply embarrassed by your child several times between her birth and her wedding, you just aren't paying attention. It's our jobs as mothers to respect our toddler's needs for comfort zones. The rest of the world might tease and ridicule, but Mommy should let her little one understand that she is on his side and will support his attachments and habits to the best of her ability.

If the thought of sending your child off to college with his bankie upsets you or if you can't imagine living through a ride on public transportation during which your toddler not only picks her nose but *eats it,* then you may be too fainthearted for this job. Humiliation should come as no surprise to you now. After all, aren't you the woman who spent an entire afternoon in Nordstrom's with baby urp dripping down her back? Wasn't it you who got all dressed up in a silk summer frock, went to a grown-up party and had her breasts leak so profusely that you looked like a contestant in a wet T-shirt contest? And how about that plane ride when you held your little infant in your lap and he had a projectile poo poo that covered him, you and the seat AND had a stench that sent the other passengers running for the air masks? All right, then, let's just calm down and remind ourselves that motherhood is the most noble job on earth, and that we're so tired and distracted that we don't really have the energy to get good and mortified.

If you think that everyone is looking at you and your toddler, may I humbly suggest that you're a little self-obsessed? Remember, we are all nothing more than bit players in other people's drama; unless, of course, you are the stuff of which tabloids are made. The only people outside your immediate family who notice whether your child is still sucking his thumb are those competitive mothers who spend their lives measuring their success by other people's *perceived* failures. You and I both know that these women are generally friendless, have crummy sex lives and wrinkle earlier than the rest of us, and so are to be pitied rather than feared.

5. Encourage adjustments that make your life easier. Going back to the example of my Girlfriend Allison and her son with the taped music, Andy, a suggestion might be to shorten the tape. Andy's loving dad must have used every second of the ninety minutes the tape provided. After a couple of years of this bedtime ritual, it would be difficult for the parents to suddenly edit out sixty minutes of magic music, but by that time Andy was old enough for them to mention the idea and see how it flew. I suspect that the affection for the songs was not based in their musical value, but rather in the fact that Allison stayed in the room with Andy until the end of the tape. Perhaps she could offer to rub his back or read him a story and then play a few musical selections at bedtime.

If you are reading this book at the beginning of your toddler tour of duty, pay close attention to the Andy/Allison example. Bedtime rituals are as valuable for the parents as for their babies, but only with the firstborns. Unless your kids are born ten years apart, you simply won't have the time or the energy to repeat the little nighty-night song and dance once another baby enters the picture.

I know moms who devote forty-five minutes of their undivided attention to their toddler's bath, give a little massage before putting on the pajamas, let the kid pick out his attire for the night (as if he were Hugh Hefner), listen to an entire *Bananas in Pajamas* CD, read a story and then sing a lullaby. At my house the ritual is slightly more free-form: Kids double up in the bath, wash each other's hair (sometimes without pulling it), put on the pajamas I've laid on the bathroom floor, come to me for a hair combing and a dental check, and then they all call to me for at least twenty minutes, begging me to tuck them in again, get them some water or get the toilet to stop making that funny noise.

The Fear of Raising Serial Killers

The last major reason why toddlers' parents feel pressure to "cure" them of their obsessions, rituals and attachments is the suspicion that Jack the Ripper was a thumb sucker and Lizzie Borden may have been reluctant to take to the potty. Hey, they *may* have been, but my suspicion is that it was entirely coincidental. It's possible that some of the greatest socio-paths of our times were head bangers or bottle lovers, but then, so were a great number of our world's most healthy, happy and well-adjusted individuals. A recent survey of my own Girlfriends, all of whom are smart, candid, loving and funny and without any known police records, revealed that at least 70 percent of them still had a "lovey" from their toddlerhood or occasionally retreated back into their cuticle biting or eyebrow tugging when under stress.

I don't want to go too far out on a limb here and suggest that every single variation of toddler behavior is completely normal. Some children have obsessive-compulsive disorder, are under so much stress that their little lives are sheer misery or have medical conditions whose symptoms are those tics and twitches that the Girlfriends are going to such lengths to justify. There may be a hazy line between acceptable and unacceptable toddler behavior, but you should never make the determination alone. While you should always start with your pediatrician, my Girlfriend Melanie and I both caution you not to disregard your own intuition and accept all things the doctor says as gospel. Another great source is your child-care provider or preschool teacher. They are able to observe your child without looking through that parent prism that adds fear and guilt to every glimpse. Also, unless they are as new to this job as you are, they will have the accumulated experience that comes with sharing toddlerhood with lots of kids from lots of backgrounds with lots of bizarre behavior. Your Girlfriends can also be a great resource, especially if their kids are older than yours. Few things are more reassuring to a mother than hearing about a child who was wackier than your own and is still living a rich and happy life, unless it's learning that a mother you thought had a master's degree in parenting spent the toddler years in an even thicker haze than you did.

Does Father Know Best?

I know that I am leaving a key person out of this advice directory, but the Girlfriends and I have a lot of ambivalence here. Should the daddies be consulted when the mommies are concerned that the thumb sucking is getting out of hand or that the attachment to a Raggedy Ann is getting in the way of playing and eating? In our house, the paternal response to any of my concerns or worries is dread and panic. Perhaps because I am Secretary of Health, Education and Welfare (not to mention Transportation) for our family, my husband believes I actually know all there is to know about my domain. Then again, I am also in charge of paying the household bills, and I can't make a move without him questioning my competency there, so I don't know why he is so trusting where the kids are concerned. The only explanation I can think of is that he is certain he would be stricken and die if anything were wrong with the kids so he would rather not know about any glitches or concerns.

Toddler behavior is also a rich vein for marital discord. My husband and I have called in the Howitzers over such issues as whether a toddler's constant motion and failure to heed even the simplest directions might mean attention deficit disorder, whether little boys chronically holding on to their "dingalings" meant they were masturbating, and whether the word *masturbating* was obscene when used in a discussion about our children. If my husband had his way, no one in this house would ever have to go poo poo or have a bowel movement; she would simply have a "tummy ache" that was miraculously cured by a visit to the potty.

The dynamic between parents varies as greatly as toddlers' personalities. In some families it is the dad who brings a calm and perspective to child rearing. Sometimes we moms are too close to see the behavior clearly, and, yes, I'll admit it, some of us are just plain hysterical. Marriage counselors and therapists might sensibly suggest that all child-rearing business be shared equally between both parents, and that may work for you. All I can say is, if after some trial and error, you discover that one of you is slightly better at navigating the bumpy parts of parenthood, spare the more fragile of your team and reach out to the bigger network of friends and professionals.

When Will This All End?

Most people learn to end or limit most of their Comfort Zone behavior right about the age they start school, since it soon becomes apparent that their classmates don't tolerate thumb-sucking bankie carriers in the cool crowd. By divine coincidence, at about the same time, the world no longer seems quite as daunting as it did a couple of years before. In other words, a combination of growing confidence and a strong desire to fit in with one's peers generally results in a child who is much less dependent on the Comfort Zone.

Sure, you may have very strong recollections of your parents "breaking" you of some of your habits, like hiding your pacifier, or slapping your hand every time you tried to stick your thumb into your mouth, but I bet you kept up the behavior longer than they knew by hiding it from them or finding a slightly more socially acceptable version of the same thing, like biting your nails or clearing your throat a little more often than is strictly necessary. Since I'm not the boss of you, I can't forbid you to intervene in your child's annoying habits and obsessions, but I can beseech you to honestly appraise your own recollections of childhood and see if you really think it's helpful for a parent to forbid or take away a toddler's access to the Comfort Zone. I've tried it myself, and I will confess now, the price my child and I had to pay was too great for me to ever want to put either of us through it again.

Here is a checklist you might find helpful when you think you've had it up to here with whatever "zoning" behavior your toddler has chosen to comfort himself (and, as it happens, to drive you nuts):

1. Accept that this behavior, annoying as it can be, is completely normal and age appropriate. If it's any comfort to you, it can be taken as a good sign when your child shows that she is feeling overwhelmed by toddlerhood: It means that she is smart enough to understand the ramifications of leaving babyhood behind. This is a big leap for her to make, and it's good that she is seeking coping skills now because she will need to be able to trust in herself that she will always find a way to get through rough times. That said, it is also completely normal for us parents to become obsessively aware of these behaviors and to worry that they are the sign of a deeper problem. Perhaps they are a sign, and we'll get to that in a moment, but most of the time they are nothing more than what Dumbo's magic feather was to him; he really can fly without it, but he doesn't know that yet (nor does he need to know).

2. Check for a medical explanation. Before you work yourself into a lather trying to identify some deep psychological explanation for your toddler's habits and twitches, make a visit to the pediatrician. For all you know, sweet little Sarah has her finger up her nose because she's searching for the popcorn kernel she stuck up there a couple of days ago. Same thing with the ears. Toddlers delight in putting little things into bigger things, whether it's stacking cups or popping peas into body orifices. If you have a new baby as well as a toddler in your household, be particularly aware of this insertion fetish. My Girlfriend Mary Lou recently found her three-year-old, Marty, putting quarters, one at a time, into the five-month-old's mouth as if she were a toy bank. Fortunately, no Heimlich maneuvering was necessary, but Mary Lou is still checking the baby's diapers for spare change.

Another medical explanation might be allergies. You're talking to an allergy pro here, since two of my kids have had runny, itchy noses, little coughs and asthma for several months out of every year. I couldn't have broken them of their eye rubbing and perpetual sniffling habits no matter how desperately I might have wanted to. Here's the tricky part of allergic behavior: It may start out directly related to the discomfort of the allergy, but it can then continue on long after the allergy symptoms have been relieved because it has become enjoyable in its own right, but more about the enjoyment factor in a little bit.

Getting back to medical causes, a good pediatrician will look for anything from intestinal parasites to head lice to dietary deficiencies to explain all the scratching, poking and fidgeting that your toddler might be engaging in. As much as we hope with all our hearts that there is no physical ailment, we understand how disappointed you will be if you are told that your sweetie is in fine health and her little habits are of her own creation. That means there is no wonder treatment in store and you, like the rest of us, will have to wait for this stage to pass.

3. Help your toddler to ease the stress. Even toddlers old and savvy enough to understand that they have certain habits that drive other people crazy often can't give the habits up because they have taken on a role beyond just feeling good. They have become "magical" in their ability to take the sting out of certain situations or to keep the boogeymen at bay or, in some cases, the habits become alternative behavior to engage in when what the toddler really wants to do is forbidden or disapproved of. Without being too obvious, make a mental note of the situations and events that trigger the habits. Does your little girl start sucking on her hair with enough vigor to choke herself while you dress and feed her in the morning? Perhaps she's anticipating having to separate from you when you drop her at the sitter or day care, and hair sucking is like taking a toddler Valium for her.

One of my own little darlings, in preparation for sleep, used to wrap his head in a bankie that was so dirty and worn that we couldn't even tell what color it originally was. There was something so intoxicating about the familiar smell and texture of the blanket that he could transcend the environment and go to sleep anywhere. The blanket might have started out simply as something soft and warm, but it took on its magical talisman powers when we Southern Californians were awakened from deep sleep to a humdinger of an earthquake. The blanket became a lifesaver to that child because sleep was beginning to look like a pretty scary place to go. If truth be told, I was jealous of that blanket myself because I, too, hated waking to shattering glass and swinging light fixtures, and I was yearning for something to wrap my head in, too.

Without making too big a deal of it, try talking to your toddler about how difficult some parts of his day might be for him. I always found it helpful to talk about some other child, often an older sibling, whom the toddler admired, telling a short story of how the bigger kid felt worried or upset about something; like how a big sister I happened to know was scared to death of the chimney sweeps in *Mary Poppins*. Don't feel like your little story has to have a moral or a solution at the end. What really counts is your conveying that the feeling of "lack of comfort" is common to everybody.

*Remember, we're not looking for a way to stop the behavior here; we're trying to take some of the sting out of the stress. In the long run, relieving the anxiety will be the very thing that allows your little sweetie to let go of the Comfort Zone for longer and longer periods of time.

4. Don't shine a light on it. Look, I get it that certain toddler behavior is so unnerving and often downright gross that we sometimes can't resist doing something, ANYTHING, to put a halt to it. Still, this is never a good idea, and here's why: It is against the Girlfriends' Guides Rules of Parenting to use shame as a disciplinary tool. (That is, of course, until your kids are bigger than you and you're desperate to get the upper hand at least once a semester.) The whole point of the Comfort Zone is to avoid bad feelings, so why on earth would we want to heap more discomfort on a little kid who is already in the thick of it? If you feel you will burst if you don't at least mention that keeping one's finger in one's belly button all day is off-putting, at least promise me that you will discuss it with your toddler at a time when she is not engaged in that behavior. Even young toddlers with limited vocabularies will get your drift and consider your point if you make it without judging them.

5. Help the toddler find another way to cope. My Girlfriends and I have noticed that we can break down this kind of toddler behavior into two groups: the stuff they do when they are anxious about some sort of change or challenge ahead of them, and the stuff they do when they are bored and spaced-out. Examples of the first group could be a child who rocks back and forth in his bed before surrendering to sleep or who tugs on her hair when it's time to try out the potty again. Examples of the second group would be the legions of children who pop a thumb into their mouth as they are bending their knees to sit in front of the television or those cuties who lie on their mats at rest time in preschool and pick their noses as they wait for this interruption of play to end. No matter what group you think your toddler's behavior fits into (or even if he has habits for both groups of situations), our advice is to treat it all the same. Think about it, boredom or waiting can be quite stressful to a toddler who has more pent-up energy than the Energizer Bunny.

If there is something so upsetting or injurious to your child that you feel you absolutely must modify the behavior, don't forbid it, but rather help them adjust it to be more bearable for all concerned. If your child has unconsciously pulled at his eyebrows so incessantly that his face is as bald as Uncle Fester's, try substituting some other thing for him to do with his hands like playing with a Rubik's Cube (don't expect him to actually get the colors lined up like they do on TV) or bending a Gumby doll half to death. I gave one of my children a string of worry beads (once he/she was past that choking stage) to take the place of his/her zipping and unzipping a sweatshirt jacket. I'm not going to guarantee you that the substitution will work immediately, or even at all, but it's worth a chance because it's your way of saying it's all right to need a Comfort Zone, and you are willing to help your child find a safe way there.

My Girlfriend Karen crashed headfirst into this situation when, three years after giving birth to precious Kathleen, she had a second baby. Kathleen is very bright and she deduced very early on that her parents would not be particularly pleased if she were to bop her new baby brother in the head or carry on about her lack of affection for him. Karen and her husband were terrific about making sure Kathleen got lots of extra love and attention, and they certainly would have tolerated it if Kathleen had started spewing slurs about the darling boy (which she never did), since they understood how hard it was for her to make room for this intruder in her previously perfect life.

Kathleen instinctively wanted to be a good girl and to love her new brother, even if she did wish someone would take him back to the hospital where they got him, so she found new behaviors to let off some of the steam she felt about this dimpled little interloper. She became a nose rubber. She had already discovered the relief of rubbing her nose, having just gone through a flu that seemed to have her congested from June to December, so it was easy to see why she turned to that familiar sensation again when she felt out of balance. She was nice to her little brother, she pleased her mommy and daddy, and she occasionally rubbed her nose so vigorously it turned pink.

While Karen was a wise mommy and bit her tongue rather than say anything to Kathleen about the nose business, she did something equally wise and made a point of taking her little girl out, just mom and daughter, for an hour of rough-and-tumble beach play nearly every afternoon. She rolled with her in the sand, chased her near the surfline and kicked over castles that they made with plastic buckets. They did anything Karen could think of to help Kathleen let off steam. Several months later, when it became apparent that baby brother was not only staying, but that he was kind of wonderful, after all, the nose rubbing gradually disappeared. Co-incidence? Who knows? All Karen knows is that it made her feel better and seemed to help Kathleen, too.

6. Help your toddler see growing up as a good thing. Nothing is more natural for a toddler than having occasional second thoughts about taking the big toddle right out of babyhood. Who can blame them? Babies are usually found safe in Mommy's arms or somewhere else very close to her. They don't have decisions to make, they don't have to master buttons and potties and how to sit still, and they certainly don't take as many tumbles as a toddler does. Come to think of it, all that falling down and off of things can really start to take a toll on a kid, don't you think? As little Kathleen's experience showed, having a real living, breathing baby come into your life while you're already feeling a little ambivalent about this whole growing up business can make matters worse. Every day, right before your eyes, there is plenty of evidence why being the baby is the better gig. Look, between us Girlfriends, I often notice men still longing for infancy, so it's easy to see why a toddler, with his more recent memories of the good old days, might have that longing, too.

Ah, but we smart mommies know that growing up brings all sorts of fun opportunities and privileges. It's our job to point them out on a regular basis. My Girlfriend Marie Ann, who has a kindergartner, a preschooler named Jody, and a new baby, is busy these days extolling the merits of being three-going-on-four to her preschooler who wants to live in the bassinet with little Toby. One hit has been starting ballet and tap class. Jody loves the teacher and enjoys the dancing, but what really rocks her world are the crushed velvet leotards with matching bias-cut skirts that stand out straight when she twirls. Everybody knows that no baby on this planet can have a skirt that does that!

Mommy to the Rescue

It helps an awful lot if your portrayal of the rosy future clearly includes YOU in all the fun. Since toddlers are most anxious about losing their strong attachment to mom, growing up and getting the "privilege" to go away for playdates or to start preschool is not all that enticing. My Girlfriend Annette, who is a genius in many areas of her life, including parenting, noticed this ambivalence in her daughter Ronni. Annette helped save the day by instituting "Sparkly Saturdays." Since Annette is a very senior executive in a major corporation and must work long hours occasionally and sometimes travels abroad, she committed to a schedule of Saturday morning manicures for herself and little Ronni. Since Ronni always picks the brightest polishes in the palette, Annette started calling their manicures "sparklies." After their grooming is complete, they often walk up and down the street letting the polish dry and window shopping. Ronni would be the first to tell you that babies can't have sparklies because they're too small and they might put the polished finger in their mouth and they don't know how to sit nicely in the manicurist's chair and say thank you.

When my fourth baby reached the second half of toddlerhood and was showing signs of wanting to return to my womb, one of the tricks that got me through was letting her help with chores around the house. Don't wet yourself laughing here, Girlfriend! Toddlers think washing dishes and stirring things in bowls are very exotic endeavors, and now is not the time to burst their bubble. My little domestic goddess had a special talent for folding things, don't ask me why, so when she needed to be needed as a "grown-up," I would give her a pile of hand towels and washcloths from the dryer and have her fold beside me while I did something, anything, else. She was so proud of her creases and the way the towels stacked nicely, and I made a big deal of her skill and artistry. It reminded me for the hundredth time that mastery of a big kid skill is one of the most wonderful feelings in toddlerhood.

Several years ago a job I had sent me to Nepal of all places to work on a documentary. Don't stop reading; I promise not to bore you with my travelogue! I mention it now because I was stunned at how four-year-olds walked the streets with tiny babies in their arms, and quite competently, I might add. They explained that it was their responsibility to care for their younger siblings, and they took great pride in their job. I'm not saying I would trust any baby of mine to the care of your average pre-K kid, but it did occur to me that Nepal might have less trouble with this toddler ambivalence thing than we do because they understood toddlerhood as staying close within the family, but moving up a rung in seniority. Have I integrated what I've learned from my world travels into raising my own four darlings? Of course not; they would still let me feed them and brush their teeth for them if I'd offer.

And yet, it's worth pondering whether toddlerhood is anxious-making for our kids because it's so ill-defined. We all know what babies are, and we all know what school-age kids are, but the jury's still out on that three-year holding pattern known as toddlerhood. Perhaps we could help our little ones through this transition if we paid closer attention to their need to grow up while still knowing that they can run back into Mommy's or Daddy's arms when they need a hug. My kids have this mantra that they have repeated to me since the day they could form a sentence: "No matter how old I am, I will always be your baby." And I say, "That's right, even when you have babies of your own, you're *always* going to be Mommy's baby."

Eating (Or Not)

We're mothers. We feed children. It's our job. With infants, our role in the universe as the provider of manna is relatively simple because there are only two basic kinds: from the breast and from a bottle of formula. One simple food, with a little water for variety and hydration, and all nourishment needs are met. It's a thing of beauty. Sure, you can struggle with the decisions about breast over bottle, milk-based over soy-based, cereal versus fruit as the first solid food, but you're the only one struggling because your baby is pretty happy with whatever you choose. And, best of all, he can usually be relied upon to consume whatever you feed him, at least until you start introducing solids, but even those introductory solids are generally bland and benign. Besides, feeding babies solid food is first and foremost a spectator sport for the parents and other loving relatives. Who really cares whether that cereal makes it all the way past the esophagus; the fun is in watching the baby try to get any of it past his moist and messy little mouth. When that infant becomes a toddler, however, the struggle becomes a duet; you're fighting to get certain foods into him and he's fighting just as hard to keep them out. Alternatively, she's fighting to get her hands on forbidden foods while you fight to hide them from her.

Perfunctory Disclaimer

I mentioned this once before in *The Girlfriends' Guide to Surviving the First Year of Motherhood*, but it will make me feel like I'm completely up front with you if I say it again: I am not, nor are my Girlfriends, nutrition experts, and we would all feel a heck of a lot better if you didn't rely on us for any hard science. We don't really know our enzymes from our electrolytes, and we do not purport to be authorities on anything beyond our personal parenting experiences. This chapter is not about keeping our toddlers in any "zones," discovering the toddler gourmet within or the merits of baby food combining. Our goal, simply put, is to encourage you not to kill yourself when you haven't gotten anything but corn dogs (albeit lowfat turkey corn dogs) and watermelon into your child in two weeks. It's not about simple versus complex carbohydrates, it's about not getting a complex yourself when your toddler sticks his simple carbohydrate (read: carrot) up his nose. There are certain mealtime behaviors that are as common in toddlers as runny noses, and in this chapter we hit most of them. If we can throw in a suggestion, a useful tip or even just a joke, then we'll all feel much better.

Why the Fuss?

Food is a battlefield for most toddlers and their parents because of the simple element of choice. Choices have to be made about when to eat, how much to eat, where to eat, how to eat and, most critically, what to eat. Inevitably, Mommy will have an opinion where these choices are concerned, and almost as inevitably, her toddler's opinion will be "NO!" Is it "NO" because they really can't face a plate of salad or is it "NO" because that's the opposite of what you want? Probably both. Toddlers are often suspicious of new foods just on principle, AND toddlers are little humans struggling to wrest some of the power over their little universes from their omnipotent mommies. If you haven't noticed how often your toddler doesn't want to do what you suggest, then you just aren't paying attention, Girlfriend.

This wicket becomes particularly sticky when we moms add our own insecurities and ambivalence about food to the equation. We offer wholesome meals three times a day, since that's how we think we're supposed to do it, and when our toddlers don't play along, we feel this irresistible urge to force them. We are the bosses here, we reason, and it's up to us to determine the eating habits of all people too young to know not to eat chalk or put food in their ears. Right, Mom. It's time for that lead a horse to water analogy again.

Choice pops up in such subtle ways that we often don't notice it. For example, you serve cubed chicken pieces, applesauce and peas. Your little gourmet eats the applesauce in one handful, pops in a few peas and completely rejects the chicken. Do you remove the plate, wipe her face and hands and announce that the meal is over? Not in a million years. You start gently, "Did you taste the yummy chicken Mommy made for you, Molly?" No response. "Take three bites of the yummy chicken, Molly, then Mommy will give you frozen yogurt for dessert." No response. "Please, Molly, just do this one little thing for Mommy; take one taste and you can have frozen yogurt with sprinkles on it for dessert." The chicken and its melamine plate land on the kitchen floor with a clatter like plastic cymbals. "Molly, no dessert for you! No throwing food in this house! Now, how about a bologna sandwich instead of chicken?"

You know this drill as well as I do. Who do you think is wielding the power here? We moms have about as much backbone as an earthworm in these eating crises. Even though it's apparent to all of us that this whole exchange could have been avoided in several ways, this is where most of us end up. Once again, out of a lethal combination of our deep desire to be perfect mothers and our general lack of experience with toddlers, we end up in a sort of feeding quicksand: The more we struggle to stay afloat and succeed in the eating wars, the deeper we sink into the mire.

Just think of that scene in *Oliver* when the hungry little boy actually overcomes his terror to ask for "More, please" of the dreadful gruel he was served. You didn't see little Ollie ask if he could have chicken fingers instead. He knew that gruel was the meal of the day and there were no choices in the matter. I'm not suggesting that you just pass out the Blue Plate Special to your toddler every day and tell him to like it or lump it, even though that was considered completely acceptable parenting up until very recently. No, I'm saying control the choices by limiting them to two things you can live with. When lunch time is near, try asking "Which would you like, chicken fingers or a tuna sandwich for lunch, Big Boy? If they respond by suggesting yet another dish, try to stick to your guns and repeat the offer of tuna or chicken. The message is this: "Mommy wants to serve you a healthy meal that you'd like, but she'll be damned if she is going to spend two hours every day offering more 'specials' than the waiters at Tavern on the Green." If your toddler rejects your choices completely, take a deep breath, muster your self-control and calmly announce that lunch will not be served as planned. This will be physically painful for you because most of us mothers live in mortal fear that our children will starve to death if a single meal is missed. Trust the Girlfriends when we tell you now: THIS IS ABSOLUTELY NOT TRUE.

How Much Is Enough? How Much Is Too Much?

Still, you're muttering, you can't just neglect a toddler's dietary needs: This is the time of such explosive growth and essential brain development. You're right! And this is another sand trap for us parents yearning to shoot par. We want someone to prescribe just the right nutritional and caloric intake for our toddlers. Unfortunately, feeding toddlers has not yet been reduced to a science, and we moms have a lot of ad libbing and intuiting to do in this area.

Since toddlers don't spew out data on whether they are getting enough of the "right" things to eat, we mothers watch for more subtle indications. We call our sisters and ask how much our nieces and nephews ate when they were this age. We read books and magazines for dietary prescriptions for the different stages of toddlerhood. We ask our pediatricians, nurses, Mommy and Me group leaders and the lady handing out free samples of SpaghettiOs in the supermarket. Then we combine that information, uninformed as it may be, with our own gut feelings about how our toddlers are eating. We start by trying to get a protein, a vegetable and a carbohydrate on the plate and then hope for the best. We watch in anguish and frustration as they eat the bread, take one bite of the ground turkey and smear the creamed broccoli all over the high chair or toddler table.

One of the most compelling indicators of whether our children are eating properly is their appearance. I'm not saying this is a good indicator or the only indicator, just the most common. A toddler so slender that you can play his rib cage like a xylophone sends most moms into fits of worry that he's hovering near starvation. A toddler with so many folds of fat around her wrists that it looks like she's slipped rubber bands around them has many of us searching the grocery aisles for Toddler Lean Cuisines or Slim Fast in disposable baby bottles. The Girlfriends and I can tell you from now till we have to leave to break up a sandbox tussle that the best sign of good nutrition in a toddler is his trademark boundless energy and appetite for life, but you will still rely on his height and weight as the most tangible indicators of your darling's health. What's so surprising about that in a society where 60 percent of couples in a recent survey indicated they would terminate a pregnancy that showed the fetus had a good chance of being an obese adult? We're obsessed with body image, and we apply it to our offspring from the minute they're placed in our arms.

If you doubt what I'm saying, ask your mommy friends whether they are satisfied with how much their toddlers are eating. Then get ready for the tidal wave of emotion that will spill over the room. The fact is, mothers of toddlers secretly suspect their child is on the verge of starvation given how little and infrequently he eats, or they are phobic that Junior loves his food so much that he's going to take after the "big boned" members in his daddy's family. I have been in mommy discussion groups about toddler eating habits where at least one of the moms melted into a puddle of tears over her failure to get her daughter to accept the concept of "three squares a day." I have also been asked countless times by mothers of two- and three-year-olds whether a child's protruding belly meant that he was getting too fat.

Then, if there isn't enough anxiety caused by our own covert comparisons of our toddlers to the other toddlers we encounter in the course of a day, every six months or so we take them to the pediatrician who informs us that our little angel is in the "57th percentile for height and the 99th percentile for weight." What the heck is that supposed to mean? Is our deep desire to have "normal" children the same as wanting them to be "average"? That's a big N-O if you accept my anecdotal research on the matter. Every mother alive wants her boys to be taller than the national average, and heavier would be okay, too, because that just means he's strong and healthy. As for toddler daughters, mothers are still known to crow about their daughters' stature (another Uma Thurman in the making?), but any weight percentile over the sixtieth gives them panicky flashbacks to their own pudgy childhood or one spent ostracizing the girl who was. Once again, our love for our children combines with our desire to correct all the wrongs of our own childhoods to make us completely mental about our toddlers.

What Does a Healthy Toddler Look Like?

The answer is, pretty much like you and/or your mate looked at her age. That's right, a lot of it seems to be in the genes. Some toddlers look like the stereotype: rounded bellies, chubby thighs and short pudgy arms. Others, however, are as lean as Gandhi and look like they've been assembled with Tinkertoys. More to the meat of the issue (yeah, I get the pun), they are usually equally healthy. One of the most surprising things about our toddlers' physical appearance is how little it ultimately has to do with how they look at age six, age ten and age sixteen. My Girlfriend Candy's daughter Fiona towered over her elementary school classmates, but by puberty, she seems to have peaked at a very petite five feet two. My Girlfriend Laura's son David, who couldn't have weighed more than fifty pounds fully dressed and after a bar mitzvah buffet when he entered sixth grade, stretched up to over six feet tall by high school. Go figure!

Can You Tell by Looking?

I wish I could suggest "moderation in everything" and that would do the trick, but it rarely does. My darling skinny husband has scratchy old

8-millimeter home movies of him being chased around an amusement park near Coney Island with his mother begging him to eat while she pursued him with a drippy ice-cream cone. Clearly, she was convinced he was famished. From the look on his face, you would have sworn she was chasing him with a stun gun, he was so uninterested in eating that cone. Now, at the age of forty-five (I married a *much* older man!), he is the darling of cardiologists from coast to coast because of his lack of adipose tissue, but you'd have never convinced his mom that failing to get a few licks of that ice cream in him was anything short of child abuse.

My own personal toddler tale of parental feeding lunacy can be conjured up in three simple words: Blue Pleated Skirt. For the Easter of my fourth year, my mom bought me a navy blue pleated skirt, a middy blouse with a sailor collar and white patent leather Mary Janes and matching frilled anklets. I'm not even going to get into the part about how she set my flossy little toddler hair in brush rollers (look for them in the Cosmetology Hall of Fame) and styled it with heavy aerosol hairspray, since it's redundant after *Mommy Dearest.* Anyway, after I was dressed in my darling little Shirley Temple outfit with my Doris Day hair and ready to get into the car to go to Sunday school, my mother whispered some advice that has stayed with me to this day, "Hold your tummy in so that your skirt hangs nicer."

Okay, it's not that unusual for parents to look at the protruding tummies of toddlers and wonder if they they indicate potbellies for life, but for heaven's sake! Has anyone ever heard the term *projection?* Let me tell all of you wondering mommies once and for all: *Toddlers' tummies protrude because of an immaturity of the abdominal muscles, not because they are overflowing with fat.* I'm not saying I needed that ice-cream cone my mother-in-law was pushing, but I'm pretty darn certain I wasn't a candidate for Jenny Craig yet, either.

I share these painful and oh-so-vivid memories of my youthful spouse and my own reasonably well-preserved self not to involve you in our personal issues, but to show how two perfectly well-intentioned mommies just couldn't leave well enough alone because one of us looked like he had a total body fat of less than 3 percent and the other of us looked like she was on her way to living to eat rather than eating to live. As it turns out, neither my husband nor I is very tall nor very wide and we've spawned a foursome of kids who will all probably be able to fit in clothes straight off the rack (unless, of course, this video game addiction doesn't wind down in the next couple of years).

What Do Toddlers Actually Eat?

You may not agree with me now, but one of the most amusing things about toddlers is the neck-snapping speed with which they change their likes and dislikes in all things, particularly food. This can be crazy-making for those of us moms who don't have the time or inclination to prepare entire meals that were acceptable yesterday but rejected today, but it does keep things interesting. Nearly every toddler's mom, like my sister-in-law and her first child, has a story about how their toddler lived on dry toast and apple juice for what seemed like six months, and then one morning refused to even allow the toast on her breakfast plate for fear it would contaminate the egg sitting nearby. Then it's on to the next food fetish, like scrambled eggs and creamed corn for another agonizing (at least for the mother) few months. (By the way, that toddler is now twenty years old and staying with me for the summer. I still have to contain my ecstasy when I see him dive into a Caesar salad or have second helpings of grilled sea bass, we were so traumatized by his eating habits seventeen years ago.)

Mothers can make themselves crazy trying to determine which foods are "appropriate" for their toddlers. If you care to take a broader look at the misconception that there is proper toddler food and all the rest should be rejected, just consider what you feed your child compared to what a mother in the Arctic Circle or a mother in China feeds her toddler. These kids don't just spend their childhoods eating bologna sandwiches and carrots sticks and then suddenly develop a taste for seal blubber or curried rice and dried fish. Toddlers can thrive on all sorts of diets that don't appeal to you, so try to keep an open mind. Try not to impose your food prejudices on your child as you introduce him to the smorgasbord of life.

Just because lima beans stimulate your gag reflex doesn't mean you need to scowl and make furball noises when you serve them to your little one.

Now that I've encouraged you to consider the universe when trying to help your toddler find a satisfying and healthy diet, let me pull back a little bit: Some of the most amusing things I read in parenting books and magazines are recipes to "keep your toddler's diet varied and interesting." What a bunch of hooey. I know we've never formally met, yet I am willing to bet that you have more important things to do than subscribe to *Toddler Gourmet Magazine*. As I suggested with my illustration of international toddler palates, these little people don't require as much imagination and preparation as you might think to be culinarily satisfied. If the family meal can be modified to suit your toddler, then by all means, serve him the house special. Otherwise, try to keep meal preparation as simple and efficient as possible. Most toddlers are slightly obsessive/compulsive and definitely resistant to change. If anyone needs variety or interest in a meal, it's the mother who prepares it and is certain she will have a psychotic episode if she serves one more meal of buttered noodles, sliced bananas and peas. The Girlfriends' advice to you is, if you hit the lottery and discover a reasonably healthy meal that your child likes, try to stick to variations on that theme. Most nutritionists recommend that you don't repeat each meal ingredient for ingredient because you can compensate for any nutritional limitations by substituting, say, rice for the beloved pasta at one meal and papaya for banana at the next. Then again, if he doesn't go for it, relax and follow his regimen; he'll change it before it stunts his growth or shrinks his brain.

Meals as Early Education

There is a lot to be learned during toddler meals besides eating. For example, this is the beginning of the tradition of "breaking the bread" in a social setting. That's why parents should rarely, if ever, leave their toddlers on their own to eat their meals. I don't just mean you should supervise them to make sure they don't choke or leap from their high chairs; I mean you should try to spend time sitting with them, talking and making the meal relaxing and fun. This is a tall order for those of you who have a new baby in the house, too, but it's truly worth trying to schedule a baby nap and a toddler meal to coincide at least once a day.

Those of you who are particularly stouthearted can even try including your toddler in your family meal, although I personally found this experience gave me a gastrointestinal disorder. It was much more enjoyable for me to have a private lunch with my toddlers while everyone else was otherwise occupied than to try to get a dinner on the table, keep my toddler from pouring his milk into the dog's mouth from his sippy cup, ask my husband how his day was in a halfway sincere way, keep the older kids from kicking each other under the table and trying to remember to chew my own food before swallowing it. Still, with more and more of us working during the day, a private luncheon with our toddlers can be pretty hard to come by. If that's the case in your family, the Girlfriends suggest a compromise meal. Perhaps your sitter or you can serve dinner to your toddler between five and six o'clock, then, when the older members of the family are ready to sit down for your meal, invite the little one to join you for dessert or a little extra pasta or even just a glass of water. That way he will get to be part of the family rhythm and ritual without the trauma of getting overtired or overhungry, and you will be able to digest your meal because you'll know your child has already met his nutritional needs for the day.

Mealtime is also when we teach our children that eating is an activity all to itself and should be respected as such. Perhaps if we didn't consider eating an adjunct to watching television or playing with toys (or talking on the phone, Girlfriend!), our kids would be more aware than we are about how much they have eaten and when they are full. I live in a glass house as far as eating habits are concerned, but I would humbly suggest that you don't eat your meals over the sink or out of the refrigerator when your toddler can see you. Our message to our children should be that good food is good for us and good fun in moderation. It is not something we begrudge ourselves or adopt as a hobby, but what we do out of respect for our bodies. Then again, there should be no such thing as cellulite and PMS, so I may be whistling into the wind on this one.

While the Girlfriends profoundly respect the educational value of toddler meals, I must confess to one pet peeve. I've noticed some parents are so eager to create toddler *bon vivants* that they use their mealtimes as mini-enrichment programs. I have been in several mommy groups where one or another of the moms announced with pride that her little Harry just loved sushi or Thai food, as if it indicated a sophistication and taste beyond his years. I suppose the implication is that any child who is still scarfing up Kraft macaroni and cheese is culturally disadvantaged or even backward.

Risk Rejection and Keep Offering the Good Stuff

The most essential bit of reassurance we can offer you, the mother of a toddler food fetishist, is this: As far as we Girlfriends know, no child has ever died from a voluntary lack of certain food groups. You and your mother may swear that she's cruising full speed ahead toward a glacier called Eating Disorders, but Mother Nature will compel her to eat what she really, really needs if it's made available to her. And therein lies the moral of this story: Even if you know that your child will never qualify as a member of the Clean Plate Club, try to offer a variety of nutritious foods at least three times a day. I'm not saying you should waste money and food by preparing large quantities of things like navy bean soup and cauliflower when you're reasonably certain your toddler will gag if he tastes them; just go ahead and toss a small portion of the nutritious stuff that you and Daddy are eating for dinner on your toddler's plate on the off chance that he'll eat it. You may be pleasantly surprised. Then again, you may end up with salad on your wallpaper, so be prepared for anything.

The Dreaded Veggies

I will never, ever understand why Mother Nature made Brussels sprouts taste like dirty sneakers and chocolate cream pie taste like heaven and then asked us to eschew the pie and force the sprouts. What did we mothers ever do to deserve a sentence like that? And it's not just a battle to be waged once and then forgotten. Oh, no, we, like Sisyphus, have to push those vegetables day after day with no amount ever being enough to hold the kid for the rest of his life. Sure, proteins, legumes and carbs are of concern to us moms, but they never wreak the same emotional havoc as vegetables. This food group taunts us because its nutritional value is indisputable, but it comes hidden in food textures, tastes and aromas that make most toddlers dive under the nearest bed. A vegetable is no longer just a simple thing like a carrot or a stick of celery; it is the standard by which me measure our parenting success. Our toddler may count to a thousand, use the potty with skill and flair and possess the gregariousness of George Hamilton, but if he lives on turkey dogs and yogurt, we are as shamed as if he were a crack addict.

I don't think I know a mother of a toddler (at least an honest one without major delusional disorders) who thinks she is doing a good enough job in the fruits and vegetables area. I've spent so many hours in mommies' groups where every mother in the room has wept in silent solidarity with the hysterical mom sharing her tales of a child who refused to eat anything that was green or orange, that I can't help but feel my heart leap with joy any time I see a toddler, any toddler, swallow a pea. After raising four toddlers, who on any given day would *still* choose pizza over anything, I can't even watch a TV show without searching the dinner plates in every meal scene to see if all the major food groups are adequately represented. I know other kinds of children exist; in fact yesterday, my Girlfriend Carol's daughter went without eating lunch because pizza was all that was served. She actually waited good-naturedly until Carol arrived with little Ziploc bags of fresh carrot sticks and some multigrain roll with a little cream cheese on it. I think she may have even asked for water to wash it down, but by that time I was so busy chasing my caffeinated kids, who'd been sipping colas all afternoon, that I couldn't stop to notice. These wonder children may exist, but not in my house.

What They Don't Know Won't Hurt Them

If your toddler sounds a little more like my kids than Carol's, you might be interested in some veggie psych-outs that the Girlfriends and I have collected over the years. These are little tricks we have discovered for getting those vegetables into our suspicious toddlers without their knowing. Starting with the premise that most kids don't like seeing the veggies on their plates, it makes sense that disguising them is a good place to start. One of the all-time great disguises is soup. I am the last one to extol the virtues of cooking, since I can't even find a spatula when I need one and my measuring spoons were long ago turned into bath toys, but I will go out on a limb here and encourage you to make your own soup stock.

Relax; this is nothing more than filling a big pot with water and throwing in every vegetable in your crisper drawer. Don't worry about whether your toddler likes any of these ingredients, because most of them will be thrown out or so well stewed that they won't be noticed. After an hour or so of simmering all these wonderful foods in a pot, the glorious nutrients are released into the stock. After they are all limp and well-souped, remove the veggies and add cooked chicken or turkey pieces and some rice, pastina or noodles and serve it up. Whatever you've got left can be refrigerated or frozen for later use such as pureeing those veggies your toddler will eat without disguise. I've relied on variations of this soup-stock-stew-sauce magic fortified liquid to get some really ghastly (at least as far as my toddlers were concerned) green and orange foods into them, and it always left me with a pleasant afterglow that was as satisfying as any sex I could recall.

Another very clever ruse for those of you yearning to ply your toddlers with unpopular vegetables is the shredding technique. This approach calls for grating the carrots and zucchini and broccoli on a cheese grater or disintegrating them in a blender or Cuisinart (see, you knew that wedding gift would come in handy some day!) and mixing them into meat loaf or burgers. Since both those dishes are really more about the ketchup or other condiments than about the meat product itself, you can really smuggle some good vegetables past the palate patrol. Remember, don't ruin a good thing by going overboard here. If your burgers look distinctly orange or have green chunks sticking out, you have not only succeeded in ruining that particular meal, but you have set up a scenario of mistrust on the part of your toddler. If you get a teaspoon's worth of the forbidden food into a burger, consider your responsibility as a manna provider met.

Still another ruse is the one used by my Girlfriend Alison. She belonged to the Cult of Velveeta. Just as ketchup or seasoned bread crumbs can mask the taste of the more benign vegetables, Velveeta, that famous cheese food, got Alison's boys to dig into a plate of beans or cauliflower with gusto. Knowing my kids, they would have licked off all the cheesy parts and left the nutritious stuff untouched. Hers, however, were good sports and had a simple belief that good foods, if tolerable to ingest, would make them big and strong. I suppose the question eventually arises: When is the disguise so unhealthy that it negates the value of the veggie it's trying to hide?

I don't really know the answer to that. I remember when my husband told his mother, one of the all-time great cooks, that he was giving up all salt and sugar from his diet; her famous eggplant parmigiana went to hell in a hand basket. As she explained to me in tears, eggplants are born bitter and it's up to us mothers to give them their magical taste. Look, if vegetables were so deliriously delicious in their natural state, why do you think onion dip and ranch dressing were invented? Anyway, I don't have any pat answer for this dilemma. If your instinct tells you that the veggie-to-vehicle ratio is reasonable, it probably is. Still, it doesn't hurt to discuss your individual child's diet with your pediatrician, especially if he or she thinks calories and cholesterol are concerns.

Vitamin Supplements

Then again, your sensible doctor might just tell you to relax and give your toddler a Flintstone's vitamin (or some comparable multi) every morning. Many pediatricians are firm believers in the value of sustaining a toddler's nutrititional needs during times of dietary intolerance. I have friends whose children have been on supplements of one kind or another since infancy. I usually keep a supply of tasty orange-flavored chewable vitamin C on hand and feed them to my troops during flu season, just in case Linus Pauling was right. My pediatrician is also a firm believer in making sure my daughters get enough calcium in their diets, since we all know that bone density and growth is largely established at puberty, and he prescribes a benign-tasting liquid supplement for me to slip into their food unnoticed. Dentists, too, might have some recommendations for supplements in toddlers, like fluoride, either in the form of little tablets or often in bottled water from companies like Sparkletts. Ask the pros, then do what your best instinct decides. You can make your toddler, and you, neurotic if you start going too far with this supplement business. Have confidence in the food you serve, even if it isn't always spa cuisine; your child will make it through this agonizing food stage and be a lot more cooperative in a year or two.

Sugar and Toddlers

I just have to get on my soapbox here about sugar. I am willing to bet good money, especially if this is your first child, that you have all sorts of highfalutin notions about protecting him from that dread substance, sugar. Sure, we moms aren't big fans of pesticides, fatty foods or foods that have been so processed that they no longer share the same molecular structure as their namesake, but sugar has emerged as the boogeyman of our generation. We read the small print on baby-food labels, we limit juice intake and we do our darndest to convince our snack-obsessed kids that popcorn-flavored rice cakes are comparable to Oreos and Popsicles. I remember taking my firstborn to a birthday party and snottily declining the cake on the premise that sugar would not pass my beloved's lips.

You know what? I'm not going to get in the way of your sugar boycott. You're absolutely right; processed sugar is junk food and is best avoided for as long as possible. But as your Girlfriend, I feel compelled to tell you that one of these days, your little purist is going to get a lick of ice cream or a sip of Kool-Aid, and he will think he met his Creator. You can control first babies and toddlers and keep them hermetically sealed for the first couple of years, but sooner or later, some sugar pusher (often a grandparent, I must warn) is going to give them their first high. Then you have to learn the art of parental pragmatism, which goes something like this:

A little bit of anything isn't going to hurt her.

Let me share with you the story of my first child and his best friend. I begin by confessing my son saw me eat peanut clusters while I nursed him. I don't live on sweets, but if I am going to indulge, it's going to be chocolate and it will probably have nuts. My treasured friend, the mother of my son's best friend, didn't even have sugar for cooking in her house. She bought the occasional "health food" cookie (which her darling daughter pronounced "tookie," to our great delight and amusement) or passed out the whole-grain graham crackers sweetened with fructose, but you couldn't find a Chips Ahoy in her pantry if your life depended on it.

My son knew that his food—everything from Fruit Roll-ups to cheddar cheese crackers—was stocked in our pantry beside Mom's candy, a case of diet soda and Daddy's chocolate snaps. Amazingly, he didn't turn into the junk-food junkie that all this exposure would suggest. It didn't occur to him that simply because adult food commingled with kid food he was entitled to everything in the pantry. On the contrary, sweets seemed to be pretty insignificant; just another type of food that had its time and place.

His healthy friend, however, turned into a sugar hoarder. She never went ape for the ice cream and chocolate stuff, but she couldn't sleep if she didn't have several red Twizzlers and gummy bears hidden under her bed and behind her toy box. She lives about three minutes away by car, but until she was about nine years old, she never left our house without packing a "to go" bag of Ritz Bits, Fritos and whatever the "tookie" of the week was to sustain her through the journey. This little scout would take her Halloween loot, immediately bury it or stash it under doll collections or in pretend kitchens, and ration it out till July. She knew what every house offered the trick-or-treaters (and which houses she wouldn't bother with next October). My son, on the other hand, while no example of better living through clean living, was very blasé about piñatas (which I hate on principle), Halloween and Christmas stockings. I still steal two thirds of his take from him a day or two later, when he has forgotten about it.

The moral here, at least while I'm on this soapbox, is that there is a risk when we parents designate certain foods more "powerful" or "evil" than others, especially when those foods are promoted so heavily on TV that whole cartoons are designed around them. You are already quite familiar with the contrariness of toddlers, so why in the world would you want to bait them by telling them certain foods are absolutely off-limits? This isn't like saying running into parking lots or putting fingers into electrical sockets is forbidden because those acts are ALWAYS against the rules. The sugar rule, however, unless you intend to stalk your child, is going to be broken again and again by very well-intentioned and loving people (including, when you are desperate to get out of a grocery store without living through a scene of *The Possessed*).

There is one last thing I want to say about sugar before dropping the subject for the rest of the book: All the recent scientific studies indicate that sugar does not make children hyper. Don't everybody scream at me at once; I understand if you think you have lots of anecdotal evidence that eating a Hershey bar turns your toddler into Dr. Jekyll, but I don't happen to believe it was the Hershey bar's fault. If it is, then your toddler's pancreas isn't doing its job, and you should consult your pediatrician to check for diabetes, hypoglycemia or some other medical explanation. Mothers across the country have tales about birthday parties where cake and ice cream were served and they were left with unguided missiles for children; missiles that eventually crashed and burned. That may be true, but it's only fair to consider whether all that socializing with other little bundles of dynamite, intense stimulation from Moon Bounces, or controlled terror at the appearance of Beauty and the Beast facsimiles might have played any role in the emotional Chernobyl that toddlers usually experience after a party.

There, I've vented my spleen on the sugar issue. The only advice I can add is for the health of the parents as well as the child: Keep most of the junk food out of the house—no one needs that kind of temptation.

Who's Feeding Whom?

Far more amusing, at least in hindsight, than *what* our toddlers eat is *how* they eat. Keep in mind that these little creatures were recently completely dependent on some loving outside person to make sure that their food got to their insides. Now, consistent with their developmental eruptions and fireworks, they have gained the coordination for and the satisfaction of serving themselves to a great extent. You might think that this growth and achievement would be so liberating for parents that there would be a cheer heard through the land. But listen, not a sound.

That's because there is a very large learning curve between being a spoon-fed baby to knowing which butter knife to use. During the three years of toddlerhood, children aren't so concerned with how they get the food into their mouths as they are with getting it there. Even then, they aren't particularly interested in taking the most expedient route from plate to mouth: They may want to mush it around a little, see what happens when they put it on their head or try giving themselves a facial with it; and that's just the stuff that they haven't already dropped on the floor. Eating, especially for young toddlers, is a lot like John Belushi's cafeteria scene in *Animal House*. They want to know how much food they can stuff into their mouths at one time, what it looks like when it has been chewed and spit back out and if two-fisted eating is twice as good as one.

How you and your toddler will peacefully coexist during these meals is a very personal matter to be worked out between the two of you. Let's start with the premise that you should encourage your emerging human to feed herself as much as possible; this is a combination of fine and gross (emphasis on the gross) motor skills, and they are going to have to learn to do it for themselves one of these days. Besides, anyone who has seen *9 1/2 Weeks* knows how recreational food can be.

That said, let's get a little more real. First of all, many of us mothers know that, if left to manage themselves at each meal, our children would spend an hour or two just fingerpainting in the yams. Second, since discipline is a very new concept for toddlers, just giving them the order not to spill their yogurt onto the floor is usually not particularly effective; there need to be constant surveillance and reminders. And last, while some toddlers are neat and tidy not only at mealtime but throughout the day, most of their peers go through more costume changes in a day than a Vegas showgirl, and no one really needs to sit back and watch her little one paint on his T-shirt with beets. Clearly, some parental control is required for those of us who don't have one of those neatniks, endless free time, or a kitchen that can be hosed down after every meal.

How much control that is varies from mommy to mommy. Living in sunny California, and never finding a bib that provided everything I needed from a garment, I often took my children's shirts off at mealtime to avoid that extra load of laundry. I also owned two of what they call "splat mats" in the children's mail-order catalogs. They are those plastic squares that are large enough to be placed under the high chair or booster seat and catch 90 percent of the spillage from a toddler meal. Having two gave me a chance to take one outside and rinse it off while having a fresh one at the ready. With those two basic precautions taken, I pretty much left my kids to have at it at mealtime. I am one of those people who think that toddlers, by definition, are humorous, and a baby with nectarine pieces styling its hair in a pompadour just cracks me up.

Not so for some of my favorite Girlfriends and relatives. I am not exaggerating one bit when I tell you that my sister-in-law used to prepare for a toddler meal by setting out one or two dampened (with water about 98.6 degrees) paper towels and one or two dry towels right beside them. She would then keep the toddler's food on the dining table next to her; NOT ON THE HIGHCHAIR TRAY, and she would spoon or fork each bite into the child's mouth. After every single bite, I kid you not, she would wipe the child's mouth, first with the damp towel and then with the dry. Every single bite! And guess what? Her mother did the exact same thing! Neither of them could stand the sight of a child with *schmutz* on its little mouth or hands. I have to confess that, whenever I would take my kids to visit them, I would serve them things like SpaghettiOs and not even give them utensils, just to see my in-laws squirm. They were so sweet and respectful of my mothering turf that they never so much as sneaked a wipe in, but you could see the beads of sweat forming on their hairlines.

Toddlers on the Town

In case you haven't noticed yet, there are many things that are more easily done with a baby in tow than with a toddler. Airplane travel leaps to mind, but a close second is dining in a restaurant. Whether it's because we don't have a sitter to free us up for a meal out or because we think it's "fun" for our toddlers to eat saltine crackers and terrorize the other diners while waiting for a half-portion of macaroni and cheese that she won't like, we frequently pack up the family and dine out. Unless you are eating in a place that gives toys with its meals, provides paper and crayons to young clients, or is in other ways expressly "child friendly," this is never a good idea. Pizza parlors, the local diner or a casual place with outdoor seating may be okay, but that's probably about it for tots in restaurants.

On behalf of the food servers, restaurateurs and fellow diners, I just have to tell you that eating near toddlers has nearly everyone reaching for the Mylanta. Look, I'm a mother, too, and I know how superior your toddler is to the general riffraff found in the toddler community. I know how well behaved he nearly always is, and I'm also completely convinced that the other people in the restaurant will be enchanted by his cowboy boots, matching hat and holster, *with gun*. You have to believe me when I tell you that if people wanted a kiddie show while they paid $30 for a meal for two, they would have gone to Disney World.

It's time someone told the besotted mothers and fathers of this country that taking children who still eat with their hands to dine in restaurants is cruel and unusual punishment, both for the other diners and for the child. Kids this age have no patience and get claustrophobic in a booth. They are also guaranteed to spill any drink within reach, wield the knives and forks like instruments of torture and push their feet against the dining table hard enough to make their own seat tumble backward in a horrifying clatter.

Kids in restaurants can also be dangerous. As a former waitress, I have horror stories of small children running wildly around the tables and colliding with a food server who was carrying a pot of coffee or a tray of four bowls of steaming soup. Even parents who don't have a cocktail with their meal seem to be inebriated when eating out: They think that the rest of the patrons are *de facto* baby-sitters, and that their darling dervishes are fine as long as they don't go out the front door. This is not only naive, it's disrespectful, and, as your Girlfriend, I'd like to point this out to you. Unlike air travel, where you don't really have any other choice except to drive the million miles to Grandma's house, eating out is almost always optional. Unless you have recently sustained a kitchen fire and have no other way to feed your child, there is always the choice to leave the kids at home. Besides, no mother has ever in the history of parenthood successfully digested a meal shared in public with a toddler. Give yourself a much-needed and well-deserved reward and save restaurants for those rare moments spent with other grown-ups.

Safety First, Last and Always

Because food is such a fun and total-body experience for toddlers, there are some typical behaviors you really have to watch out for. These little darlings are notorious for mistaking nonfoods for food, confusing ears and noses for mouths and believing they can swallow what they can't chew. We can't stress enough how important it is for you not only to expect this behavior but to prepare for it.

The first and, for my money, most important act of preparation you can take as a parent is to learn the Heimlich maneuver and CPR. Toddlers, like babies, consider their mouths one of their most tactile organs, and they don't consider any experience complete without tasting the fascinating new thing. Also, now that they have a nearly complete set of choppers, biting or chewing are also favorite parts of the getting-to-know-you ritual. Nearly every mother I know has a choking incident in her early parenting experience, and while most of them turn out all right, there is no reason not to hedge your bets for when your turn presents itself.

As you probably know, the Heimlich maneuver is a life-saving technique to get a choking object out of a person's windpipe. You've seen how it's done on adults; the rescuer stands behind the choker and forces his fist up and under her rib cage. While the principle is the same for children, the techniques have been significantly adjusted to allow for their smaller and more fragile bodies. A good class at your local YMCA or community center will give you two or three ways to dislodge choking objects from a little one. Different symptoms or objects require different techniques, so you must educate yourself, and anyone else who cares for your toddler (like spouses, sitters and grandparents) in all of them. While you're at it, a refresher course on infant and child first aid and CPR is a good idea, too.

Most medical-type parenting books (as opposed to the Girlfriends' Guides, which are almost exclusively anecdotal and emotional) recognize the risk of choking in toddlers and they list certain foods that present such a risk. Some things, like hard candies and hot dog slices, are obvious risks. Other foods, however, look safe and inviting and yet can lead to catastrophe. Grapes are one of the first foods that come to mind. They seem so wholesome and healthy, but they are slippery as all get out and often slide right past the teeth into the throat. Go ahead and serve grapes; after all, they are one of the few universally loved toddler fruits, but cut them into quarters or halves first. Peanut butter is another food that surprised me with its hidden dangers. Have you ever gotten peanut butter stuck on the roof of your mouth and been unable to dredge it out? Imagine that happening to a two- or three-year-old. Not only can't they move the peanut butter, their tongues get stuck, too, and when they can't take a deep breath they panic. That, of course, takes matters from dodgy to disastrous.

There are lots of other foods to reconsider when introducing them to a toddler's diet, whether they are chunky, sticky or stringy, but I would like to take this moment to mention the most serious cause of choking of toddlers in this country—**Balloons**. I know that, technically, latex globes and their particles are not considered food, but lots of toddlers find the springy, chewy sensation of a piece of balloon as fun and satisfying as a wad of gum. Besides, I can't pass up this opportunity to share a message that could save your infant or toddler's life.

Pieces of balloons have a way of spreading out flat when swallowed and completely blocking a child's windpipe. Because they are so lightweight and the way they adhere to moist surfaces, they often don't dislodge with the Heimlich maneuver or other choking responses. The best cure here is a pound of prevention: After a birthday or other balloon celebration, make sure that you claim all balloons and pop them in an area not frequented by your child. After you've killed the balloons, take all remnants, from strings and ribbons to pieces of latex, and throw them in the outside garbage. As whimsical and romantic as a bunch of balloons can be, they can be lethal. Consider kites or banners or even mylar balloons for your next celebration, at least until your little one is old enough to know better than to put strange things in his mouth.

Once again, the refrain of this chapter on toddlers and their food is to relax and trust Mother Nature. All the Girlfriends and I promise you that your toddler will not starve to death or have his development stunted simply because he refused to take you up on your offer of nutritious food. Stand back (and try to keep your own food issues back there with you), and realize that learning to feed oneself is even more essential to a child's development than potty training or sleeping in a bed. Relax and let the mastery take its own pace. It will be years before your sweetie is invited to dine at Buckingham Palace, and I promise you, well before that time, he will have stopped throwing his Tater Tots at the hostess. *Bon appétit!*

chapter five

Discipline

What Is Toddler Discipline?

As the mother of a toddler, you may already feel you say "no" more times in a day than you take a breath. I recall with stinging clarity the nights I would lie in bed at night and berate myself for a day spent denying my toddler things, stopping him from going where he wanted to go and interrupting all manner of rude or hazardous behavior, from nose picking to eye rubbing. Why, I moaned, why couldn't I have found a way to make the day more fun and positive for my child and me? In hindsight, I see that part of this agony inspired me to try harder to find smarter disciplining techniques, and part of the agony went with the territory.

It's a stunning discovery for the mother of a former baby who was pretty much incapable of criminal action (except for colic, which we all know is a felony), to find herself the mother of someone who constantly walks the line between crime and punishment. Mothering a toddler is a completely different sport from other kinds of mothering. Not only is there an overwhelming need to exert some sort of control over what looks like chaotic, irrational behavior, but there is also the need to start shaping your little baby into a HUMAN BEING. Both of those things require you to teach boundaries, consequences and self-control. Take it from the Girlfriends, none of these things will be fully learned during toddlerhood, so you shouldn't set unrealistic standards for you or your toddler. On the other hand, if you don't start now, it will be even harder for them to learn when they're older.

"Because I Said So."

Think of some types of discipline as memorized facts; something like the multiplication tables. Fact number one, no shoes on the bed. Fact number two, no hitting the new baby. Fact number three, no throwing food. You don't really have to waste your breath trying to explain to a person with a vocabulary of thirty words *why* these things are against the law, any more than you have to explain *why* three times five is fifteen. It just *is*. Later, when they are older and itching to question your authority and they ask exactly why it is that shoes aren't allowed on the bed, you have two options: You can either explain the need for clean sheets and the cost of laundry detergent, or you can resort to the Mother's Coda: "Because I said so."

Explaining really is the curse of the modern mother. Children, particularly toddlers, are rarely if ever interested in long-winded rationales. Think of them as editors of a huge daily metropolitan newspaper and yourself as a cub reporter: They only want the essential facts and will edit out anything that goes beyond that. I used to get frantic when my first two kids got to be about age three and asked the inevitable question "Where do babies come from, Mommy?" Immediately the room would spin and in that maelstrom I would try to carefully put together an explanation that was both age appropriate and factual. It was only by my third and fourth kids that I learned the answer that was most satisfying to a three-year-old and a three-year-old's mom:

"From the hospital, honey."

I've used this one successfully twice now, and they've never followed it up with another question, so it must have worked for them.

Mommyspeak

I talk to my children pretty much like I talk to my husband. That's not to say that I talk down to him, but rather that I talk up to my kids. People have teased me about it before, and perhaps it is a bit jarring to hear my half of a conversation and then to realize that I'm directing it to a person shorter than a yardstick, but I've never mastered that new mommyspeak where the parent refers to herself in the third person and has an arch in her voice that makes her sound slightly pained but unable to yelp out loud. You know, something like this, "Chuckie, sweetheart, Mommy's crystal vase has a boo-boo now and Mommy is very sad. Mommy loved her vase and hopes that next time Chuckie decides to empty the toilet water on the floor, which is good work, darling, Chuckie thinks to use his bathtub bucket instead."

Talking to your babies and toddlers is a marvelous and essential thing and children love it, particularly when you seem to be enjoying it, too. Why in the world should we get into the habit of spending most of our conversational time lecturing about proper behavior? It makes conversation seem like its primary function is to pontificate, and nobody likes that, except maybe the Pope. These are the magic years when language is the stuff of stories and jokes and moral support for a little person who is trying to cope with the strain of leaving babyhood behind.

My philosophy, after my education at the School of Hard Knocks, goes right smack against a lot of what you may be hearing or reading from so-called parenting experts. Partly out of humility, and partly because I don't want you to send a lynch mob out after me if my advice proves disastrous to you, I must take this moment to remind you that I have no degree in this area and I encourage you to check with the experts, read as much as you can find time for and try everything within reason. Then, if all that fails, come back and do it my way. You see, my philosophy is slightly skewed by the fact that I was raising toddlers for nine years (trust me on the numbers; four kids, each one a toddler for about three full years, and my kids roughly two years apart in age). One very important person overlooked by the many parenting authorities who espouse this overly talky, self-esteem-preserving discipline is US, *the beleaguered mommies*. Hey, we have feelings, too, you know!

There is something so artificial about us moms pretending to be all-knowing and all-tolerating. Outraged, terrified, grossed out, these are all emotions that any mother of a toddler feels washing over her like overlapping waves on the shore of her psyche. We aren't detached and professional in our mothering. We are deeply vulnerable, hopelessly devoted and slightly guilty that we don't know more about this mothering business than we do. It's sheer folly to think that today's mothers, who often work outside the home, live nowhere near their family support system of mother, sisters and cousins, and never even took home economics can just stitch together a seamless parenting plan based on books, talk shows and vague recollections of our own childhoods. The Marines are wrong; *this* is the toughest job you'll ever love.

Get Real

So does all this mean that I think mothers should run around shrieking, whining and pouring out our frustrations and resentments to hapless little toddlers? Of course not. I don't think there is any excuse for lashing out with anger or blame at the toddler (at least 99 percent of the time), but let's be real here; holding all these feelings in for three years can send a gal running for the Tagamet. The trick is to let a little emotion trickle out here and there with the intention of not letting it all compound like the national debt. A statement like "It just cracks me, Tommy, that my vanity skirt is covered with red lipstick. Now I have to throw it away or buy something off the home shopping channel to remove those stains!" honestly expresses your feelings, acknowledges that the toddler may have some understanding of the crime and the reaction, and lets you blow off some steam. After you've said that, unless Tommy then runs up and kicks you in the shins, the matter can probably end with you being more careful to put your lipstick in one of the babyproofed bathroom drawers you spent so much time and money on.

I also happen to think that maintaining a placid exterior toward your toddlers, particularly when it's not your true nature, sets them up for a monumental shock when they meet the real world. A mommyspeak mommy might gently pull away and say something benign like "Mommy doesn't like her hair patted like that," after her two-year-old has ripped a handful out with delirious glee, but if he tries that nonsense with anyone else, he's just asking for a punch in the nose. Why let him think that the world is neutral to his actions? One of the most important lessons a toddler is learning during this stage is his effect on his environment. If his parents act timid around him, he'll grow up thinking the whole community can be bullied. If his parents constantly admonish and disapprove of him, he will think the world will squash him with judgments. If he lives in a family that HE KNOWS loves him unconditionally, and sometimes doesn't much like his behavior, he can learn to adjust the behavior. Sounds simple, doesn't it? I just wish it were.

Keep in mind that the irritated emotions are certainly not the only ones that need expressing. When you and your toddler have a good, funny or endearing moment, make sure you take the time to notice it and rejoice in it. Don't get into the very lazy habit of only noticing the flare-ups and not the connecting moments of calm. Jump up and down with glee for the good behavior and squeak or glare or say "NO!" vehemently for the not so good. Otherwise you're just faking it, which we all know from our experience with orgasms, does us absolutely no good and only lets our loved ones live in a fool's paradise.

"Danger, Will Robinson!"

The second kind of discipline is the kind designed to keep life and limb together. This is when we teach our toddlers the nature of certain objects or situations that may be a danger to them. I once read about a culture in which crawling babies and toddlers were allowed to go right up to the campfire and stick their hand or foot in, if they were so inclined.

The theory was that, once burned, they probably wouldn't go too close to the campfire again in this lifetime. Much as I respect cultural differences, this one just doesn't work for me. I figure, if I am the mother and I understand about fire, it's my job to pass on my wisdom to my child so that she doesn't have to relearn everything.

One step removed from letting toddlers put their hands in the fire to experience it firsthand is what I call the dramatic re-creation. I think that my own darling daddy was the master of this way of educating young minds. I remember him calling to my younger brother and me one hot summer day when we were about three and four years old. He stood us in front of the room fan that he had just purchased to move some of the unairconditioned air around and turned it on. Then he took a nice long pencil and stuck it through the protective grid and into the blades. It snapped with such force that you could actually smell the fresh wood exposed. "That," he said, "is what will happen to your fingers if you put them into a fan." Not only did I never put my hand within a foot of the fan, I never even went on that side of the room again until summer was over and the fan was safely back in the garage.

My Girlfriend Marta once took advantage of a juice glass breaking on her kitchen floor to show her toddler the danger of glass shards. She put on rubber gloves and picked up one of the bigger pieces. Then she took a tomato out of the crisper and showed her three-year-old boy how deeply it cut into the tomato's flesh. The drama was enhanced by the fact that tomato juice and seeds dripped everywhere in the properly macabre way blood would if the cut were on flesh. Her little Nate's eyes bugged out, but the impression was made.

Sometimes it's difficult to get such a good example legitimately, but that's why it's called dramatic re-creation; you have dramatic license to stage some of your lessons. Let's take electrical outlets for example. Even though you should have all of them covered up in your own home, one visit to Grandma's presents a world of high-voltage adventure. While I know you would sacrifice nearly anything for the safety of your little one, I think a little playacting will do just fine in this circumstance. You might pretend to touch an outlet, then react as if you'd been shocked. Be careful not to be too grand in your gestures or else your toddler will simply convulse in laughter like he's watching a Three Stooges routine. Instead look surprised and pained and repeat something like "That hole hurt me very badly. I'm never touching that hole again. I'm really mad at that hole!"

"Is That How You Would Behave at the White House?"

The last major area of discipline involves what we loosely refer to as manners. These are the unnatural behaviors that most of us ultimately adopt just so that we can play nicely with others, respect authority, and know how to eat if, please God, we should ever get invited to dinner at the White House. As far as your toddler's immediate concerns go, these are the lessons that will get him invited over for playdates, help him function in groups, allow him to be liked at school and playgroups, and, best of all (just kidding), get you pats on the back from your parents and in-laws because older people are total suckers for manners.

Children on the younger end of the toddler spectrum are traditionally eased into this area of discipline by learning to say please and thank you. After that, you will branch out into such issues of fancy protocol as using utensils rather than hands to eat and not playing "Look" with food in your mouth. If you're persnickety, you may mount a campaign against belching, but most of us just settle for the occasional "excuse me" after the deed is done.

It may take you a decade to instill even those simple niceties, but you can't wait till then to move into the more abstract and more difficult concepts: sharing, taking turns, being gentle and being truthful. It's been the Girlfriends' experience that few if any of these traits can be fully understood, let alone embraced by the whirling dervish that is a toddler. For that reason, we recommend that you don't spend too much time actually disciplining toddlers for their transgressions. You can give a two-year-old more time-outs than a professional basketball team for refusing to share his favorite intergalactic vehicle, and he still isn't going to want to hand that toy over. Better now to settle for demonstrating how sharing, taking turns, etc., look when practiced by others. Praise them when they unwittingly behave as you'd like them to, and never miss the opportunity to make a quick remark about how nice that behavior makes other people feel. Remember, empathy and sympathy are the jewels in the crown of gentility.

If Spanking Is Out, What Can We Do to Make Them Behave?

I don't know how things worked in your house when you were growing up, but in my day, the punctuation mark that ended most disciplinary lessons was a spanking. Nowadays, most of us parents feel that violence just teaches the value of superior strength, and all of us know that hitting a child in rage or frustration teaches children nothing except to stay out of your way, and is, at its worst, child endangerment.

Don't think for one moment that I haven't felt like spanking more than a few times, and I'm not particularly proud of the second choices I resorted to, like the Vulcan death grip, where I've grabbed the little offender by the arms or shoulders so tightly they have yelped. This was usually a desperate ploy to regain control in some public place where my toddler was acting possessed and all I really wanted to do was step away from him and pretend I had no idea whose child he was. As far as teaching anything, the grip was right there in purgatory with spanking and slapping.

My dad, whom I quite obviously admired as a disciplinarian (and so much more), believed in spanking. He maintained, however, that spanking was not to teach the lesson, but rather to get the child's attention so that you could then teach them the lesson. He was right; sometimes the hardest part is getting your toddler to stop his tirade or demolition derby to listen to what you have to say. There are other ways besides spanking to do this, however. The only catch is that they take more effort on your part than a quick smack. You must move immediately to your child and get down on his level so that you can look right into each other's eyes. No lesson is really heard by small people with the attention span of a gnat unless they look into your eyes and see God. Don't even bother saying anything. Just gently, but firmly, restrain them until they see that something serious is going on. Then lay down the law. If you think that you need a little more backup, pick an appropriate disciplinary action like "I am taking away the Barney video until tomorrow when I see that you can control yourself."

Whatever you do, don't get into the One More Time Syndrome. You know the way it goes: "I swear, Buster, if you pour motor oil into the bathtub one more time, I'm going to do something that will make you very sorry." If you are a mommy who prefers to give a warning before taking away privileges or giving time-outs, then make sure the warning is specific: Name the crime, detail the penalty to be paid, and explain how long the penalty will last. Being vague or too talky is the same as being mute; no useful information is being imparted to your toddler.

When I'm really on top of my mothering game, which I think happened twice in 1991 and never again since my fourth child was born, I subscribe to the cause-and-effect school of discipline. The message to the toddler goes something like this: "Oops, you have thrown Daddy's shaver out the second-story window. Your Playmobils are mine until after your nap" (or till kingdom come, whatever you like under the circumstances). The charm of this approach is twofold. First, it shocks and surprises your little one. Even if she wasn't paying close attention to you when you were talking about the shaver and the window and yadda, yadda, yadda, she's sure to prick up her ears when you get to the name of her favorite toy. Second, it forces you to avoid idle threats. Sure, it's a far smaller expenditure of calories to sit on your behind and just wag your finger with warnings than it is to get up, enact the penalty, explain the reason again, now that you have their attention, and leave them to their crying and protesting after, but it's really the only thing that works. If you think about it, it's really how the world works; you spit into the wind and it hits you right in the eye, no warning, just cause and effect.

My Girlfriend Franny is great at it. She will stop any activity, even a phone chat with really tasty gossip, to direct all of her attention to a misdirected child. If her toddler son was throwing sand up in the air at the playground and dusting the other kids playing nearby, she would crouch right down beside him to intervene, state the rule, and then watch for any fallout. And fallout there will often be, since toddlers are notorious for their rebellious streak. Rare is the discipline scenario that ends with

Mom laying down the law and Toddler promising to be a law-abiding citizen. They either test you by throwing *just one more* handful of sand up, crying hysterically or biting the kid next to them. That's why time is the essential factor here: You must be prepared to stay crouched in the sandbox like Franny until all the variations have been tried out and the child appears to be reformed. Having said that, let me tell you that if you achieve that kind of effective discipline 20 to 30 percent of the time, you are doing a great job. No one I know has the kind of time on her hands required to be a toddler's personal guru. Sometimes we just dash into the sandbox, grab the kid, put him in the car and go home. Other times we pretend not to notice until someone else says something. But if we get the message across 30 percent of the time, we're really communicating.

The Truth About Time-Outs

I've mentioned the use of time-outs as a form of discipline, not so much because I think they're so great, but rather because they're so in vogue these days. For those of you who aren't familiar with time-outs, they go something like this. A child who is caught committing a kiddie crime is stopped, told that what he did was wrong, and then put in a holding place like his bedroom or a chair in the corner to take some time out to think about the error of his ways and adjust his attitude before becoming part of the family group again. Perhaps equally valuable about this technique is that is allows us mommies to take a migraine formula Excedrin and gulp half a cup of coffee before we blow our tops higher than Moby Dick. Hopefully, by the end of the time-out, which varies in duration based on the child's age, the egregiousness of the crime and the Richter measurement of the parent's quaking anger, the child has reconsidered his behavior and vowed to stay on the path of righteousness.

The most important thing you should know right now about time-outs is that they are not for everybody. First of all, younger toddlers as a group have not yet developed those skills of introspection and resolution that make for successful time-outs. Try putting an eighteen-month-old in a playpen for a time-out, and he will either wail loudly enough to make the paint crack or he will quietly find a way to stack his stuffed animals high enough to form a stairway over the side to freedom. Either way, he has passed his time-out minutes by doing everything but understanding the unacceptability of his behavior.

Older toddlers can grasp the concept that they voluntarily did something that was against the rules and there is a price to pay, as well as an attitude shift required, before joining the general public. Some three-year-olds have a very developed sense of right and wrong and will feel very badly about disappointing you. They will sit remorsefully in their rooms until you rescue them from their guilty consciences. Once again, however, I think that time-outs, even for older toddlers, must be applied with much premeditation on your part.

With my first child, I was very naive about some of the intricacies of time-outs. The crime escapes me now, but I remember marching my little three-year-old, who was in tears even though he had no idea what a time-out was, upstairs to his room. I told him again why he needed some time alone to think and take a chill pill, and then I closed the door behind me. From that single time-out I learned three critical rules about successful time-outs:

1. Bedrooms are the worst *places to send most kids for time-outs because there is too much fun stuff to do in there.* Where's the deprivation in being sent to a room with clouds painted on the ceiling, an entire collection of still-in-their-boxes-for-display-only Barbie dolls, enough stuffed animals to rival FAO Schwarz, and maybe even a TV set with a complete set of Rugrats tapes? Sure, they don't get the profound pleasure of your company, but hey, they'll struggle through.

2. When your child has a time-out, you have a time-out, too. Think about it; toddlers are not yet big subscribers to the Honor System, and just because you tell them to stay in their rooms doesn't mean they will do so. Oh, no. The only way you know that you are successfully timing-out your little trespasser is to park yourself somewhere near the door to the time-out room. That way you'll be able to see any escape attempts and be alerted to any strange sounds, like when my Girl-friend Shelly heard some knocking around and then a window open—Bentley had tied together karate belts and was planning to skinny down the wall of the house.

3. Time-outs shouldn't be too long. How long is too long varies from child to child, of course. They should be long enough for the crying to stop, since that's usually when the thinking begins, but they shouldn't be too much longer than that or else you will walk in to find a sleeping child. Not that a sleeping toddler is a bad thing, quite the contrary, but if you'd hoped to end the time-out with a joyous, loving reunion, or even with lunch, for that matter, your plans will have to change.

Participatory Time-Outs

It has generally been my experience that toddlers get little more out of time-outs than the pain of isolation. Granted, isolation is a very impor-tant weapon in a mommy's limited arsenal, since children would often prefer you yell and scream at them rather than leave them alone. Still, since the two of you are momentarily "grounded," anyway, why not get the most bang for your parenting buck? Toddlers are, quite literally, just a few steps removed from babies. Their frustration, anger and confusion are often far bigger than their ability to comprehend. Think of yourself when you were pregnant. Remember how you would interrupt your own raving to say, "I have no idea why I'm still screaming and crying, but I can't make myself stop"? That's the same rocky emotional terrain that toddlers often travel. Sometimes they can't change gears by themselves, and they find the experience frightening. Ask any PMS sufferer and she'll second that emotion.

Rather than sit outside a closed door the whole time, try sitting quietly beside the penitent. Sure, she has been whisked away from the knife drawer she found so compelling or from the wooden blocks she was throwing into the aquarium, but she has not been abandoned. Don't speak until she has finished crying or arguing. I'm pretty confident that your failure to respond, or even look in her direction during her demonstration will curb her enthusiasm for it. If you notice her slowing down, ask her if she can talk to you quietly. If she starts screaming again, tell her that you will sit there beside her and wait as long as it takes for her to get a hold of herself. Be careful not to scream yourself; your tone of voice is very important here because you should be soothing and reassuring her out of her hysteria, not fueling it by fighting back. Go silent again for a minute or until she winds down a bit more. Then quietly start talking to her about her mistake, for example: "Julia, it is rude and unkind to spit, and every time you spit, I will make you stop playing and come sit here quietly with me. I won't play with you, I won't read to you and I won't laugh with you until you understand what you did was wrong. After you understand, I want you to apologize to me."

Now, some child psychiatrists will challenge me on the apology requirement. They may say that the child doesn't really feel sorry or understand the meaning of the words "I'm sorry." Tough. Part of successfully living in this life is learning to apologize without having the words get stuck in your throat and nearly choke you (like some people I know) so practicing early and often helps lubricate those muscles. Trust me, you won't get some namby-pamby kid who is constantly sorry for every little thing he did, because you will save the time-outs and the sorrys for the important stuff. Later, you may end up, as I did, with a five-year-old who says "I'm sorry" the minute he gets caught in any crime, as if it has some magical eraser quality, but I never fell for it and neither will you. By the way, if I've upset anyone with my attitudes about apologies, I'm really sorry. . . .

Pick Your Battles

As you may have deduced from my mixed reviews of the various disciplinary techniques available to moms of toddlers, I find it far more effective to avoid the issue of discipline as frequently as possible by choosing only a handful of things that are rule breakers deserving of mandatory sentencing. This takes some advance preparation on the parents' part, like mutually deciding the Code of Behavior (and agreeing to stick to the party line, at least while the kids are present—you can save all arguments about who's the worse parent till right before bed, like the rest of us, and then wonder why your sex life has lost its old oomph), removing temptation from the toddler's path and agreeing to be deaf to any grandparental advice that messes with your plan.

It was with great parenting pride that my mother told me, more than once by the way, that when my brother and I were toddlers she never had to adjust her home in the slightest way to accommodate us. She left cigarette lighters, ashtrays, various brightly colored glass objects and several magazines artfully spread in a fan motif across the coffee table, and she swears we never touched them. Of course, my parents' generation was not only of the spanking species, but also of the subgroup known as hand slappers.

Go ahead and call me indulgent (my mother does), but I just don't have the time or the inclination to want to fight with a two-year-old about magazine touching. If I were to start there, I would have to care when my toddler opened the one kitchen cabinet not babyproofed and pulled out every bit of Tupperware I've collected over fifteen years of marriage. What are we non–hand slappers supposed to do, take ten nonexistent minutes out of our chaotic days to perform the time-out ritual over something as insignificant as our little guy collecting all the shoes from our closet and making a railroad out of them? Who the heck really cares?

If you can't just remove the things that inspire a toddler to get into mischief, then learn the value of diversion. Mothers are either born with it or quickly discover it during a crisis; the technique of averting disaster by introducing something else that, we hope, is equally fun and interesting, minus the sharp edges or electrical cords. My gosh, if we were to harness the sterling sales pitches and double-talking we moms use trying to get a skeptical toddler to give up the pliers dad left on the kitchen table in favor of some soft, boring educational toy with no pieces small enough for a three-year-old to swallow, we'd all be as rich as Ron Popeil.

My most recent toddler, Jade, could be lured back from the edge of the Empire State Building with something as simple as a Skittle. Of course, by the age of four, she had already had her first dental filling, so the temptation to rely on candy had to be curbed. Short of outright bribery with candy, toys or treasury bonds (not that it doesn't have a very valid place in the lexicon of child rearing, but more about that later), an experienced mom understands that the most successful distractions are those that involve mommy's participation. In other words, the only thing compelling enough to get a toddler to give up a tube of MAC Russian Red lipstick is Mommy offering to give a pony ride all around the house. Trust me, there isn't a toy in that toy box that will hold a candle to a good, staining lipstick, so don't even look. Another suggestion is to allow the toddler to do something that is normally off-limits. My kids would drop a hot curling iron in mid-duel with the offer to learn how to crack an egg or mix dirt and water or squirt the hose. Look, you and I both know that it would be a lot easier to unload the dishwasher or return at least one of the fifty calls on your voice mail if your little one could just deal herself a hand of solitaire and sit quietly, but you're the mother of a toddler, and if dreams were dollars, you'd be a millionaire.

Changelings

And now for a particularly fuzzy area of parenting: coping with a toddler who isn't misbehaving or endangering himself but simply having trouble deciding whether he should stand up or sit down, eat or drink, laugh or cry (sounds like PMS again, doesn't it?). Being a toddler means being a changeling, a creature in flux. They are not quite babies and not quite people. I will remind you of this unsettling situation several times in the Guide, but I bring it up in the Discipline chapter because a lot of seemingly naughty behavior is really changeling behavior in disguise. I remember a day when I was trying to do forty hours' worth of errands in two hours' time with my toddler daughter in tow. After one of the stops, I opened the backseat car door and picked her up to put her in her car seat. You'd have thought the seat was on fire! She arched her back and screamed so loudly I felt like someone stuck needles in my eardrums. She squirmed her way out of my arms and threw herself on the floor of the car. What did I miss? How had I hurt her? I was both panicked and annoyed, since the clock was tick, tick, ticking my precious errand time away and my daughter was lying with her legs flailing out the car door and her upper body cemented to the floor below her car seat.

"I get in myseff!" she wailed.

"Not this time, honey," I replied. "I'm in a hurry and you need to get into your car seat quickly or there won't be time for McDonald's." (See, there's that bribery thing again.)

"NOOOOOOOOOOO!"

She won. I had to set her on the pavement, let her climb up the running board of my huge mommy-mobile, get into the car seat, take three minutes to figure out how to turn herself around to face forward and then another three or four trying to get her arms through the straps. By this time my blood pressure was so high I was sure I was about to stroke out. All this, and I still had to keep my McDonald's promise!

Was I mad? Oh yessiree, Bob, I was good and mad. Was my daughter misbehaving? I don't think so. I think that she needed to master that car seat entry as much as I needed to finish my errands. To this day, I still can't think of any appropriate disciplining I should have done. The only lesson I learned was not to schedule myself so tightly when I have a toddler with me. Better still, leave the toddler at home and do the errands in half the time, then pick up the toddler for the more pleasurable outings like the carwash or the bookstore. If you simply haven't got the safety net of a sitter or the ability to bail on some of your errand obligations, here's a suggestion: Go over your planned itinerary with your toddler and show her that the day is evenly divided between "Mommy stops" and "Toddler stops." That means that after the ATM visit, you owe her a visit to the pet store where she can buy a goldfish or pet the puppy on display. Then, after sitting fairly quietly while you get your legs waxed for the first time in a year (ouch!), it's her turn to go the the community fountain and to make wishes and throw in all the pennies from your wallet. Make it clear that this day is going to be fun for both of you (the old win/win negotiating tool), and encourage her to help list her "chores." If you share the plan with her, it can be a lifesaver in a couple of ways; first, she will know what to expect out of her day and have a "contract" from you to prove it, and second, she will get another lesson in that sterling toddler accomplishment called "taking turns."

You mommies of toddlers know what I'm talking about. Have you ever given your little one a box of juice only to have him throw it across the kitchen simply because you already put the straw in for him? You can stand there all day and explain that this box is already open and that next time he can put the straw in, but he won't buy it. My Girlfriend Phyllis's toddler daughter applies the "I do myself" approach to those individually wrapped slices of American cheese that kids love so much. If Phyllis unwraps the cellophane before giving the cheese to her daughter, her little one rejects it outright because "It's BROKEN." Take it from a tired veteran, this is not a battle for your engagement. Take the "strawed" juice box, put it in the fridge for later and give him a new one to straw himself. Eat the broken cheese slice yourself (or feed it to the dog—they love the stuff) and give her an intact slice. Life is too short to do anything but.

The lesson here is that changelings do things on their own time, and rarely is it the same rhythm as yours. They may cheerfully participate in your agenda for several months, but don't get spoiled and complacent, because sooner or later they will rebel. They don't do it to tick you off, they do it because they MUST. It takes time to master the zillions of things that people who are not babies must do. Try to stay calm and allow the little ritual, whether it's buttoning her own sweater for two hours or pouring the kibble into the dog's bowl and spilling it all over the porch. In the long run, it takes longer to fight with your toddler about the buttons than to leave her to them. Better still, a really experienced mom knows not to buy any clothes with buttons for the next three years (unless, of course, they are going for a visit to Grandma's house, hee hee hee . . .).

This is a hard lesson for lots of moms, whether we work inside or outside the home (or both!), because we are constantly juggling the desire to spend time with our kids with our deep, abiding need to keep groceries in the house, pets vaccinated and cars gassed. Besides, baby-sitters can be few and far between, and who wants to waste precious sitter time on errands when there are still so many movies we haven't seen yet? As a charter member of the Do As I Say, Not As I Do Society, I'm just going to remind you one more time that the essence of motherhood is juggling, and very rarely will you manage to keep all the balls in the air at the same time. Get used to tripping over balls, Girlfriend; it's your destiny.

The Infamous Temper Tantrum

Mention a toddler to most people, and they immediately picture a small, enraged person rolling and kicking around the floor like the victim of a voodoo curse. You're familiar with the picture: They hold their breath, they scream without pausing to take a breath at all, they hit and kick anyone foolish enough to enter their zone and it all seems to be in response to having heard the word "No," or something like it. When a temper tantrum strikes, it seems there is nothing a conscientious adult can do but walk away and act as if they have never before laid eyes on the little demon. Do I even have to mention that most of these alarming demonstrations occur in public where the parents are guaranteed to suffer the most helplessness and humiliation? Those little toddlers are cunning, aren't they?

There are as many reasons for tantrums as there are toddlers, but they usually are a result of two distinct emotions: Frustration or Tyranny.

Frustration Tantrums

We've discussed how difficult it is for these little changelings to master their ever-expanding universes. Think about it from your own perspective; imagine one of those days when you can't get your pants zipped, you open a yogurt in a rushed lunch hour and it splatters all over your navy blazer, your husband doesn't seem to understand a word you say to him and then you dent the car because you forgot to look backward before going in reverse. If a day like that doesn't send you running straight for a martini or at least a Calgon bath, then you are unbelievably evolved and no one I would really feel comfortable having for a Girlfriend. If you don't feel like the universe is conspiring against you and that everything is beyond your reach, then I worry that the brain damage of postpartum depression was more extensive than we originally thought.

When your toddler has a meltdown based on having had it up to here with his life, this is the time for you to don your asbestos suit and rush into the blaze. He needs your comfort as well as your help in getting out of fourth gear. If you think it's scary to *watch* a toddler have a tantrum, imagine what it must feel like from *his* point of view. How is a two-year-old supposed to know that this total loss of control will pass and that he will live to see a happy moment again soon? He hasn't got the wisdom of your experience, and he has no reason not to believe that he has become possessed and that it's permanent. And, if you stand bug-eyed and yelling at him, he will think he's not only possessed but rejected, too. Ouch!

The very first thing you do when your toddler has a frustration tantrum is to pick him up and run from the food court of the mall, the checkout line at Toys "R" Us or your mother-in-law's best friend's living room. Do not, I repeat, do not attempt to coax or threaten your toddler out of his tantrum in hopes of returning to your former pleasurable activities. You have a grenade on your hands, and the pin has been pulled. Your job, Soldier, is to save the civilians by removing the grenade at all costs. Try to hold him tight against you so that you don't suffer too much injury, but how you get him out is not critical. The most important thing is to remove him from all staring eyes and all fragile things that he could hurt or that could hurt him. Don't waste a moment worrying about the impression the two of you are making or being embarrassed by this display. I maintain that a mother who is not frequently humiliated by her child is not getting her money's worth out of parenthood.

Aim for the car or a private room or even the backyard. Who knows, the sudden change of venue could be just enough to shock him into taking that rage down a notch or two. Once you two are someplace relatively private and safe, and if the Exorcist behavior continues, stay nearby and repeat that you are there and that he will be fine. Be calm and steady, but don't be a fool; if he tries to use his rage on you, grab his flying fist (or foot or box of juice) and hold it firmly while saying "NO!" I don't think that it's a wise move for the mother of a frustrated, freaked-out toddler to use abandonment as a disciplinary tool. It's almost like saying, "You're stuck in quicksand, honey, and I don't want to get anywhere near that, so you're on your own." Look, *I* wouldn't forgive you, and you're not even my mother! The goal here is to regain composure and the reassurance that Mommy is here to help when these crises occur. Other than that, there isn't really much need for a lesson or lecture. This kind of tantrum is like lightning or an earthquake; no one really knows what they mean or why they happen, they're just a force of nature. Once they have been survived with all parties intact, get back to having fun as quickly as possible.

What a mother really wishes to achieve when it comes to tantrums is the ability to distinguish a genuinely frustrated tantrum from its evil cousin, the Tyrannical Tantrum.

Tyrannical Tantrums

Just like every dog has his bite, every toddler has his tantrum. In other words, the first one is excusable because there is no premeditation; the dogs and toddlers are both as surprised by their outburst as their victims. But, depending on how the folks in charge deal with the first tantrum, such outbursts can be an acquired toddler weapon to be deployed with agonizing frequency. These are the kids who give toddlers a bad name, the ones who engendered the term The Terrible Twos.

So, how do you know if your child is sincerely responding to changeling frustrations or if she is simply yanking your chain when she shatters into a million pieces? Unfortunately, it's usually little more than an educated guess. Sometimes your guts, also known as maternal instinct, will tip you off. For example, say you have a well-rested, healthy toddler who has developed a taste for cookies and the tantrum occurs when you insist that a healthy lunch precede all cookie ingesting. If you have ever (and I mean *ever*) given in and begrudgingly handed out a cookie to stop one of these furies, I can pretty much guarantee you that you have a tyrannical tantrum on your hands.

The other fairly reliable indication is the frequency of the tantrums. If you find that you're dealing with one a day, for example, it's more likely your little darling has developed a nasty habit. When your mind is completely boggled, you can also ask for the observations of those people who spend significant time with your toddler to determine what kind of tantrum you have on your hands. Teachers, day-care providers and fathers who spend significant time alone caring for the little one are much more equipped to give an accurate reading of your child's motivation than are other friends and family members who tend to see all tantrums as equally deplorable and deserving of prompt and firm discipline. As much as it might burn your hide when your great-aunt claims your child's outburst means she is spoiled, don't take her diagnosis too much to heart. You are the Boss Mom here, and you may know that your little girl is acting maniacally because she's getting an ear infection, not because you are the most indulgent mother in the universe (even if that is also true). Don't let embarrassment or panic force you to make a premature judgment. Like we said before, spirit your little one away from dear old Auntie and make your game plan in the relative calm (and I mean calm in the loosest use of the word) of being alone with your Tasmanian Devil.

Keeping in mind that we moms often live much of our lives at wit's end, it can take a lot of self-control to deal appropriately with a tantrum, especially a tyrannical one. It would be so much simpler and satisfying to scream right back at them when they let loose, and, while I don't think that this is a lethal mistake, it doesn't go far toward teaching your toddler to stop the tantrums, unless, of course, you scream loudly enough to make his ears bleed. And, if you scream your lungs out and then feel guilty and hand out that cookie as a peace gesture, then you've simply taught your toddler that the price of a cookie is a tantrum plus some temporary hearing loss—a good deal if the cookie is an Oreo.

Ideally, none of us would ever have tried to avert or interrupt a tyrannical tantrum by giving in "just this once." Just this once is all it takes for the little tyrant to embrace the tantrum as his most effective way of influencing you. If you are a part of the "just this once" gang, don't worry about it; we Girlfriends are charter members. It's still not too late to learn to cope and then nearly eliminate these tantrums. That's the nice thing about parenting; you can change direction when you find that the path you've been on is leading to a dead end. Children do, indeed, like predictability and consistency, but they are intelligent and evolved enough to understand when the rules have changed, especially if you announce the change in advance, and if you don't change every single time you get frustrated.

The General Rule

As my Girlfriends and my kids all get older, a general rule about discipline seems to be taking shape:

When the kid is grounded, the mom is grounded, too.

What we mean by this is: You will never be effective disciplining your child if you don't stop what you're doing and give the discipline your undivided attention. Sure, there have been some legendary mothers throughout history who could rule a country and raise a toddler simultaneously or write the unifying work for all modern anthropology and raise a toddler, but they are the exceptions. One of my favorite "split screen" mom stories is Eddie Murphy's skit about how his mother could be talking on the phone, detect toddler misbehaving somewhere within radar range, take off her shoe, hurl it at her offending child, have it return to her hand like a boomerang, and slip it back onto her foot before the child even knew what hit him or the caller missed a beat. My sister-in-law swears her mother could do the same thing, and I must tell you, there are times I wish we still wore those great aerodynamic shoes of the fifties instead of squishy, heavy running shoes.

Anyway, now that shoe bonking, spanking and other forms of corporal punishment are considered an unfair parental advantage, the only really effective tool you have left is your ability to endure deprivation and misery longer than your toddler. When, for example, the cookie crisis begins, you have to have the intestinal fortitude not only to endure the tantrum without caving in and giving him the damn cookie, but to let him know that every time he devolves into tantrum behavior, you will move him somewhere in the house where he can't talk to any humans, can't play with his toys and can't see television. Yes, this goes directly against the Frustration Tantrum prescription, but that is because the lesson to be learned about the Tyrannical Tantrum is that it entitles the toddler to absolutely nothing pleasurable. Trust me, most toddlers find a total lack of interaction much worse than physical punishment. I call this secret weapon "Sensory Deprivation."

Just because your child is supposedly sitting quietly, learning from his mistakes, doesn't mean you are free to open the mail or have a long telephone chat. There is something intangible yet effective about hovering just out of sight with a stern and serious attitude enveloping you like a cloak. I don't know if it's because they can feel your vibes or simply because it shocks the heck out of them if they get up and come looking for you, but it works. It keeps your toddler focused, and even more importantly, it keeps *you* focused.

**SICK KIDS ARE CRANKY KIDS (SPECIAL NOTE)

Keep in mind this observation of the Girlfriends who have gone before you because it can help you tolerate some otherwise intolerable behavior *and* it can definitely spare you a ton of guilt and remorse:

Toddlers who act particularly perverse are often toddlers who are about to become sick.

I can think of at least five times when I put a child in a time-out zone and considered putting him or her up for adoption only to have them throw up on me or, worse, to find out later that they had double ear infections. We aren't telling you this to make you a wimp and your child a hypochondriac, but simply to encourage you to make sure that there is no physical reason for your toddler's outrageous behavior.

How Do I Know If My Toddler Is Spoiled?

When in doubt, just assume your toddler is spoiled; we Girlfriends know ours were. The problem with that label is that it suggests standards that applied better to our parents' generation than to our children's. First of all, most of our children are not afraid of us. That in itself is a big generational difference. Second, more than half of us moms work outside the home and we are often either too tired or too guilty to mete out the serious discipline. If we only get to spend three or four hours a day with our toddler, we don't want the majority of time to be spent in misery. The third, and for my money, the most significant contribution to a nationwide epidemic of toddler spoiling can be reduced to three little words: Toys "R" Us. Never before in history has there existed a toy store that so closely resembled a supermarket. Nowadays, when a mother is stir-crazy or wants to indulge her little sweetie, she can spend an hour or two mindlessly cruising up and down the aisles with her toddler gobbling up the eye candy. Mother and child can actually have some peace and quiet—that is, until they finally reach the checkout counter and the child realizes he's not going home with all that cool stuff. For that, I refer you back to the Tyrannical Tantrum section.

"Do As I Say, Not As I Do"

You can curse like a sailor, pick your nose or eat nothing but Doritos for breakfast, lunch and dinner around a baby and he will not pick up your bad habits. Once you have a toddler in the house, however, you'd better be ready to see your worst behavior mirrored. Every one of us Girlfriends has heard our little angels say, "Shit!" when the building blocks tower has tumbled, and we can only imagine what worse utterings have occurred when we weren't around, like in Sunday school or a preschool assessment meeting. Remember, toddlers are us without the social restrictions. Boy, is that a scary thought.

Everybody knows, at least anecdotally, that screamers tend to raise more screamers, drinkers tend to raise more drinkers and food obsessors tend to raise more food obsessors. Well, Mom, this is where it all starts. If you wish your child to behave in a certain way, the very best thing you can do is behave that very same way. From now on, your child is watching you and emulating you. You are her hero, her protector, the one who knows everything. You cannot expect her to do anything less than try to be you, at least until adolescence, when temporary insanity takes over.

It will occasionally strike you as almost eerie how your toddler displays so much of both his mother and father's behavior. Some of it has to be genetic; how else would all little boys know to watch TV with their hands in their pants? But much of it is a direct result of mimicking behavior that you may not even be aware of. One of my daughters, for example, has since the age of four felt obligated to point out any lint, boogers or food on anyone else's person. Let's see, who do I know who could have taught her that. . . .

In the long run, it will not be the little quirks your toddler inherited from you that really matter. Your challenge lies in not setting examples that can ruin his life. What follows is a list of the most important behaviors to cut out of your life before they are woven into the fabric of your toddler's life:

1. Don't smoke.
2. Don't hit or allow yourself to be hit.
3. Don't demean or allow yourself to be demeaned.
4. Don't lie.
5. Don't hate.

If you can master those things as well as toss in all the good stuff like:

1. Love freely.
2. Be enthusiastic.
3. Honor commitments.
4. Read together.

then you're already miles ahead in the parenting game.

Discipline and the Modern Marriage

My Girlfriend Tina and her husband are experiencing a little friction around their otherwise groovy house now that their daughter is two and a half years old. It seems that their previously delightful little moppet has learned some new party tricks. The first one involves throwing a hard object whenever she says the word "No." Recently, Tina looked up to see a hairbrush heading her way, and a few nights later she watched as her little girl hurled bottles of nailpolish one by one against the bedroom wall. Last, but not least, she refuses to sleep anywhere but right smack between her parents in their bed.

Their toddler's tricks are not the cause of the friction, however. What Tina and her husband are fighting about is whose job it is to fix their "broken" angel. In that inimitable way of toddlers, Tina's little girl saves her most annoying behavior for those hours after the sun goes down. That means that Daddy gets home from work just in time for the show to begin. He's tired, he wants dinner, he wants his wife's romantic attention and what he gets is the apple of his eye slapping him when he asks her for a kiss or howling like a coyote when he turns off the *Beauty and the Beast* video. On through the evening it goes until the little one climbs out of her crib for the fourth time at midnight and her parents' exhaustedly allow her to resume her place of honor between them.

She's been in her mom's care all day, so clearly this is Mom's fault. If Mom were doing her mom job, Daddy's little girl would have learned to sleep in her own bed and control her anger during the normal work day, not on his time. Isn't that why they agreed that Tina would work in the home for the first three years of their little sweetie's life? What is she doing all day if not teaching and molding their child? It must be bonbons and soaps! Does that mean that Dad has got to take over *every single* important job in the family to make sure they're done right?

This is as normal as macaroni and cheese, Girlfriend. The first reaction most parents have to the violent emergence of individuality that is characteristic of a toddler is shock. The second reaction is to blame anyone in sight, usually your co-parent. It is so unthinkable that yesterday's precious baby has turned into today's James Dean that our temptation is to think that something has gone terribly wrong. Somebody must have broken her! Since it's unthinkable that we broke her ourself, it must be our mate's fault.

It's nobody's fault. The sooner the two of you understand that you are both blameless here, the better for your marriage. Don't let your uncertainty get in the way of remaining a team with your mate. You need to give each other moral and physical support through these parenting years, so don't drift apart now, Girlfriend. As your toddler grows, it will become increasingly important, too, for you to present a united front. Older toddlers are sophisticated enough to know when mom and dad aren't allied on the rules, and they will start shopping for the parent who gives them the answer or indulgence they want. That is a felony in the Parenting Penal Code, so don't even let the toddler consider the possibility that when Mommy says no, Daddy might say yes. Remember, if you do your job right, this little human will one day walk out of your house for good. It might be nice if your mate stayed behind with you.

Welcome to the Circus

I have yet to meet anyone of my parenting generation who thinks she has this discipline business down cold. In fact, it seems to be further proof that parenting is life's biggest ad lib. Sometimes when we compare our children to their peers, we sigh with relief that they seem no more spoiled or repressed than the rest. Other times, however, we feel as if our toddlers are ruling their lives and ours like Mad King Ludwig ruled Bavaria. And still other times we go to bed at night in tears because it seems that all we did was say "No" or give time-outs all day long.

I can't even tell you that it gets easier with the second, third or fourth child because in my family, each child required a personalized behavior code and methods for enforcement: One child crumbles if anyone raises a voice around her, another bites her nails nervously if corrected, and still another doesn't seem to hear me unless I am yelling six inches from his ear. Not only that, but just when you think you have a handle on one developmental stage, the kids have the nerve to move on to another, still uncharted, territory. For example, just when I thought we had the separation anxiety bit handled at preschool, my child moved into caring whether she was popular with the other students or not. Wait a second! I hadn't gotten to the part where Mommy was replaced as Best Playmate in the World with little Johnnie and Jackie, who weren't yet including her darling in their games. And from what I hear, all of this worry is positively anemic compared to the red-blooded terror of raising teenagers, but let's not get ahead of ourselves.

The one thing we can know with certainty is that part of our job as parents is to teach them how to function in this world. Toddlerhood is the first real foray into this world, so toddlerhood is the time to start demonstrating such things as cause and effect, respect and self-control. Take it slow and steady, learn from your own mistakes and don't get frustrated. Remember, you're the Boss Mom; you really do know what's best for your child. Confidence and consistency are at least as important as the actual forms of discipline you use, so cultivate them both in yourself. You're toddler will be taking their cues from you long after toddlerhood is a hazy memory.

Top Ten Things to Do When Your Toddler Drives You Nuts

10. **Next time your toddler has a tantrum, video it.**
    There's a lot to be said for that directorial detachment.
    Besides, you'll have it for evidence if he ever tells his
    therapist his neuroses are your fault.

9. **Turn the radio on loud and dance.** It will shock your
   toddler into a moment's silence and let you release a little steam. Who knows? Junior may end up wanting to
   dance with you.

8. **Call a Mommy/Girlfriend.** The two of you can commiserate about how hard motherhood is and how fathers
   haven't got a clue.

7. **Go outside.** You and your toddler may be getting cabin
   fever and not realize it. If it's a nice day, spend an hour
   in the park. If it's a crummy day (and it usually will be
   in this situation), put the toddler in a stroller or take
   him by the hand to do a lap around the block as
   quickly as you can.

6. **Turn to TV.** Put on a show or video that your child
   adores and sit nearby practicing your deep breathing
   and meditation skills.

5. **Have a (healthy) snack.** Maybe you are a little hypo-
   glycemic and all you need is a little lift in the old blood
   sugar.

4. **Take the toddler's side.** Tell him in completely adult
   sentences all the ways in which he is justified in being

grumpy. Start like this: "It's really hard being you because of that whole diaper versus potty thing. Then
there's that inability to fully articulate your needs or
concerns. Plus there is always someone like me around
trying to sneak vegetables into things you thought could
be trusted to taste good. And then again, there's always
the sensitive issue of height . . ."

He might find it amusing to hear so much about his favorite subject — himself — and you might actually feel a
pang of empathy.

3. **Find a playdate, FAST.** You know how we Girlfriends
   feel about safety in numbers. Take some of the heat off
   you and put it on some unsuspecting neighborhood toddler who couldn't care less.

2. **Read her *Guess How Much I Love You* (McBratney) or
   Love You Forever (Munsch).** She'll like the story, and
   the sobbing you'll do will feel great.

1. **Go away.** Beg or pay someone to baby-sit while you get
   as far away as you can. If you can talk your mate into a
   rendezvous, you can share a glass of wine and try to recall why you wanted to be parents in the first place.

The Potty

What's the Big Deal About Potty Training?

Really, what is the big rush to get babies out of diapers (that can be folded up and disposed of with nary a glance) and onto potties (that have to be flushed and cleaned, and are often missed entirely until aim is fine-tuned)? Something about a child's second birthday gets a mother's blood pressure up as she feels all of civilized society staring at her, making sure that she accepts the potty-training baton and completes her lap successfully.

The toddler can be completely uninterested, uncooperative or unable, and still we mothers reprioritize our frantic lives so that we can devote hours of every day to going to the bathroom, talking about the bathroom and fretting when our little one hates the bathroom. And, assuming even the most enlightened of businesses doesn't have a two-year maternity leave policy, more than half of us mommies are back at work outside of the house when this task presents itself. Unless you intend to bring your toddler to work with you and try potty training in the staff's ladies' lounge, distance alone can be problematic.

If you ask me, the big deal is all based on the assumption that potty training is a microcosm of parenting; if we do a "good" job at potty training, then we are most likely doing a "good" job as parents. And God knows, all of us beleaguered parents are yearning for any sign that we are doing our job right. That's the problem with parenting: There are no annual reviews, no report cards, no promotions and, as I far as I can tell, no bonuses to let us know when we are parenting well. Parenting toddlers presents a particular challenge to a parent's self-esteem since the little one hasn't yet *mastered* so many skills as he is *in the process* of mastering. Few of us can point to our toddlers and say, "He's playing that Bach piece perfectly, I thought it would take him months!" or "She finally has a firm grasp of Hemingway, so now I can relax about her being ready for pre-school." My thesis here, Girlfriend, is that we are searching for that one little success for our children to demonstrate to the universe that we are, indeed, up to the job. Pretty tall order for excrement, if you ask me, but potty training seems to be the crucible for toddler moms.

Housebreaking

If you start with the premise that using the potty is a nice, tidy habit that you, the older, bigger, smarter one, can impose on your toddler, the younger, smaller and equally smart one, you are setting yourself up for a mighty big fall. You know the old line about how you can lead a horse to water? Well, it's even more applicable to toddlers and their potties. You can start out with an absolutely clear and sunny attitude about this potty business. No pressure, no expectations, maybe just a ceremonious purchase of a pair of frilly panties or little Jockeys with fire trucks on them. But it never ends there. Potty training is not a complete parenting experience if it hasn't included tears, promises, threats and disappointment (for you, I mean). It can end up taking on so much emotional baggage that you wish you lived on some tropical island where children ran naked and did their eliminating behind the nearest coconut tree. You might recognize this tropical island fantasy as one of the seven early warning signs of parental breakdown, if only you weren't already so distracted.

The Secret of the Holy Grail

I'm going out on a limb here, but I think it's safe to presume that you have already experienced a premonition of disaster regarding your toddler and the joys of indoor plumbing. Otherwise you'd use this valuable time to look for the credit cards Junior hid around the house when you gave him your wallet to keep him quiet so that you could place that J. Crew catalog order. Therefore, I won't waste one more sentence before getting down to the *bottom* line, so to speak, of potty training:

They all learn to use the potty before kindergarten.

In other words, even if your toddler is as resistant or indifferent as the far end of the spectrum allows, she will still learn what she needs to know by the age of four. Yes, your life can be more embarrassing if you are still sensitive to the judgments and remarks of others, and it can be more troublesome if you have some spiffy little college-prep preschool in mind for her that requires "full toileting responsibility." But other than that, and of course, several hundred more diaper changes, when your child learns to use the toilet is no big deal in the scheme of things. In fact, even the slowest converts to the porcelain bowl are often predictable enough that you can enroll them in an elite preschool on the assumption that they will not have a bowel movement until you bring them home at noon, thus keeping your secret safe.

This information alone should reassure you enough to let you pass a magazine stand without immediately zooming in on the parenting section to check for any headlines promising a cure for diaper dependency, but it won't. I know it won't because my sister-in-law used to give me the same reassurances, and I still fretted. There was one thing I simply had to know, and no one was giving me the straight poop, so to speak:

When should a mother start worrying that her child has completely flunked potty training and needs professional help?

After eight years of asking myself, and any Girlfriend I could collar, this very question, I would like to give you the answer I was so desperate for:

A child can still be gifted, well-adjusted and socially successful and be iffy about potty training until the age of three and a half. By age four, if they are having any potty problems more serious than the occasional accident (as in once every two or three weeks), you need to call in the National Guard.

Even then, there is no reason to panic. Still, as the parent in this situation, you should keep your pediatrician up to date on your problems and progress so that any medical conditions that might interfere with bladder or bowel control can be identified or eliminated (why does every word I write in this section seem like a pun?) as a reason. Little girls, for example, frequently get urinary tract or yeast infections that can make them feel the urge to pee pee all the time or make peeing burn. And little boys have their own internal wire-crossings that can fail to wake them at night when they need to use the potty. Never let your own embarrassment or worry that you have done something to damage your child keep you from seeking your doctor's advice. Relief might be as simple as an antibiotic or even a nose spray for a nighttime bed wetter, and won't you feel like a doofus if you deny your child all the help he or she deserves?

In Praise of Three-Year-Olds

Since it is our collective belief that completely terrific toddlers have celebrated their third birthdays and are still wearing paper undergarments, we Girlfriends would like to suggest several reasons why potty training a three-year-old can be *even better* than training a younger toddler. That's right; we'll show you how really smart the two of you are, mother and toddler, to have saved this spectacular achievement for your fourth year together rather than letting it pass by before your little one was even capable of discussing it with you. (Besides, who needs Girlfriends who can't put a good spin on these endless mothering crises?)

The significance attached to toileting and the third birthday is understandable. After all, I can't have been the first mother to have looked in my trusty child-rearing guide's index under *toilet training* only to discover that it is mentioned in the section devoted to one-year-olds. I still remember how I broke out into a sweat and my hands began to shake. Then again, there are those proud other mothers, particularly your own, who reminisce with pride about turning their toddler's diapers into kitchen rags before they were in spitting distance of their second birthday. I'm not saying that it is unheard of for a toddler who can barely say "mama" to master the intricacies of the potty, and if you have one such child, we heartily congratulate you and suggest you review the chapters on hitting or bad eating habits. The rest of us should be resigned to potty training children who are sophisticated enough to ask why you and daddy have hair down there and they don't.

Keep this little anecdote in mind: As the proud owner of a swimming pool, and an avid swimmer myself, I was one of those overly excited mothers who searched far and wide for a swimming instructor to make my toddlers "pool safe" as soon as they could walk themselves down to the pool (which was also surrounded by a fence and covered, I might add). Sure, I met a couple of crackpots who insisted that the only cure for non-swimming was the sink-or-swim scenario created by dunking the unsuspecting toddler and having them rely on some faint genetic coding that would inspire them to rise to the surface and paddle like small frightened puppies. I never even let those Navy Seals onto my property, but I did finally meet a swim teacher who eventually became the miracle worker who taught all four of my little fish to swim and love the water. (I swear I'm going to make a point here, and soon.) He explained, with great wisdom I think, that a child's brain must have been functioning for three years before enough synapses and connections have been formed for him to understand the concepts of:

1. intending to do an action;
2. knowing the skills required for that action;
3. putting those skills to work and
4. having the problem-solving skills to put a Plan B into effect should the first plan get botched.

In swimming, that Plan B could come after getting water up his nose or not taking a deep enough breath or having his bathing trunks fall off. In children too young to ad lib, these could all present crises that end with a sputtering child being swooped out of the pool by a hysterical parent. In potty training, too, there are very real reasons for the pottier to stay light on his feet, er seat. First of all, potties do not grow throughout our landscape like crabgrass. Unless you refuse to leave your own home and the familiar toilet it provides for up to a year, your child will have to learn that most famous of Plan Bs called "holding it." Unless, as I mentioned earlier, you are like my Girlfriend Sonia who carried a potty in her over-sized L.L. Bean canvas bag everywhere her toddlers went, there will be some time lag between when your child expresses the urge and when you find a toilet that is probably skeevy but will do in an emergency. A three-year-old will work with you on this one and probably not just let loose wherever he is standing.

Three-year-olds, bless their little hearts, are also capable of understanding the urgency in your voice when you say, "Mommy will put you on the nice paper seat, but you mustn't touch a single thing." They will behave all through the pottying, then use both of their hands to boost themselves off the toilet seat, leap to the floor and put a finger up their nose. This is your cue to tell a story about the invisible germs that live in public places and how we must wash our hands, as well as keep them out of our nose and mouth, as much as possible.

You know, you never really get to say your child is completely potty trained if she has not mastered these fundamentals of toilet hygiene. Wiping up after is as critical to a job well done as the peeing and the pooping, if you ask me. You will pass on your particular family traditions here, believe it or not. For example, if you are a toilet paper folder, you will teach your offspring to neatly line up all those perforation lines to make a tidy square for wiping. If not, you will simply give the toilet roll a spin or two and crumple up a small handful for the trainee. Don't be in the least bit self-conscious about your peculiarities in this matter. After all, you are creating the habits of a lifetime.

Modern science (is there any other kind?) has dramatically shown us that germs and infections that don't fly through the air rely on their ability to hitchhike on the hands and fingers of the great unwashed. If you want to cut way down on colds and flus, not to mention pinkeye, teach your toddler that no visit to the potty is complete without a good vigorous hand wash. Even if there isn't any soap available, rubbing the hands under running water gets rid of millions of those vermin. Here's a little hint to help your little one, who I presume is not yet wearing a chronograph watch, get in a good hand-wash session. Teach him to sing the first verse of "Twinkle, Twinkle, Little Star" while washing and finish on the line that follows "like a diamond in the sky." It works as a measure of time and as a weapon against boredom.

Last, but certainly not least where preschool and day care are concerned, a three-year-old potty master understands waiting his turn. Sure, there might still be the hand in the crotch and the voodoo dance of urgency, but they will generally wait, especially as that three-year-old becomes three and a half. Since, featured and beloved as they are, preschool potties are not one to a customer, learning this lesson will put your toddler in good stead, not just now but for a future of airplane rides and cocktail parties when there's never an available loo when you need it.

Six Degrees of Potty Training

One of the reasons for so much anxiety about potty training, at least as far as we Girlfriends are concerned, is that the term itself is imprecise. One mother can say her child is potty trained and mean that she will urinate in the potty every hour and fifteen minutes when her mommy puts her on it, but still uses a diaper when sleeping or pooping. Another mother, like two of my Girlfriends, Sonia and Shelly, will have children who completely master the pee pee part of potty training, including staying dry all night, but who will run to Mom with a diaper or Pull-Up for her to put it on them for the daily poop. I'm talking about kids who were old enough to stand there and say "Hurry up, Mommy, it's coming!" while their mothers were struggling with the diaper tabs. Even the most gung-ho books about potty training (you know, the ones that say all two-year-olds should be doing it for themselves) allow that there's a world of difference between being "day-trained" and "night-trained," and that the latter takes far longer to achieve with most kids. Still other toddlers are completely potty trained as long as they never leave the house, since they only associate their home potty with elimination. Then let's not overlook our last large group of reluctant pottiers: those kids who were well on their way to perfect pottying until 1) the new baby came, 2) the family moved, 3) they started separating from Mommy at preschool, 4) they missed an episode of *Blue's Clues,* or 5) anything else that could possibly rock a toddler's world.

The lesson here is that potty training is best viewed as a gradual progression of a mastery of several skills. There will be progress, and there will be apparent setbacks, but you must trust that the whole show will be ready to take on the road before the fourth birthday.

Semantics

Several of the books I frantically devoured during my toddler tours of duty took great pains to teach us the politically correct terminology for teaching former babies to use the toilet. One made a big deal out of the need to call this process "toilet learning" rather than the "potty training" of our mothers' native tongue. I guess this was a distinction deemed critical by the authors so that we parents wouldn't confuse how we taught our children with how we housebroke our dogs. *Learning* somehow implies a more liberal and patient approach to the task, while *training* is a more apt description of those of us who lure our little ones to do the deed with rewards of M&M's or doggie biscuits. Since I never really succeeded in teaching anyone to use the toilet where and when I wanted them to, and since I find little use for political correctness in the dirty job of mothering, I am going to stick with the quaint and cute term of "potty training." You'll learn soon enough that you'll have far more profane ways to refer to it over the next few months.

Even more heated in the potty wars is discussion about what to call all of the operative parts and processes involved in using the toilet. Does a toddler of the new millennium say, for example, "I make pee pee" or "I go potty"? Does she carefully wipe her "bottom," "booty," "tushy" or does she go right for jugular with the word "buttocks"? The most dia-bolical challenge of all involves the P word and the V word. The trend in some circles is to take a healthy and straightforward attitude toward anat-omy and begin using the textbook terms for "privates" right from the beginning. This can provide moments of tremendous anxiety and light-headedness among those who are not part of this trend—usually your parents and your in-laws. Nothing blows a grandmother's mind more than hearing her precious grandson announce in public that "he can make his penis squirt," unless, of course, it's hearing her granddaughter share "I have a bagina!" If you ask me, there is an ethnic component to whether a person is comfortable with explicit terms or prefers saying things more "nicely." Perhaps it's because certain groups of people have such clever euphemisms, often from their native tongues. My New York Italian mother-in-law believes that all good mothers call their little boy's penis a "pesce," because it's an endearing (and Sicilian) reference to a little fish swimming in the bathtub. Get it? And few self-respecting Jewish grandmas would prefer the word "butt" to the Yiddish "tushy."

This time the Girlfriends and I come out on the side of the Grandmas. The anatomically accurate words do sound a bit aggressive, don't you think? It's not that we're weak and can't look a little penis in the eye and call it by its name; heck, we do that every time we change a little boy's diaper. It's just that we think that there is absolutely no need for anyone who speaks the English language to ever have to utter the word "bowels."

Those of you who are entirely new to potty training may think that those mothers who have strong feelings about the proper choice of words are making much ado about nothing, but just you wait. You'll soon see that there are good reasons for investigating the standards and practices in your toddler's community of friends. What good is it to teach your child to ask his day-care provider whether he can go to the bathroom to "void" (as I swear a girlfriend of mine was taught by a finicky mother) when all the other kids are being told it's time to go "potty"? It can't help but be useful for potty trainees to share a common potty language.

When to Introduce the Potty

There's a classic skit from the old *Honeymooners* where Ralph and Norton teach themselves to golf. The first line in their how-to manual directs, "Address the ball."

"Hello, ball," replies Norton.

That's sort of how I feel every time I bring the little plastic potty out for a new round of training. "Children, I'd like to introduce you to your potty." I think I bought my first white plastic free-standing model when my firstborn was nearly two. I had heard stories of children using the potty at eighteen months, but I disregarded them as some sick form of competitive mothering. I put the potty on the floor in the playroom on the assumption that we would be spending a lot of time sitting there, and a little access to TV or books might be useful. I was right, we sat there for months: We watched various potty-training videos, I would trim his nails, I'd read books to him and he would sit until there was a ring around his bottom. Once or twice he would unknowingly make pee pee in the potty, but that was more a function of time spent there than of his making the connection intentionally.

I did notice with all of my children that their affection for their novel new seat dimmed noticeably when I started letting them know that I had expectations for their time seated. Call it performance anxiety or rebellion; whatever it was, they stopped sitting on the seat as soon as it became clear it wasn't about storytime and games. There were months at a time when the potty became just another piece of furniture collecting dust.

You probably haven't even decided whether you'd like to start with a portable plastic potty for your trainee or if you'd like to cut right to the chase and put them up on the family toilet (with a rubber ring on top to keep the little one from jackknifing closed and falling in the bowl). As I said, I never had much luck with the baby potties, not only because my kids didn't take to them, but because they were usually too tall for them by the time they understood what was expected of them in that regard. (Just *kidding!*) No, I didn't care for those little white pots because they were too close to the floor for me to comfortably keep my toddlers company, because I didn't much like cleaning them, and because I knew that I would inevitably be out in public without a potty when my trainee declared she wanted to make pee pee. What was I to do then, when the only available facility was in a restaurant and required a paper sanitary cover; hope that she understood the translation?

My darling Sonia, however, was always prepared to keep up with potty training; she carried that damn potty every time she left the house. One of her kids would get a little red in the face, and Sonia would be up in a flash, dashing to her car to get the potty. She'd set that sucker down on the lawn in the park, in the parking lot of the mall, even behind the supermarket, to preserve consistency for her trainees. I used to walk away from her and pretend I didn't know her, but she'd punish me by making me hold the full potty in the car when she drove us all home. I will always torture her about this, but she must have been on to something because her kids were, indeed, trained several months ahead of my own. Between us Girls, when we were out and about and away from our potty (which was always being hidden by one of the other kids anyway) and my trainee announced her need for relief, I always whispered to my eager beaver, "Go ahead and go pee pee in your Pull-Up. Mommy says it's okay just this one time."

Note: If you do choose a seat to place on a grown-up's toilet, make sure that you provide a steady step or box for your toddler to climb aboard. Remember, the ultimate goal here is to leave all toileting to the toddler; so if she always has to ask you to pick her up and get her situated, you've insinuated yourself way too deeply into her business. By the way, my experience with both the floor potties and the toddler toilet seats has been that they come with a detachable shield sort of thing on the front. This brilliant invention was clearly designed to keep little boys from spraying the shower door from their perch on the potty. Guess what: Those shields are a groin injury waiting to happen. They make it impossible for a toddler to get onto the seat without hurting some very sensitive body parts and should be thrown away with the box the potty came in. Little boys, who as we already know are developing a fondness for their little penises, will usually be very cooperative in pushing the little soldiers down between their legs if they sit to make pee pee.

Potty Ready?

In my book, and this *is* my book, no mother should take a single step toward potty training until her child is old enough to communicate his or her readiness, IN WRITING! Well, perhaps that's a bit extreme, but I wouldn't even think of potty training a toddler much before their second birthday (okay, third) unless he or she absolutely begged to learn. Trust me, most don't. In the meantime, there are some generally accepted signs and behaviors that just might signify that using a potty is looming on your toddler's horizon.

Clue Number One: The Desire to Be Clean (As If!)

In the potty training books that I devoured, the most common indicator that a toddler was ready for the potty was his growing awareness that a wet or poopy diaper wasn't as comfortable as nice dry underpants. Evidently, the mythical children of these books were tidy little creatures who could be tempted to give up the convenience and familiarity of the diaper for the improved hygiene offered by the potty. Boy, the promise of a visit to a bidet would probably send these tykes into rapture. My Girlfriends and I never had a kid among us who expressed fussiness about a soiled diaper. The best explanation for this, aside from the fact that we live in Malibu and are slightly more earthy than other people, is the preponderance of disposable diapers. According to their own advertising, they "wick" the icky stuff away from the baby's bottom. If you ask me, all this wicking has simply served to make a dirty diaper a slightly more inviting place to be.

The silver lining for us moms, however, is that an extra year of diapers isn't quite so oppressive if you don't have to dunk them in a toilet and then launder them yourself. Believe me, there will come a time when your child has been using the potty for months and you will yearn for the convenience of disposable diapers again. Which would you rather do during a car trip at night when your toddler says he needs to go potty RIGHT NOW: stop in some dingy gas station or put a nice clean disposable on him and let him do his business in the safety of your car, rolling smoothly down the freeway at 70 mph? Here's the news on that one: As reluctant as they might have been to give up the diaper a few months ago, now that it's been given up, it ain't comin' back, Mommy, no matter how much you beg. Just bring your Lysol spray with you into that scuzzy gas station bathroom and don't touch anything.

Clue Number Two: Monkey See, Monkey Do Do

Having a toddler in your life is like being stalked. They're in the closet with you, they sit on your lap when you try to use the toilet, they're right between your knees when you run to answer the phone. Just about the only time that a toddler isn't within five inches of you is when there is some mischief calling him away like a siren's song. You are probably already seeing your little one imitate your actions by holding the plastic phone between her head and shoulder (just like you) and blabbing away, or you may have discovered your toddler just in the nick of time as he picked up your razor and prepared to shave his beard like daddy.

It's only natural for your little stalker to eventually become curious about your most private bodily functions and, one would hope, ultimately want to emulate you. If this is your first child, and if she's not spending a lot of time in day care or with other kids who already use the potty, the job of setting a good example falls to you and your mate. Trust me, this comes more easily to some people than to others. In my household, for example, my husband still pales and leaves the room if I continue our morning conversation while I sit down and take a pee. Needless to say, he's not sending out invitations for guests at his bathroom show. I, on the other hand, have to be reminded to close the door when I use the bathroom. Guess who devoted her life to letting our toddlers see how one sits on the potty, wipes properly and courageously flushes the contents away? You got it: ME! It's now been so many years since I've used the bathroom without visitors that when I find myself in there alone, I get a little anxious.

Anyway, in defense of the beloved father of my children, he did step forward to take his two sons under his wing for the male bonding lesson called the Standing Pee and the advanced course called "Two Taps or Three?" For all you moms out there who are taking care of business on your own in potty training and every other parenting regard, let me rush to reassure you that this is in no way a required course; rather it's a very old ploy for getting the child's father to put the remote control down for one minute and relieve the mother of the uncertainties, anxieties and the tedium of potty training a toddler.

Believe me, as a single mom, your job is NOT to prevail upon any squeamish cousins or brothers you might have, or worse yet, to let your toddler walk into a men's rest room to check out the action. God forbid on that one. My oldest son is ten and I still stand outside the door of men's washrooms screaming in the door, "Is everything okay honey?" to my son. I've had men good-naturedly yell back out the door, "Yes, sweetie, everything looks just fine, indeed," but my son knows from experience that if he doesn't answer me every single time I yodel in, he must suffer the consequences of having his lunatic mother burst into that male bastion. Your little man will see others similarly equipped (meaning male, but small and hairless) soon enough in day care, Sunday school or preschool, all proudly displaying their potties side by side with open doors so that using the toilet is as social a gathering as high tea.

Clue Number Three: Toilet Talk

I'm not referring here to the great affection older toddlers have for saying "nasty" words like "poop head" or "pee pee face," but rather their ability to understand and respond when you introduce the subject of learning to use the potty. As we mentioned in the section In Praise of Three-Year-Olds, most of life's lessons are most easily taught when the child is old enough to learn by a combination of listening, observing and understanding: That's what makes potty training different from housebreaking a puppy.

Your toddler may bring it up herself by asking when she will be old enough to wear "big girl" panties like her favorite cousin. Or you might bring it up by asking whether she has any interest in using the potty like you. You two can talk about the benefits of living diaper-free for days or even weeks before you do anything about it. What's most important, especially if it was you who brought the subject of the potty up in the first place, is that you refrain from any hard-sell techniques. If you act like this is something that's really charged for you, then you've already taken it out of the arena of natural phenomena and put it into the basket of "things we save to tell our shrinks." Once again, do as I say, not as I did: Resist the temptation to contaminate this simple task with layers of people-pleasing, bribery and disapproval.

The Psych-Out

My Girlfriend Lani and her two-and-a-half year-old daughter Chelsea are spending most of their quality time together in the bathroom these days. On one hand, Lani is thrilled because all this interest in the potty suggests that her days of changing diapers are numbered. On the other hand, she is beginning to see that just because a toddler is willing to take a seat doesn't necessarily mean that she is ready to close the deal. The truth is that toddlers are very cunning little creatures, and if you act like their brave forays to the potty are the most thrilling and irresistible occurrences in your home, they will soon learn to take advantage of you. "Sit wit me," your little trainee might command, "I go potty."

"Yes, of course Mommy would LOVE to go to the potty with you, you clever little darling," we sing rapturously. So we sit on the edge of the tub, or, in my husband's case, pull the step-up stool from the sink to sit knee-to-knee opposite our trainee of the moment, and encourage (but not too much), amuse them (so they don't jump off and leave), even turn on the faucet in hopes that the age-old belief that hearing the sound of rushing water makes everyone's bladder instantly release is actually true.

We DO NOT talk on the phone, cook a meal or read a paper because that would make going potty seem boring and unimportant. Get it? They have found the perfect ruse for getting our complete and undivided attention, which is never in sufficient measure as far as most toddlers are concerned.

"Almost" Only Counts in Horseshoes and Hand Grenades

Most toddlers go through what I call a coy stage when they tease you about their potty proficiency. They seem to understand the concept and can even be counted on for several consecutive days to behave just like real potty-trained people, but this is just part of the game called Mommy Is a Sucker. Remember, there is a tremendous emotional component to using the potty, both for the toddler and the parent, and the experience just wouldn't be complete without some neuroses. Why else do you think

Freud had so much fun with this stage of development? So, either in the interest of injecting some variety into their life, to keep you paying very close attention or in reaction to some insecurity about this growing-up business as a whole, the toileting toddler might be overcome at any moment by potty amnesia.

For example, you may have a little one who has been going pee pee in the potty for weeks, but insisting on wearing a diaper to do the big job. Then one day he won't ask for the diaper, but will head for the potty room. You, careful not to make too big a deal out of the huge event you know is about to happen, wait just outside the door where you are ready to leap to his aid should he request it. A couple of minutes later, out he comes with a relieved look on his face and into the bathroom you race to examine the fruits of his labors, so to speak. Well, there it is, on the floor *beside* the potty, just like a cocker spaniel leaving a calling card.

My Girlfriend Mary's little boy went through a stage when he only went pee pee and poo poo in the backyard. She was frantic with insecurity and the fear that the neighbors would look over the fence and see her child acting like a barnyard animal. Since it was not my son fertilizing the lawn, I could calmly and patronizingly tell Mary that she should be grateful that there was no mess for her to clean up. If I really wanted to tick her off, I could remind her that this behavior was human in its most natural state and that her son was simply in touch with his primitive self.

Should you be annoyed and frustrated by this toilet teasing? Well, heck yes! You clearly have better things to do with your time than figure out the best way to clean a poop off the floor without squishing it all over the place or to have to search for your child among the shrubbery. But should you *act* annoyed and frustrated? Absolutely not, at least not in front of the tiny offender. Any experienced mother will tell you that a strong reaction of any kind just makes the situation ten times worse. The first thing you will probably want to do is put a diaper back on your toddler to avoid another mishap occurring before you've had a chance to clean up the first. Then mention matter-of-factly that making potty *outside* of the potty is simply not done. The last thing you want to do is frighten or embarrass a little one who is going through a rather scary developmental spurt. Believe it or not, they might really just be testing to see if the rules of potty training are rigid or if getting close is good enough. And, if your toddler does understand the rules but is playing with them to engage you, a big emotional reaction to pooping on the floor will just encourage him to do it again. Far wiser to close the door to the potty room for later cleanup and lead your toddler to an activity that the two of you can feel happy about, like sudsy hand washing. Or, if you have a backyard reliever, remind yourself to stop and smell the roses together, as long as you take a few steps downwind.

*Note: Do not, however, take this kind of attention-getting behavior as indisputable evidence that you are failing to devote enough time to your little one; a toddler's need for attention is deeper than the Black Hole of Calcutta and we moms just do the best we can.

Social Pressure

A child with a potty problem can be as socially challenging as a dotty old aunt to a family that has not gone through this process before. You must constantly contrive to keep your little secret. Take Mary, who wouldn't let her son go to the park, to preschool or to any grassy area for fear that his fertilizing would take place there, too.

Sure, I could make fun of Mary, but I was the mom who put cotton training pants *over* Pull-Ups to disguise the fact that my little girl wasn't toilet trustworthy when I sent her off to a preschool that required it, and who picked her up every day before she had lunch with the rest of the class because I knew her body clock better than Greenwich knows Mean Time and I knew she was due for a Number Two by noon.

All I can tell you is that each of my children seemed to have an internal schedule with some secret date circled as the day they would grasp the mysteries of the potty. Sure enough, when that day came, they knew and not one minute before. My job, as it turned out, was to stay calm and trust that the date would come, either because of my help or in spite of it.

One time, in the days when we still believed that potty training was something we could impart to our child, my husband and I got into a fight; he maintained that nothing was more important than being there for our child while he struggled with this new challenge. I, however, insisted that, on the old you-can-lead-a-horse-to-water theory, the two of them would be knee to knee for the rest of the night. We were at such an impasse that I went alone (and hugely pregnant, thank you very much) to our friends' daughter's bat mitzvah while my husband the father played a board game called Crossfire (it's indelibly etched in my brain) with our child as he sat the night away on the pot. I was right, by the way, about the horse not being forced to drink part, but I'm still not sure about my disloyalty in leaving my guys when they were in full crisis mode.

What I Learned the Hard Way

So disastrous were my attempts to potty train my first two children that I absolutely refused to live that nightmare ever again. That meant that my third and fourth children were as undirected in their discovery of the potty and its pleasures as Dr. Livingston in the bush. Guess what! They were successfully potty trained (self-taught, of course) at the EXACT SAME AGE AS THE FIRST TWO HAD BEEN WHEN THEY OVER-CAME MY INTERFERENCE.

Do you know what that means? It means that the three days I spent locked in the house putting my first toddler on the potty every forty-five minutes while simultaneously filling him with juice and water so that his visits would be fruitful meant bupkis. I can still recite, in either gender, all of *Once Upon a Potty*, so many times did I read it to my fascinated two-year-olds. Cute as they and their orifices were (check out the pictures of where the poo poo comes out of little Prudence and Joshua!), those fictional pottiers never succeeded in making my own little cuties see the merit of potties over stinky, heavy diapers.

Yes, there were moments when I considered using my superior size and strength to put the potty candidate on the seat against his wishes, but that always seemed a little too much like corporal punishment. Besides, he would just stand up and run away, probably to pee pee in the corner, if I were to bully him about something he considered deeply personal and none of my business. If one of the kids did ever voluntarily sit on the potty, however, I was not above all sorts of "encouraging" tricks. I once even put a toddler's fingertips in a bowl of tepid water hoping that it would make her go; after all, it worked on Caroline Adamson at my thirteenth birthday slumber party when she was sound asleep and we made her wet her sleeping bag!

I am clearly a proponent of the "first do no harm" school of potty training. While I don't think it does a toddler or her parent much good to rush, cajole, bribe or shame her into using the potty, I do think there are certain simple things you can do to help nature take its course.

1. Make sure that your toddler eats and drinks the stuff required to make using the potty as easy as possible. Sure, broccoli or a small Caesar salad might not pass your toddler's palate, but you can still get some fiber into that finicky diet by giving her an apple or pear every day. (See, I told you Grandma was right.) Those yummy little cubes of cheese that are the snack of choice in many preschools and day-care centers can constipate little ones, so it might be wise to substitute Goldfish crackers or something less binding. Of course, water, water, water is the magic potion in healthy elimination. Spike it with a little fruit juice as needed. The concept is that you shouldn't wait until they say they are parched before suggesting a cup of water or half and half (1/4 apple juice to 3/4 water as we call it around here. Toddlers don't understand fractions yet). Remember to take a drink yourself every time you serve your toddler; you will be setting a good example and, besides, you are probably dehydrated anyway.

2. Avoid all clothes with suspenders, snaps, zippers and buttons when dressing your toddler. Look, it's hard enough to recognize the sensation that you need the potty, stop whatever fun thing you'd rather be doing, remember where the potty is and then begin the struggle to escape your clothes like a little Houdini in a straitjacket.

3. Remind, but don't nag. One of the most compelling character-istics of toddlers is their fierce concentration on whatever activity they are currently involved in. Quitting that activity to go potty can make a toddler's brain feel like a transmission stripping gears. By the time the adjustment is made, it may be too late. Sometimes you can help by making a casual comment like "I have to use the potty, do you want to come with me?" Don't, however, put any pressure whatsoever on your toddler to fulfill some toilet quota you have in mind. They will even-tually smooth out the bumps in their transitions and get to the potty on time, every time.

4. Pay no attention to other toddlers' potty habits. If you think your toddler is more accomplished in his pottying than his peers, there will be too much temptation on your part to gloat and pontificate about your successful teaching techniques. Girlfriends don't like that in other Girlfriends.

More likely, since you're still here with me reading this chapter twenty pages later, you think your child is the only toddler in your community who is clueless about using the potty. You listen with envy to mothers effusively telling miracle stories about how all they had to do was say that if little Janey used the potty, she could have Barbie panties and she never wet herself again. What you aren't hearing are the stories of the mortified mothers like my Girlfriend Lori who has been dangling the promise of coveted ice-skating lessons as an incentive to get her three-year-old out of Pull-Ups. So far, every time the bargain is mentioned, Lori's daughter replies, "That's okay. I skate later." Just keep in mind two principles about competitive mothering: First, mothers don't always tell the truth. Second, and most important, there are absolutely no studies showing that learning to use the potty early gives your child a better chance at getting into an Ivy League school or becoming an astronaut. In other words, it's mean-ingless except for its wear and tear on you.

5. Take that advice about fear of flushing seriously. I got it in my head early on that stories about children freaking out when they saw their pee pee or poo poo flushed away were simply that: more of the mythology of potty training. I didn't even want to allow for that possibility on the theory that I would just be training my toddlers to be neurotic. Well, chalk another one up to experience: I was so wrong about the fear of flushing.

It appears that there are two forces at work that make flushing traumatic: the noise the toilet makes, and the way it sucks those precious eliminations into oblivion. If you have one of the newer water-saving toilets, you, too, are probably scared half to death by the loud gush of air and water efficiently cleaning out the bowl. I know I am. And the part about the affection your toddler may feel about his "stuff," while best *explained* by psychologists, is best *respected* by us parents. In fact, in the beginning of your potty training odyssey, it might be best to just leave the potty unflushed until a later time when your trainee isn't around. As they get a little more blasé about the whole thing, you can ask them if they want to make it flush themselves. They seem to like having some control over the situation, not to mention the fact that, to a curious, water-obsessed toddler, flushing a toilet can be as amusing as squirting a garden hose.

Don't Reinvent the Wheel

In my never-ending quest to find the solution to my potty-training dilemmas, I tried several of the approaches that you've tried or are considering as your next full-court press. I am willing to share my failures with you, my Girlfriend, in hopes that you will spare yourself and your toddler a lot of unnecessary frustration. I will understand completely if you cannot rest without giving them a go, since we all tend to feel that activity of any sort is preferable to just sitting around hoping for something to happen, but please just hear me out about a few of the most popular "training" methods.

1. Intensive training. There is a popular potty-training book making the rounds that suggests you can train your toddler in a weekend if you follow its simple instructions. When I saw this book on the shelves a few years ago, I nearly wept with relief. I had been praying for nearly a year for some-one, anyone, to spell this potty-training task out for me in a way any idiot could understand, and my prayers had been answered.

The premise was that trainer (read: Mommy) and trainee (read: Tod-dler) had to commit to spending two or three days going to the potty once an hour. That didn't sound very difficult when I read it, so I set about clearing our calendars to make sure we could stay close to our family toilet. The first couple of times, no problem. No pee pee or poo poo either, but the book said that was okay. In the meantime, I was to encourage lots of fluids so that one of these hourly visits would have to be successful. No problem.

About five hours into this program, and my toddler and I want to kill each other. He is bored silly by being cooped up with me all day, drinking water and sitting purposelessly on the potty every hour. I am cranky be-cause I, too, am bored and also very aware that I will accomplish nothing else in a day broken into twenty-four potty-interrupted chunks. My hus-band volunteers to take over a couple of shifts for me, turns on a football game and completely misses the next scheduled potty visit. Now I want to kill both of them.

By dinnertime I start to hyperventilate because we haven't made any real association between sitting on the potty and actually using it, and pretty soon it will by my toddler's bedtime. Will that mean that all Saturday will have been a waste? Will we be starting from scratch on Sunday? Can I really face a Sunday of twelve to fourteen individual vis-its of five minutes each to the potty? Do I really care this much? No! Let's all go to bed with a double diaper on (remember all those fluids throughout the day), and let's spend Sunday at the beach having fun! End of story: We are a Pampers family, but a happy one, for at least an-other six months.

2. The M&M's approach. Don't ask me where this one came from; I just know that potty-training Girlfriends all across the country know exactly what I'm talking about when I mention that particular candy and its role in teaching toilet habits. Gosh, I bet the people from Mars Candy

Company never dreamed that they would end up making any bigger contribution to child development than tooth decay and a little sugar buzz, but here they are on the forefront of toddler education.

The M&M's theory is Pavlovian: Your toddler does something good, like using the potty, and he gets a reward, like a piece of candy. Ideally, your toddler will like the candy reward so much that he will pattern his potty habits to get maximum amounts of candy. My best guess is that this particular kind of candy was chosen for its universal appeal and because it's about as small a piece of candy as you can give. We mothers may be desperate, but we're not about to hand out Hershey bars every time a little pee pee hits the mark.

Here are my problems with this approach to potty training: First, I have this vague distaste for anything that associates using the toilet with food. Sure, if we didn't eat food, we wouldn't need the toilet so often, but I prefer to have an hour or two of separation between the oral gratification and the ultimate elimination. Besides, there's that whole germ thing that eating near a bathroom signifies, no matter how thorough the hand washing may be. Second, I'm not sure that toddlers need any special "prize" for doing what comes naturally. Certainly later in life there won't be anyone handing out candy as she comes waltzing out of the ladies' room (unless of course, she's in a restaurant that continues that quaint tradition of attendants handing out mints and hairspray). This is bribery, no matter how you slice it, and that gets a little too close to interference and control over your toddler's plumbing if you ask me. Last, but not least, do we really need one more excuse to sing the praises of the empty calorie? I love chocolate as much as the next one, probably more, and I've never been one of those sugar-free mommies, but between holidays, birthday parties, grocery-store pilfering and visits with grandparents, I think there are quite enough candy handouts for toddlers.

3. The charts and stickers technique. As its name suggests, this technique involves a more subtle approach to the reward concept. On its surface it looks rather enticing: positive reinforcement and no nasty sugar bugs. Plus, it presumes a certain calm and rational communication between the parents and toddler since it's supposed to work in a nonjudg-mental fashion: Your toddler stays dry and clean for a specified period and he gets a star or happy face on his chart. I guess for those kids who find stickers a little unexciting on their own, the idea is to offer the opportunity to earn toys or privileges in exchange for a certain number of stickers. Here's where the rub begins; no toddler I know will humbly accept the denial of a sticker, especially if he knows it's all that stands between him and a new bottle of bubbles. He might want to blame his wet pants on his baby brother (as I did in my toddlerhood), he might hide his pants altogether to destroy any sticker-invalidating evidence (as my brother did in his toddlerhood), or he might just cry and cry over his failure to ac-complish this goal he had his heart set on. Don't you feel like crying yourself? This is just too much to lay on a toddler. Learning to use the potty is not about succeeding or failing, Mom! It's about gradually mas-tering all the small, individual skills required to take responsibility for one's most personal habits. Once again, I plead with you, BUTT OUT!!

It All Comes Out in the End

I'm sorry, but I couldn't resist bringing this bronco back to the barn on yet another potty pun. You see, the joke is on us parents and we had darn well better laugh about it every now and then. Chances are, you will be involved in the potty process for several months, if not for a couple of years, and, as in all parenting matters, it's wise to pace your-self. Your darling little toddler will gradually accept this responsibility as surely as he learned to walk and is learning to talk. You can gently en-courage him in all these things, but if you think you're the Great Edu-cator here, you're a tad deluded. As we've mentioned before, Mother Nature loves you and thinks you're one swell Mommy, but she doesn't depend on you to do all the heavy lifting in this parenting experience. She has a backup plan that is nearly fail-safe if we stay out of its way and allow it to happen; and it's called growth. Your toddler's growth will bring the awareness, the interest and the ability to take care of himself; so much so that he will one day be able to live without hearing from you for days at a time. Trust your toddler, trust Mother Nature, and trust yourself to be able to survive this.

chapter seven

Sleepy Time

*T*he *Guinness Book of World Records* (or some other such authority) states that the longest period of time a human being has remained awake was about four days. Mothers must not have qualified for the competition because I can swear there were weeks on end when I parented and wifed every minute of the day and spent every darkened hour patting someone on the back, rocking someone, singing to someone, chasing someone down the hall, giving someone another glass of water or making idle threats to someone about taking away all toys if someone didn't go to sleep within three seconds. I can't speak for every mother on the planet, but in my little social set, we Girlfriends are allied in the belief that we are sorely deprived of sleep.

In infancy, the problem, though agonizing for the parents, is relatively simple: The baby wants to eat or be held at least once every two or three hours and the parents usually wish otherwise. Toddlerhood, however, introduces a much broader spectrum of variations on sleep and why we can't get any. First of all, toddlers can escape. At least infants just lie in one place while they fret. Most toddlers are not nearly so respectful; they just get up and walk away from their sleeping space, even if it involves climbing over crib rails and tumbling to the floor. Secondly, toddlers have a very rich fantasy life. Floor lamps suddenly look like Godzilla, monsters lurk under the bed and in the dark, life-size Minnie Mouse dolls look like characters from the movie *What Ever Happened to Baby Jane?* (Well, at least to me they do, so I can only extrapolate from there into the toddler mind.) A third head of the Toddler Sleep Hydra is that tiresome old potty training thing again. Some toddlers, few I know personally, however, are learning to stay dry through the night, and that can entail getting up to use the potty after curfew. There are also such enchanting toddler nighttime nuisances as nightmares, night terrors, sleepwalking and early rising. The Girlfriends don't necessarily have all the solutions to these little trials, but we will at least acknowledge and address them in this chapter.

Last but not least among the toddler sleep "challenges" is their sudden realization that Mommy and Daddy are still up "having fun" even after the little one has been put to bed. Infants believe something along the lines of "When I sleep, the world goes dark." Toddlers, unfortunately, are much more perceptive than that. Their motto is "If there's a party going on anywhere in this neighborhood, count me in!" They are now at an age when they not only have fun, but they *remember* the fun they were having and don't appreciate bedtime's interruption. Unlike infants, who live almost entirely in the moment and have little or no understanding of cause and effect, toddlers are completely clear about the fact that playing tag is a blast, and that lying alone in bed precludes tag and any other really groovy game. Not a good foot upon which to build a relationship with bedtime.

Toddlerhood is also when cribs are given up for "big boy" or "big girl" beds. As thrilling as this transition can be, it is rarely spontaneous or without some upset. If we have learned anything in the preceding chapters of this Guide, it's that toddlers, like Rome, were not built in a day. You will be flipping through the pages about now, looking for the one that tells you exactly how old a toddler is supposed to be when the crib-to-bed transition is begun. Don't bother: Our only suggestion regarding age is that the change is made some time between diapers and driver's licenses. But more about that can of worms later.

Let's Put Things in Perspective

When you think about it, we members of Western Civilization have a very unique and somewhat odd approach toward sleep. We split up the family into solitary units, put them in rooms all by themselves and then expect them to put themselves to sleep without any fuss. I bet if we were to go to some country like Somalia and explain our theories about teaching sleep skills to our children, they would be appalled and disturbed. Separate a child from the rest of the family and leave him alone in the dark?! Appalling! There are war criminals who have shown much less cruelty!

Until quite recently, most of the world has slept together like a litter of puppies. The concept of the "family bed" was not invented by hippies and members of the La Leche League. For starters, most people did everything in a single room—eating, socializing and sleeping—because one room was all they had. Staying warm was a terrific incentive to pile in on top of each other to share their body heat. Mothers in other cultures often breast-feed much longer than we do in America, so it made sense to keep the baby conveniently near. And, although I am no anthropologist, I just can't help but think that people who sleep in the profound darkness of towns without all-night diners, night-lights, and *Nick at Night* are far more sensitive than we are to the fears that can come when you can't see around you.

All this is a way of saying that I think that we may occasionally be working against good ol' Mother Nature in our efforts to teach our toddlers to abide by the family's sleeping laws. Perhaps I'm just trying to make myself feel better about the fact that my husband and I haven't spent an entire night alone in ten years, if you don't count those hospital stays when the successive siblings were born, but I happen to believe that being apart from your loved ones when you're lonely or stressed out is unnatural.

Does that mean that I want to embrace the "family bed" and reject Ferber and all his friends? Absolutely not! My dream is to sleep naked with my sexy mate and know that we will have privacy and quiet from 9:00 P.M. till around 7:00 A.M. I'm tired of dressing like a fireman every night, in preparation for whatever disaster the darkness may bring. If I hadn't already been committed to a nighttime costume of thermal jammies and a pair of serious slippers beside my bed, I learned that lesson when my Girlfriend Tanya, who, in spite of being the mother of two at the time, slept au naturel, and when evacuated from her beachfront home on the night of the big earthquake, had to stand nude among her neighbors on the sand until the shaking stopped. I might have appreciated the exhibitionistic thrill ten or fifteen years ago, before my belly and boobies felt the full gravitational pull of several pregnancies, but NO WAY with this body.

I'm also tired of discussing the reasons why my kids can't get into my bed, and then giving in and putting them in the sweet spot between my husband and me. I'm tired of getting kicked in the head by little people who have absolutely no slumber manners. I'm tired of little kids waking up at sunrise and asking me to make them an egg sandwich. I'm tired of getting up to use the bathroom four times a night (one visit for every pregnancy my bladder sustained), then feeling compelled to walk the halls and make sure all children (at least those not already in my bed) are safe and sound. Come to think of it, I'm just plain tired of never getting one of those delicious nights of sleep that I had pre-kids, when I didn't sleep like a mountain climber dangling beside the mountain in a harness, and I stayed asleep until my dreams were complete.

Sleeping Through the Night

Every toddler mommy Girlfriend I have, and I mean EVERY SINGLE ONE, asks me how to get their children to sleep in their own rooms all night. Clearly, this skill doesn't come easily to moms or kids. Perhaps if we lived in my mythical village in Somalia, we wouldn't cherish our sleep so much because there would be an opportunity for a nap sometime after lunch. But in our world, we have things to do, places to go and people to see, and a schedule is the backbone of the entire enterprise. There are few things worse than having a wakeful toddler the night before you are making your closing arguments in court or hopping on a plane to Detroit for a sales conference. We're not asking for much: We just want enough uninterrupted sleep to have made putting our pajamas on worth the effort. Nobody I know is holding out for the eight-hours-a-night deception; we just want to be rested enough to operate heavy machinery.

The Girlfriends and I actually found young toddlers far more cooperative at night than their older compatriots. One big plus is that one- and two-year-olds almost always still sleep in cribs. You never fully appreciate the value of that particular piece of furniture until it's gone: It is just the right mattress size for a mini-person, it has all the familiar smells and bedding from infancy (which gives it magical powers against night monsters and boogeymen; see chapter 3), and, best of all, it has cagelike sides that keep all but the most daring where they belong.

The other characteristic of young (and, in my family, not that young) toddlers that can work miracles in keeping them settled during the night is their affection for binkies, bankies and bottles.

***I need your attention here, Girlfriends! It's critical (at least if you tend to be slightly hysterical) that you understand that everything I am about to say is endorsed by absolutely no medical professionals.

We just spent a chapter talking about toddlers' attachments to things that take them to the Comfort Zone, and I don't want to bore you by repeating my belief that nearly any unharmful ticket to paradise is worth the price. So, contrary to what most pediatricians and child development books say to the contrary, I survived having four toddlers in nine years by giving a night bottle to anyone who cried hard enough for it. Yes, a *bottle,* I confess, I confess!!!! But hey, we do whatever it takes when we have four children in nine years because that's a lot of mothering and attention for this very tired mom to spread around every day and night.

I know all about bottle-mouth (those horrible cavities babies get when the juice or milk in the bottle is allowed to pool up in their mouths while they sleep), and I certainly am not suggesting that you risk your child's dental health just so that you can get a few more zzz's. The Girlfriends' Rule About Night Bottles is this: *Only water goes in those bottles.* We're talking no smidgens of juice, just because he doesn't like the taste of water.

Trust me, even a child who throws a water bottle into the hallway from his crib in disgust will quickly discover that the alternative—NO BOT-TLE—is far worse. The other thing we Girlfriends would like to mention in this regard is a clever invention called diaper liners or diaper doubles. Even the sturdiest Pamper can fill up like a water balloon when worn by someone who is drinking at night, and you will want something to fill in the leakage gaps. I suppose you could get up and give your little one a midnight diaper change to stay ahead of the game, but heck, if you're going to wake up anyway, why bother with the bottle in the first place? When your toddler and you have decided that staying dry is an integral element of your potty training program, this bottle trick will have to go away. My advice is to put less and less water in the bottle every night so that by the end of a week, your "big boy" is sucking air from the nipple. For those little ones who have found the Comfort Zone through a "bin-kie," I would suggest that you put an extra in the crib for those emergen-cies when the original falls between the railings and onto the floor.

If you are a first-time mom, you will probably spend several hours listening to your beloved sleeping, snoring, waking, getting reoriented and then putting himself (please, God!) back to sleep. You will quickly learn that babies and toddlers don't sleep like we do. They frequently stir, check out their environment, chat a bit and then go back to sleep at least a couple of times a night. They aren't like us grown-ups who fall into a coma with Letterman and wake up to the alarm with creases in our faces from the bedding.

Younger toddlers, especially those who haven't mastered scaling their crib sides to freedom, do tend to be more manageable. Just make sure that they have what they need to feel safe, assume that they will kick off their covers and therefore need blanket sleepers in most winter climates, and keep that baby monitor plugged in and turned up to high so that you can hear trouble as it brews.

Crib to Bed

We parents get positively giddy about kid beds. I don't know if it's because we inherently like redecorating, if it's because kids beds come in all sorts of fun shapes from tepees to race cars, or if it's because we're just so darn proud of how well our toddlers are participating in the business of growing up. Most of us have put a "big girl bed" into our toddler's room long before she is ready to leave her crib. I always made sure there was something to sleep on besides the crib in my babies' rooms because I often needed a place to lie down while I ministered to a three-year-old who dreamed we were all eaten by Barney or while I kept a closer eye on a baby with a fever.

Some people suggest that, if you didn't buy your child's first real bed when you bought his crib (you were so delirious with pregnancy hormones, and besides, it matched all the rest of the nursery furniture), you take your toddler shopping and involve him in selecting the bed he wants. That's a nice idea, but I'm not going to recommend it. First of all, kids never choose a bed that is easy to make, that they can grow into or that matches the rest of the room. Second, furniture shopping with toddlers sounds like Dante's first ring of hell to me. Far more manageable mommy-tot purchases are bed linens. Not only do kids love picking out sheets and pillowcases with pictures of Pooh or the guys from *Star Wars*, they can do it via catalog! And these character sheets tend to be very reasonably priced (probably because toddlers haven't learned about thread-counts or ratios of polyester to cotton in a blend). Just be careful not to select cartoon characters who are friendly in the light of day but who get freaky in the dark of night. Darth Vader comes to mind, as does Batman. I myself would run screaming from the room if I woke to look into Barbie's eyes as she gazed from my pillowcase, but this is a matter of individual taste. Perhaps the safest thing to do is order small theme prints like trucks or hearts to keep on hand just in case Belle's friend, the Beast, gets way too spooky when the lights are out.

It's been the Girlfriends' experience that putting the bed in the toddler's room before he leaves the crib helps a bit in the transition. For that reason, it's a good idea to buy the new bed sometime before you're going to employ it. Since most of us don't have kids' rooms the size of a suite at the Plaza, there might be some serious squeezing involved in fitting both pieces in, but it's worth it if you can. If you can't, perhaps you can assemble the bed and put it in another room, like the family room or a guest room, so that Junior can play in it and get used to it. The only prohibition here is this: DO NOT PUT THE BED IN *YOUR* BEDROOM. The last thing you need to do is encourage communal living when you are trying to teach the value of privacy and space of one's own. If you start by letting your sweetie nap and play in a bed right next to Mom and Dad's, you might as well just plan on it staying there until she is old enough for slumber parties and has a general disdain for all parental intrusion.

Ready for Bed

As you know, the Girlfriends don't believe that the age for moving from a crib to a bed is etched in stone (well, some do, but I'm ignoring them because I don't agree with them and it *is* my book). Some toddlers, especially those with older siblings whom they want to emulate or share a bunk bed with, will start talking about leaving the crib as early as two-ish. If that's what he really wants, we can't think of any good reason to nix it unless he still isn't escaping from his crib, in which case we suggest you take advantage of those last few months of keeping him corralled. As long as you have taken all precautions to protect against the inevitable tumble from bed (yes, even the sturdiest of bed rails will occasionally fail you) and toddlerproofed his room and adjacent halls and bathroom for the times he gets up and goes for a midnight stroll, let him fly.

More often than not, however, getting toddlers to forsake their cribs is much harder than you will have expected. It makes complete sense to me: Toddlers spend all their waking hours venturing out into the world of playdates, potty training and constant physical growth, so who wouldn't want to retreat to the beloved cave when her battery was wearing down? Beds aren't just places to sleep; they are refuges, not just for toddlers, but for lots of grown-ups, too. In fact, there's nothing I'd rather do right this very minute than climb into my bed and pull the covers over my head, but it ain't happening in this lifetime.

Toddlers, as we've already pointed out several times, don't mature in a nice, predictable, linear fashion. With these little critters, it's more like two steps forward, one step back. Same thing applies to the transition from crib to bed. Your toddler may enthusiastically tuck himself in to his new bed with Winnie-the-Pooh sheets one night, and then insist on returning to the crib for the next two weeks. Nightmares, potty-training glitches and the appearance of new babies have all been known to send those little bedders back to crib-land. Keeping this in mind, it's usually a good idea not to disassemble the crib and put it into storage, or worse, to pass it on to a younger sibling, until it's pretty evident that your toddler really is over it.

One last note about first beds in general. There is a vast and varied market of little beds that are bigger than cribs (though they often use regular crib mattresses) but smaller than the traditional single or twin bed. If you have money to burn, knock yourself out and buy a tiny bed that looks like Cleopatra's barge or Cinderella's glass slipper, but it certainly isn't necessary. This particular piece of furniture is very short-lived, and I don't think your toddler really needs one. First of all, many of the cribs that are sold these days can be turned into toddler beds through the removal of the side rails. My Girlfriend Peggy put a little step stool with hand rails beside the bed to make exits and entries easier, and her little boy slept contentedly in that bed until he was nearly four. The other thing to keep in mind, since you are probably going to have to buy a "real" bed sooner or later, is that there are all sorts of things we cautious parents do to make them safe and cozy enough for the littlest of campers.

At the top of the list of "real" bed adaptations is the bed rail. Some beds, especially bunk beds, come with a wooden plank that fits into slots in the headboard and footboard. (Please trust me on this: Even if the bunk bed comes with a bed rail that extends to the ceiling, do not put a toddler on the top bunk, ever. They don't sleep like normal people and are certain to find a way to fall off and break an arm, heaven forbid. The ladder to get to the top is dangerous enough for your intrepid toddler climber, so just omit the entire option.) Fisher-Price, Gerry and all those other purveyors of kid paraphernalia sell bed rails made of heavy-duty plastic or metal with fabric mesh providing the safety net. The rails stay in place with long extensions that slide two or three feet under the mattress.

Even if you have taken all adequate rail precautions, consider putting the box spring and mattress right on the floor. I don't know how they do it, but toddlers invariably manage to either move the rail out of the way or slide to those twenty inches at the foot of the bed that a rail doesn't reach, and they climb or tumble out. As the mother of four, I am certainly not suggesting that one or two episodes of falling out of bed are lethal, or even particularly serious. It's more the emotional ramifications I'm considering: A toddler who is iffy about this gigantic new bed in the first place could build up some active resentment toward it if it periodically dumps her overboard. Just a thought. Anyway, if the low bed idea doesn't appeal to you, consider putting a soft rug or even a pillow bolster alongside the bed for the first few months.

The Great Escape

My Girlfriend Chaney's daughter Simone started climbing out of her crib at about seventeen months. Her technique was primitive at best, meaning she usually climbed onto her crib bumpers and then just tumbled over the top onto a heap on the floor, but she did it every night and headed right for the superior sleeping quarters of her parents. Chaney thought that Simone's yearning to be free indicated that she was ready to sleep in a bed. Well, that was partly true. She wanted to sleep in a bed, but not her own. Now, at just a couple of months short of her third birthday, adorable, smart and incredibly well-adjusted Simone still doesn't sleep in her own bed.

Not only is a crib-catapulter not necessarily ready for bed, she is also not mature enough to be trusted as she wanders through the house while the rest of the family is sleeping. Most night wanderers have one destination in mind, Mommy and Daddy's room, but toddlers are unpredictable people, and it's not safe to bet on the general rule. Even those little ones who are in search of their parents may not be able to find their way safely with all the lights turned out. Trace the steps your nightcrawler is likely to take while visiting the bathroom, the goldfish or you, and do your best to remove all hazards he might encounter along the way. Keeping the hall light on (that's what dimmers were invented for) helps immeasurably, but a couple of strategically placed night-lights in the toddler's flight path are just as good.

Better still, make use of your baby monitor. Most of us mothers have a sixth sense about our kids, and when the sound of climbing or cruising is transmitted to the receiver we keep beside our heads, no matter how quiet and unobtrusive it is, we leap into action. While it's fine to awaken to your toddler standing beside your bed, it's even better to nip her nocturnal habits in the bud before she gets past her own threshold. Otherwise, she will beg to be put up for the night and you will be too tired to retaliate.

The grand finale to any toddler's nighttime stroll should be a return to her own bed or crib. It's pretty obvious that there should be no reward for crib escapes since it only encourages an endless cycle of death-defying leaps followed by a miserable night's sleep for you and your mate. No matter how tired you are or how simple it would be to just roll over and let the little interloper move in, with every night you capitulate, you must concede a fortnight of spontaneous sex and sound sleep (in no particular order). If you, like most of us parents, are committed to teaching your children to sleep independently of you, you are really going to have to take a stand as early as possible, and that time is often the first time your toddler ventures out of the safety of his little cage.

If I were you, I would postpone that milestone event as long as possible. One of the very first things you must keep up with is your toddler's growth in relation to the height of his crib mattress. Our advice is this: As soon as your little one can pull into a standing position, lower the crib mattress so that it's flat upon bottom support. The other little trick that might save you a night or two is to remove all crib bumpers and unnecessary stuffed animals. By unnecessary, I mean any creature who is not part of the Comfort Zone. These common crib accessories morph into stair steps to freedom for the resourceful toddler. Don't worry about bumps and bruises stemming from the lack of crib padding; most one-year-olds are more than capable of avoiding crib rails if they bother them, and even more are completely oblivious. Besides, crib bumpers are becoming suspect for all crib dwellers, especially infants, because there is some suspicion that SIDS might be caused by little teeny babies cuddling too deeply into the bumpers and being poisoned on their carbon dioxide.

Okay, enough upsetting talk like that; let's get back to determining when a toddler is ready for a bed.

Eviction

While I might be a tad vague about when a toddler is ready to move from a crib to a bed, I am absolutely certain of a time when he is *not* ready. The Girlfriends and I, many of whom have children two years apart or slightly less, know for a fact that it is never a good idea to hurry a toddler out of his beloved crib in preparation for the arrival of a new baby. Even if you don't have the discretionary cash to squander on a second crib, especially when the first one will be obsolete within a year, we recommend that you try to keep the new baby and the toddler's movement to a bed as separate as possible. I realize that if you are the mother of a one- or two-year-old and receive the glorious news that you're pregnant again, your frantic mind will attempt to anticipate all of the logistics of having two kids in the house. One mistake you will almost certainly make is to assume that your new baby will need a crib the day she comes home from the hospital. This is yet another example of postpartum amnesia, as newborns almost always sleep in bed with the parents or in a bassinet beside Mom for the first couple of months. That bassinet time can be invaluable in providing some precious time for your firstborn to adjust to the newest family member without making the crib connection in any way. In fact, lots of toddlers start to appreciate the privileges that come with toddlerhood after a couple of months of observing an infant's limited life, and enthusiastically move on to more grown-up behavior.

There Are Monsters Under the Bed!

One of the biggest differences between toddlers and babies is that toddlers recognize a monster when they see one, and they don't forget it even after it's gone. We're not necessarily talking about monsters like Godzilla or King Kong (although that particular ride at Universal Studios sent my first toddler into therapy). Often the monster that haunts the toddler by night is his friend by day. You may have taken your little girl to a Disney on Ice show or even to a birthday party that had a dressed-up character making balloon animals and had the time of your lives. Then at about two A.M., you might have heard a shriek for Mommy that would wake the dead. She's afraid of Gaston and thinks he's hiding in the bathroom, or Bert and Ernie had unattractive eyebrows and reminded her of your husband's scary uncle when she was alone in the dark.

My oldest son was the master of "friend by day, foe by night." He didn't just tolerate dangerous characters in his waking hours; he begged for them. The big fad when he was about three was Ninja Turtles, and, believe it or not, they were on a concert tour. (How does a turtle play an electric guitar with those claws, that's what I want to know.) Our son insisted he couldn't hold his head up in preschool if he didn't attend the "concert." Naturally, wussies that we are, we nearly mortgaged the house to scalpers to get tickets to that ridiculous event. Let me tell you, I wish I could have gotten my hands around the throat of any one of those reptiles or even the ticket scalper in the wee hours after the show. They were back at the hotel or aquarium, or wherever turtles live, counting their money, and I was listening to tearful tales about this scary rat who is supposed to be nice to the Turtles, but who talks funny and has a mean face. Every night for weeks after that, I had to do a Rat Check of the entire upstairs.

My Girlfriend Melanie's daughter Mariah loved Pinocchio when she was a toddler. You can imagine how thrilled I was on a weekend vacation in Northern California when I found a beautifully carved and painted Pinocchio marionette. I bought it for Melanie's daughter in anticipation of her third birthday, which was still about three months away. What a gracious gift receiver that little sweetie was: She remembered to say thank you in a genuine way, she carried the puppet like he was her precious baby and she hung him up from the foot of her four-poster big girl bed. A few weeks later, when I was shooting the breeze with Mel, I noticed Pinocchio had disappeared. I didn't want to put anybody on the spot; I mean, it was their house and they were certainly free to hang or not hang anything they wanted. But what's a little prying among Girlfriends? I learned that my beloved Mariah awoke to find that intense painted face looking right at her. That would have been terrifying enough, but the horror was compounded by vivid images of noses growing, donkey ears sprouting and little boys turning into wood. That marionette was banished from the bedroom for good, and good riddance as far as I was concerned. In fact, as an old *Twilight Zone* fan, I'm convinced the only good talking puppet is an incinerated talking puppet.

You can try to rationalize with a toddler about the true scarcity of monsters in this world, but you'd probably just be wasting your breath. To my way of thinking, toddlers spend their wakeful nights obsessing about monsters the way parents obsess about unfinished chores and un-returned phone calls. There's just something about the darkness and quiet that inspires our minds to go on endlessly about things that seem insignificant during daylight. Besides, a toddler just isn't a toddler without truly believing in the magical ability of all worldly objects to change their nature at will. Why else do you think that Merlin his been such a hit over the millennium? If you want to test this theory closer to home, apply a complexion facial and pop into your toddler's room. He will either faint or insist you take it off that instant.

The Monster Sweep

The first technique the Girlfriends suggest for conquering all monsters and bad guys under the bed is to devote of couple of minutes each night incorporating a monster search into your toddler's bedtime ritual. Open the closet and look behind the clothes and down near the shoes; get down on your hands and knees to give a thorough check under the bed and bureau; inspect behind the bathroom door and in the tub and shower (What? You never saw *Psycho*?) Then leave the bedroom door open or install a night-light so that it's never pitch black in their room. This Monster Sweep won't guarantee against further monster sightings, but it helps secure you a few hours of sleep before being beckoned for Act II.

When your toddler comes into your room or calls to you with stories about unfriendly beasts in their room, your job as a parent (feel free to share this one fifty-fifty with Dad since he is a full-fledged Monster Killer, too) is to get right up and vanquish the beast. There's a trick to doing this properly, however. While a hug and kiss and a short listen to the scary story is completely in order, as is another, more perfunctory Monster Sweep, any greater involvement than that just ensures that you will be part of the routine *every single time*. There is a fine line between showing compassion to a frightened little person and becoming a sucker who promises to sit on the floor beside the toddler until he goes back to sleep. You and I both know that they don't really trust that we suckers will stay put, so they force themselves to stay semiconscious to be able to check on us every fifteen or twenty minutes. In a nutshell, the most critical survival skill for you, the parent, is getting up and returning your toddler to his own bed, no matter how deliriously tired you are or how inconsolable your darling is. This is the crucible of your toddler sleep crisis. If for any reason, including wakefulness, bad dreams, not wanting to be alone in the middle of the night, etc., your little one feels the need to join your party, the punch line should be a return to bed and all comforting to take place on his turn. In the end, Girlfriend, no matter how you describe it, the ultimate battle of the night is one of wills: your will to sleep uninterrupted and his will to sleep with you. Sooner or later, you are going to have to meet that conflict head-on and emerge victorious.

Overreacting to a toddler's fright provides fodder for future nocturnal visits, either because we encourage their active imagination or because we satisfy their fundamental need for entertainment. I've never met a toddler who wasn't hip to the fact that the more emotional the parent gets, the more times he can be baited into playing the game again. Sure, your toddler might well have a legitimate fear or phobia about something that haunts her dreams, and she obviously needs your help and reassurance. Other toddlers, however, just find themselves awake, alone and lonely and play the monster card to get a grown-up in there on the double. If you don't linger or spend a lot of time chatting about the experience, your toddler will eventually discover that you aren't such good company at night, and he may stop inviting you quite so often. Once again, never underestimate the value of invoking magic: I give a special kiss on the forehead that's called the Angel Guardian Kiss that has the power to guarantee good dreams and keep all monsters at bay.

Night Terrors

Before we end this section, I'd like to mention a common occurrence among older babies and toddlers called night terrors. Up to this point, I have been referring to the run-of-the-mill wakeful fears or bad dreams that toddlers are known for having. These episodes require calming the little one down, offering reassurance, perhaps conducting another Monster Sweep, and finishing with the magic of an Angel Guardian Kiss. Eventually, if all goes according to plan, the sweetie will fall back asleep in the next fifteen to thirty minutes. None of this applies to night terrors. Toddlers having a night terror often open their eyes, talk and move around as if they are awake, but possessed. The first time your baby monitor alerts you to one of these spectacles, you won't know whether to faint or throw yourself on top of your thrashing child. By the way, neither response is particularly well-advised.

Toddlers in the midst of a night terror are, despite all appearances to the contrary, sound asleep. In fact, according to some smart book I once read in a desperate moment, they are in the deepest state of sleep so they aren't even dreaming while this scary outburst is happening. The Girlfriends and I have learned firsthand that the typical night terror is announced by irrational words, screaming or crying, violent movement or wandering around the room, and a seemingly inconsolable child. We are also unanimous in our belief that night terrors are far more frightening for parents than for the poor little thing going through it. There is something about having your child look so familiar and yet be so unreachable in his upset that terrifies even the most stalwart of us.

If you ever have to deal with a night terror, hear the Girlfriends' voices in your ear assuring you "This is not as bad as it looks. You will survive this." As alarming as the episode seems, no great intervention is needed by you, nor will your toddler be traumatized in any way. As a matter of fact, my kids never even remembered that we had had a little midnight get-together when I would quiz them at breakfast the following morning. Your job here is to keep your heartbeat under 220 and direct your attention to keeping your active terrorist from falling out of bed or walking out the front door. Whatever you do, don't try to protect your beloved by restraining him or waking him up. He is too far into Slumberland for a smooth reentry to our world, and you are certain to frighten and disorient him if you interfere.

If you simply cannot sit there quietly and keep watch, and believe me, the odds are high that that will be the case, then just speak very soothingly and softly or perhaps sing a quiet lullaby that the two of you love. He probably won't hear you, but it will keep you from dialing 911 for the fifteen to twenty minutes these terrors generally last. Chances are, he will go back into a peaceful sleep after the night terror's duration and won't ever mention it again. Once again, because I never did get around to going to medical school, I would like to make a disclaimer here: While the vast majority of night terrors are insignificant except for their wear and tear on the parents, any physical or emotional upset that lasts much more than an hour should be reported to your physician because it could be a symptom of something slightly more serious.

The Bedtime Ritual

Some of us prepare for bed by taking off our eye makeup or trimming our nose hairs. Babies usually need little more than a good meal followed by a resounding burp. Toddlers, however, as believers in magic and residents of the Comfort Zone, often have very elaborate little routines that must be completed in a certain order. It's very complicated to segue from free-form adventuring to lying still in bed and settling one's mind enough for sleep. The Girlfriends are big believers in bedtime rituals, but we caution against any song and dance that is so elaborate that you become prisoner to it.

The old standby for the beginning of the sleepy time waltz is the warm bath. Not only does it perform the obvious function of loosening the dried chunks of peanut butter in the hair and Magic Marker stains from around the eyes, but it is relatively contained fun for the little hyperactives. There is something about toddlers and water that is really quite stunning: They love it in almost any variation except poured over their heads to rinse out the shampoo. If you have any business to accomplish in the bathroom, like tweezing your eyebrows or even just catching up on *People* magazine, bathtime is like a gift from the heavens. Just lean back against the tub and dig in while you let that toddler soak and play and pour and splash until you deem bathtime over or until her fingers get all pruny.

Traditionally, the next phase after grooming (and, by the way, don't use Q-Tips in their ears no matter how great the temptation) is tucking into bed and then a song, a prayer or a story. My years of experience suggest that, at least where young toddlers are concerned, you read the same story or one of a small selection of stories every single night. Sure, it can make you cross-eyed with boredom, but toddlers are great fans of repetition. Plus, if they know what to expect from each night's story, they won't force themselves to stay alert for new plots or climaxes. If the heroine ends up safe and sound and delighted with her dress of many colors every single night, your listener can relax and succumb to the fairy dust even before the nighttime anxiety rears its ugly head.

These rituals should be about enough for you and your toddler, but I have always liked the addition of a bedtime prayer or meditation. As much as I respect my religious faith, what I really like about toddler prayers is what they reveal during their devotions. My Girlfriend Carla's daughter, Jillian, recently thanked God for the blessing of her naturally curly hair and the fact that she was the prettiest blonde she knew. She also mentioned her gratitude for Lucky Charms and cotton candy. This is also the time when you learn that your toddler prays to God to rescue her from any playdates with Devon or having to brush her teeth twice a day.

Some of us desperate, humble moms will admit to one last toddler bedtime ritual. VIDEOS. While I know it is eminently objectionable for parents of our generation (in fact, if part of this Guide were R rated, I would put this section there out of shame) to rely on television for anything other than educational programming, I have to say a word or two in defense of its tremendous brain-numbing attributes.

There comes a time in many a mother's life, like when she has to go to her in-laws' fiftieth anniversary party well before her toddler's bedtime, when there just isn't anything as effective at putting the little one to sleep as yet another viewing of *Thumbelina*, unless of course, you were blessed with a child who can't watch videos without dancing along and singing so loud he wakes the dog. You can tell me from now to doomsday that TV is a bad habit and a lazy mom's out, but I am not going to let go of a good thing when I've got it by the tail. If it was good enough for Steven Spielberg, it's certainly good enough for my family, as least when we're at Def Com 4. I would never put television ahead of reading a book or chitchatting, but it sure is a grand last-minute replacement when the ritual is falling flat or there just isn't time for the whole rigamarole. Just call me a creature of teletechnology; if there was a computer program that was guaranteed to put my kids to sleep, I would buy stock in the company.

One Is the Loneliest Number

My adorable husband once explained to me that the reason he couldn't sleep well when he traveled without me was because "everybody needs a *live* thing to sleep with." (You don't suppose I was being hyped, do you?) While there are nights every once in a while when I, a mate of seventeen years and a mother for over a decade, can't imagine anything more delicious than an entire bed to myself, I completely understand what he means. It can be very hard for all of us, toddlers in particular, to deal with those lonely hours when we're awake in the middle of the night and there's no one to play with.

Insult is added to injury when the toddler is awake and there is all sorts of socializing going on, just not in his room. As tired as we adults generally are, it's rare for us to go to bed at the same time as a two-year-old. In fact, getting the two-year-old into bed is often the starting pistol for all those activities that we don't get to do when we have a toddler underfoot. We may sit down to a nice meal, we may have friends over or we may just turn on the television and veg for an hour or two, and, hey, what about that laundryfest you've been putting off till now? You can't imagine how irresistible all of this sounds to a toddler who hasn't yet succumbed to slumber.

Closing the door and/or keeping the activity level down until the toddler goes to sleep is a start in the right direction. I would never endorse fibbing to your toddler, but I don't see anything wrong with letting her labor under the delusion that when she sleeps, everyone on the planet sleeps. Most little kids sleep so soundly once they've drifted off that you can dance the limbo and sing karaoke without waking them.

In addition to keeping the decibel and energy levels moderate at bedtime, you can also help your toddler overcome nighttime loneliness by providing all necessary "loveys," as well as something to play with when the solitary confinement becomes unbearable. I wouldn't put a set of building blocks or an entire tea set in the crib or bed, but I would consider slipping in a favorite picture book. Better still, put in a book like *Pat the Bunny*, since it has amusing activities built into it including those toddler favorites, mirrors.

Early to Bed, Early to Rise

Once we've become accustomed to whatever it takes to get our toddlers to sleep, we have one last parenting challenge in the snooze department: getting them to sleep past dawn. My four-year-old still gets up between 5:30 and 6:00 every morning, and boy, does it stink. She's been doing it for nearly two years now. The only difference between her and roosters is that they crow and she asks for eggs, sunny-side up. My Girlfriend Alison's little boy wakes up demanding to play, with his big brothers, with his mom and dad, with the cat, ANYBODY—he just needs to start having fun as soon as possible! My Girlfriend Maggie's little girl is also interested in getting some companionship as quickly as possible, but she's discovered that running full speed into her parents' room screaming that the witches are chasing her is more effective than calmly suggesting a predawn game of Chutes and Ladders.

This is a good news/bad news situation. Let me give you the bad news first: Some toddlers just love to get a jump on the day and will do so no matter how late you keep them up or how many naps you skip. It's funny, really, because it's such a mind game with us parents. I don't know why, but 5:30 A.M. sounds *hours* earlier than 6:00 or 6:30, and we would give our kingdoms to anyone who could help us reclaim that precious dawn sleep. If you're thinking that you'd like to train your kids to sleep until 7:00 or 8:00, you'd better think again. Yeah, I have several Girlfriends who let their toddlers stay up until 10 or 11 o'clock at night and sleep until 8:00 the next morning. This is particularly common when both parents work outside the home until late in the evening. They love having more time to spend with their child, and since they're up anyway, no problem. Well, the problem arises when you have to teach your little night owl to get up and get ready for preschool or day care early in the morning. As you know, I am a pushover in a lot of child-rearing matters, but because *I* am a morning person, I have been more willing to stick with the early-to-bed, painfully-early-to-rise routine in our house. Besides, it helps make the morning task of getting four kids up and out before 7:15 every morning just a bit more manageable.

The good new is: Toddlers really do learn to sleep later in the morning when they give up that precious afternoon nap. I always hated to say goodbye to that nap; it was such a delicious time-out for me to take a shower and slug down a couple of glasses of iced tea, but its passing often translated into a longer night's sleep for all of us. Here is some other good news: Toddlers can be *taught* to cool their jets and stay content in their cribs or beds for a half hour, sometimes more. They won't learn, however, if you respond to their morning cries by running in to their rooms or hauling yourself out of bed to chase the witches away.

Early mornings are best approached as *late nights* in the toddler-training arena, especially if it's still dark outside. Explain, in ten words or less, that it's still sleep time and that Cutie Patootie needs to go back to bed for more rest. This is the same basic technique that you use to get your child to sleep in his or her own bed at any time: few words, repetition, consistency. If you're lucky, she will either go back to sleep or she'll amuse herself with some songs and, perhaps, by taking her pajamas off. Once again, I'd like to give a plug to the makers of baby monitors since they are invaluable to mothers trying to translate their toddlers' waking noises. My rule of thumb was:

1. Deep breathing usually means sleep;
2. Quiet chatter means content;
3. Screaming means not content; and
4. Utter silence means she's escaped and you'd better get your backside out of bed immediately if you want to find her before she finds the hidden Halloween candy.

Need I even say that your toddler won't learn to sleep or quietly amuse herself in the predawn hours if you lead her back to bed two nights/mornings in a row, then cave in on the third by pulling her into your own bed and praying to God that the three of you will go back to sleep. Look, I'm not trying to judge because I personally find an early morning cuddle rather wonderful, but it's probably best in the long run (what with old jobs to return to and new babies eventually joining the family) to just keep your bed to yourself.

Cry Me a River

I'm going to go out on a limb here and assume that you don't really have a grip on the specifics of your toddler's sleep; where, when and with whom. If you do, I invite you to stick this out with me anyway because our grips on anything toddler-related tend to be more slippery than fists full of mercury. Even the most cooperative sleeper can get a bee in her bonnet or sense a change in the wind, and, POOF, you're talking about a midnight rambler. It doesn't hurt to put a few tricks up your sleeve now, while you're presumably awake, so that you have them when you're bleary-eyed with need.

Let's start with the fundamental truth: *Parents deserve to sleep alone.* Notice that I use the word *deserve* rather than *should* or *must*, and that's because I wouldn't dream of messing with your mix if your little trio of a family thinks the "lifeboat" approach to sleep, with the whole family on board, is the most wonderful thing since rock and roll; by all means, rock on. I'm just reminding you that it's clearly written in the Girlfriends' By-laws that parents have absolutely no obligation to sleep clinging to the edge of the bed or with a child's foot in their mouth, or to camp out on the extra bed in the child's room until he is old enough to go away to college. The problem here is that no matter how much you're on the side of righteousness, your child will never be the first one to support you in your decision.

The solution, Girlfriend, is hard and simple:

You must fight for the right *not* to party all night.

That means you must go to battle with your beloved child over this issue and emerge the victor. There will be more tears than you can bear, more fierce headaches than Tylenol in a bottle and more raging fights with your mate than the time you invited your mom out for a month but failed to tell him, but if peace is achieved in Slumberland, all the pain will be forgotten after the first good night's sleep.

We all know the books and theories by everyone from Ferber to Freud that give advice about how to get a child to sleep in his own bed, and we all understand the basic premise: Toddler doesn't want to sleep in own bed, Parents want him to, Parents must convince him, quickly. What we parents really want to know is: How can we convince them without making them so sad and upset? Why do all the ideas that look most promising or that are endorsed by blissfully-sleeping parents involve so much misery on the part of the toddler? Can't we just explain it to them in a way they can understand? Can't we do something to make their own bed or crib more appealing (like fill it with gummy bears and boxes of fruit punch)? Why must the entire family end up in tears?

The answer to that is: *I don't know.* I have spent nearly ten years of my life wrestling, with very mixed success, with the different approaches to teaching my children to stay and sleep in their own beds, and it only seems to work when disappointment and tears are involved. But here's some good news: I have also discovered that crying never killed anyone. We parents have got to forego the title of Most Groovy Mommy or Daddy and become Most Wise and Consistent Mommy or Daddy long enough to teach our children that there are certain behavioral rules that must be followed if they plan to join us in our larger community. Think back on your own upbringing, misguided though it may have been: Do you remember the three nights of misery that you endured while your parents made it clear to you that their bed was not your bed? Of course not. What you remember is that you never got an Easy Bake Oven for Christmas when that was all you really wanted in the world, or that your aunt Hattie had a mole on her neck that had a hair in it, or how Daddy's beard felt on a Saturday morning when he hadn't shaved. Sleeping trauma? Forget it; that's reserved for us parents, and we must remember that we are grown-up enough to take it on the chin.

Unfortunately, this isn't a painful-but-fast procedure, like a bikini wax. Rather, it is something that must be repeated whenever growth, illness, change or a scary movie intrudes into your child's life. I have kids coming into my room in the middle of the night with crises ranging from scary monsters in the hallway to pre-math test jitters to concerns about who the most popular girl in school is. From ten months to ten years, the approach is the same: Go back to bed, I'll tuck you in, and we'll talk about the rest in the morning. If that sounds like a life sentence, let me hasten to add that the tears stop at about year six. You really do know what's best for your family—you just have to be bold enough to set the rules and keep them, Mommy.

Top Ten Toddler Lessons

10. Never try to shop with a toddler at more than one su-
perstore (as in Costco *and* Sam's Club) in a single day.

9. Assume that they will swallow chewing gum, no matter
how much they protest to the contrary.

8. Always make them use the potty (once potty trained,
that is) before they get into the bath; otherwise you end
up with a contaminated bath.

7. Presume that your toddler will get an ear infection the
day before the family vacation or any plane ride. Don't
fret; just keep gallons of Dimetapp on hand.

6. Expect Santa Claus, live Disney characters and Halloween to be the subject of at least two weeks of nightmares for your toddler.

5. It's common for toddlers to prefer one parent over the
other; don't get your feelings hurt, because the prefer-
ences will change several times in the next two decades.

4. Never assume a child is "pool safe" until she can swim
a full length, take proper breaths, and apply her own
sunscreen.

3. Don't lie about whether a doctor's visit will include a
shot. It's best to plead ignorance until the exam is over,

then explain that there will be a quick shot. Promise to hold your toddler in your arms and hug her tight until the boo-boo is over.

2. No one, except perhaps your mate, wants to hear more than three minutes about the adorable thing your toddler did today. Pictures, too, are just barely tolerable and should be limited to two.

1. Keep a plastic mattress pad on your child's bed until she is about six years old. No matter how potty proficient she is, there's sure to be an accident sometime between now and first grade.

chapter eight

Fashion

Your primary concerns when dressing an infant are to maintain a healthy body temperature and to keep the baby comfy. When the baby starts to crawl, a helpful parent will cooperate by dressing her in clothes that don't restrict forward movement or get caught on things. But when the baby becomes a toddler, her clothing concerns become more like yours and mine. She still needs to stay warm and comfy, but she also needs to be able to run and play and, certainly, to make a good impression on other people. The most frightening difference, however, between dressing babies and toddlers is that toddlers actually have *opinions* about what they wear. Gone are the days of acting out your fashion whims by costuming your tractable little baby. Toddlers have favorite colors, aversions to certain undergarments and strange emotional attachments to apparently ordinary things as T-shirts or socks; and they are not going to surrender to the Mr. Blackwell in you without a good fight.

As with baby clothes, choices abound for your toddler's wardrobe. Nearly every trendy store or high fashion designer has noticed our fashion obsessions with our babies and branched off into kidswear, too. The big challenge here is to avoid going broke trying to keep up with current fashion. There really is a knack to buying things that are cute, functional, durable and appealing that the two of you can agree on. Unfortunately, it's usually only by the second or third kid that you acquire it. Here's hoping we can save you some time, money and misery with a head start from the Girlfriends.

Look for the Bare Necessities

After two or three years of selecting outfits for your toddler, having them rejected, and battling over whether pajama tops can be worn as play clothes, you will begin to understand why many mothers select their children's schools based on whether or not they have uniforms. It's so time-and-attention-consuming to keep a passel of young children groomed that you will probably have to choose between their appearance and yours. Easter Sunday, for example, requires so much effort to get the fancy duds on four clean and coiffed kids that I usually end up taking them to church with dirty hair and sweatpants on. When my friends ask why my husband and I never appear in the family Christmas card photo, I explain that we can't even get our teeth brushed on the day the photo is taken because we are so busy begging the little ones to keep their shoes tied and their panties in place.

Just like Donna Karan has always advised for us Girlfriends, toddlers, too, need certain essentials in their wardrobes to get them through any fashion challenge. Once you have acquired those essentials, you are free to branch out to sparkly red party shoes, Air Jordan warm-up suits and anything that comes in an animal print. Given that every household has different laundry capabilities (such as the need to go to a Laundromat or a phobia about fabric softeners), we Girlfriends have come up with a suggested toddler core wardrobe:

Three Pairs of Shoes. Good old sneakers are ideal footwear for every day; then a pair of nicer shoes should be on hand for those times when soil-colored footwear won't do. A seasonal shoe such as sandals for the summer or boots for the winter round out the bunch. If you are big churchgoers or have a social calendar full of white-glove engagements, then, by all means, feel free to indulge in one pair of dress-up shoes to impress the relatives.

Five pairs of underwear. If your toddler is a member of the dry pants society, you will always need to carry a spare for those inevitable accidents that even the most potty-savvy toddlers have. If getting the laundry done is a concern, then splurge the extra ninety-nine cents on extra panties; you will not be sorry.

Four to six undershirts. Toddlers are much more efficient at regulating their body temperature than babies, and you will probably find that undershirts are not always needed, especially here in California. As a matter of fact, your toddler, with his residual layers of body fat and his high energy level, will often be quite warm while you are standing there shivering. Nonetheless, grandmas and cautious moms like to know they have that layer of insulation in case of rapid blizzard onset, or, more frequently, that sudden chill that autumn afternoons and winter mornings present.

Seven pairs of socks. Normally I would stick with the magical number of four to six of the everyday essentials, but we all know the disappearing nature of socks. If you think it's hard to keep track of your spouse's big old socks, finding the mates to toddler socks, which measure about four inches long from toe to top, will make you wish that they, like Pull-Ups, were thrown away after each use.

Four to five pairs of pants (fewer if your daughter absolutely refuses to wear "boys' clothes," in which case you might consider a few pairs of stretch leggings). Lots of parents have a nostalgic preference for blue jeans, but they really aren't the ideal toddler garment, especially when they close with an exact replica of a 501 zipper. Pants with elastic waists (remember, toilet training is going to be a consideration) and that are made of a more softer and pliable fabric than regulation denim. Sure, a wardrobe of sweatpants every single day can earn your child the nickname Joey Buttafuco, but as long as he keeps away from rolling a pack of cigarettes in his T-shirt sleeve, he can probably pull it off. Besides, all sorts of mini-hip clothes now come with elastic waists—what do you think made Dockers such a hit with daddies with spreading midriffs? Try to save one pair of pants, maybe corduroys or mini-chinos, with zippers, for those times when you want to impress the family or when pictures are going to be taken.

Five T-shirts or other cotton wash-and-wear tops. It's always a good idea to keep one good white shirt on standby (keeping it safely in a drawer for those special days when your toddler will not be offered any food or given any markers, pizza or paints), but colored and patterned turtlenecks, polos and tees are better for everyday wear because toddlers can conceive of more ways to stain a shirt than Spray 'n Wash ever imagined. Better to have the markers and grape juice look like part of the overall illustration than evidence that you have another trip to the Gap in your immediate future.

Four dresses (for those of you with girly girls). One of these frocks should be what we moms (or grandmas) refer to as a party dress, but the others—simple cotton numbers like they sell in the Hanna Andersson catalog or, once again, the Gap—will get more everyday use and needn't be too fussy. A cotton or denim jumper is also a cute and versatile choice.

Four pairs of tights (girls only, unless your son wants to be Peter Pan). One black and one white, the rest optional. Tights are antithetical to most potty-training efforts, but there are times when fashion simply must prevail. Whenever possible, try to avoid dressing your toddler girl in the baby equivalent of panty hose if you aren't going to be around to help because they are so stretchy and unmanageable, they droop in the crotch and they are impossible for preschoolers to pull up and down in time for a visit to the potty. My daughters used to get all the way to the bathroom, lift up their dresses, pull down their tights and panties, and then proceed to pee pee all over the tops of the tights, which, of course, hadn't been pulled down far enough to avoid toilet contact. I understand that colder climates dictate this fashion challenge for girls who were only recently babies, but pray for an understanding preschool teacher to help you out.

Two pullovers, sweaters or, better still, sweatshirts. Every mom on the go knows that it's usually chilly in the morning when you load your toddler into the car to begin the day, and then warms up as the errands and playdates stack up. You don't want to dress your child for a Mount Everest assault when the weather will eventually be almost tropical, but a sweater or sweatshirt straddles that climate hump quite nicely. By the way, I'm suggesting pullovers because buttons and toddlers don't usually mix. (If buttons are not your personal fashion Armageddon, however, then by all means, get a cardigan or two because they are adorable, in a Ralph Lauren sort of way.) Even if your toddler can't pull a sweatshirt over his head unassisted, and has no time for buttons, he will usually submit to a quick tug on and off and carry on about his business.

One warm coat or jacket. Unless you live in Hawaii, odds are pretty good that you will encounter weather that is more than a sweatshirt can combat. While baseball-style jackets can be cute and comfy, I think a longer-cut coat with a hood is more practical. Since most of our body heat is lost via our heads, and since little bottoms and tailbones are exposed every time the toddler bends over or sits down, you would be wise to cover both ends with a proper coat. For my money the best toddler winter coats are those that have a hooded waterproof nylon shell over a warm wool or polar fleece body. The shell should be detachable from the liner so that it can function as a raincoat when needed. Keep in mind that lots of coats are made of boiled wool and lots of kids loathe the feeling of wool as much as they hate being put in a playpen, so look for a poly blend like that great fleecy stuff that is all the rage for joggers and mountaineers.

Three pairs of pajamas. There is actually some heated controversy regarding this area of toddler attire. It's not a fashion crisis on the level of, say, skirt lengths or whether gray is a viable color for real women, but rather a very serious safety issue. In most states, any article of clothing that is labeled or sold as "pajamas" or "sleepwear" must, by law, be fire retardant. If you have ever seen those *Consumer Digest* demonstrations of how quickly nonretardant pj's go up in flames, you'll be tempted to put your toddler to bed in an asbestos suit.

Still, in all candor, fire-retardant jammies are not the most appealing articles of clothing: They may look like they're made of soft flannel, but water spilled on them just beads up and runs right off, and the seams are stitched with a thread resembling fine-gauge fishing line.

For those of us who are willing to sacrifice safety for fashion, at least on those nights when we plan to sleep armed with fire extinguishers on mattresses on our toddler's bedroom floors, there are "pajamas" that go by euphemisms. Toddler "loungewear" or "thermal underwear" are usually 100 percent cotton and are as soft and cuddly as a favorite teddy bear. In my home, I sometimes shirked responsibility by selecting coziness over safety by letting my toddlers pick. Needless to say, their judgment was questionable, to say the least, but I was leaning toward the cotton jammies anyway, and all I needed was one toddler to complain about the fire-retardant thread puncturing their necks, armpits and wrists. I've never heard whether I did the right thing in my toddler sleepwear choices, but we survived intact. I just don't want to appear cavalier where your precious child is concerned.

The Girlfriends come down on the side of pajamas rather than nightgowns for toddlers. Unless your child is that infamous prodigy we have been hearing about in our Mommy and Me class and at the local coffee bar who doesn't need a diaper at night, pj's make the most sense because they add one more level of dryness and, even more charming, they make your darlin' look like a koala from the back. Pajamas also tend to stay down around the legs where they belong, while nightgowns bunch up around a toddler's neck and shoulders like a flannel boa. Since I have yet to meet a toddler who sleeps in bed in the traditional manner of head on pillow, feet extended to foot of bed and covers neatly on top, keeping warm and covered by pj's takes on extra importance.

One pair of slippers or nonskid socks. I have yet to hear a toddler complain about his cold feet, which is understandable given the fat they are wrapped in, but I still feel more satisfied as a mommy when I know those post-bath feet are protected. The most important considerations for slippers are that they be nonskid, that they stay on snugly and that they don't cost more than about $5, since they are almost always ugly and rarely get seen in public, anyway. As for those slippers with the stuffed heads of Tweety or Minnie on the toes, the Girlfriends don't recommend them for toddlers. People between the ages of one and four are not known for being graceful and nimble, and they will trip over their own feet under the best of circumstances; no need to trip them up with slippers that look like parade floats. Besides, lots of little kids are terrified of putting their feet into these combination slippers/stuffed animals—they worry that what they slip into those cunning little creatures may never come out again.

Having had my say about the essential components of a toddler's wardrobe, let's chat a bit about the folklore and prejudices that surround specific articles of clothing. As you can well imagine, mothers throughout history have tremendous emotional investments in whether their kids wear hats, walking shoes or shirts with collars. I'm sure the Pilgrims were just as nutty about buckles and the pre–French Revolutionaries about plumes. It just goes with the basic belief that our children are living extensions of our value as people: In other words, an appropriately dressed child is a reflection of good parenting, or something like that.

The Thing About the Shoes

Shoes are, in my observation, the clothing with the most entrenched and detailed belief system, so let's start there. About a generation ago any child who turned one and had not yet been fitted with proper walking shoes was deemed a victim of poor parenting. The thinking was that the little meat loaf that is a baby's foot could never support his body and develop properly unless his arches and ankles were bolstered by a good, stiff pair of shoes. For decades, most baby shoes looked like little white leather boots with laces. As a matter of fact, I think Abe Lincoln's baby portrait shows him in those very shoes. Fortunately for us, walking shoes have gone the way of shoe polish; nobody uses either anymore. Evidently, someone noticed that there are still several parts of the world where people master walking and even running without ever slipping their feet into a good old-fashioned pair of Buster Browns. Who can forget those incredible Ethiopians of the sixties and seventies who won the Olympics marathons running *barefoot*? Sure enough, Mother Nature was vindicated, as was her plan for walking shoeless.

Nowadays, any reputable shoe salesperson will tell you that it's not a good idea to put shoes on a child who is just learning to walk. Not that shoes will, in my humble opinion, seriously hamper a baby yearning to toddle, but they are no longer considered standard equipment. Putting aside the notion that the first trip to the shoe store was once a cherished rite of passage, there is no real reason for toddlers to wear them. They can be cumbersome and slippery, they interfere with the traction of gripping toes, and they cost money that can easily be spent elsewhere. I know that those little Air Jordans are irresistible, but if you can't resist, then try to limit yourself to just one pair that you can eventually put in the keepsake box. In the meantime, let your toddler feel the fresh air on his tootsies whenever possible.

If you, like I, have a phobic aversion to cold feet, or if your live in a climate where barefoot season is limited to the hottest summer months, you will certainly be tempted to find a toasty middle ground between barefoot and shod. The obvious compromise is socks, but unless you buy the kind with the rubbery grids on the soles (like those cute little ticktacktoes) and make sure that they are always on straight with the soles facing the floor, socks can turn a harmless wood or linoleum floor into a perilous ice rink. My Girlfriend Sonia and I watched helplessly during a family ski vacation several years ago while our besocked daughters played tag inside the house and her Kelly hit the floor forehead first after skidding around a corner. Let me tell you, there are about a million things I would rather do than spend my ski holiday in the emergency room. (By the way, take it from Sonia and me that cuts to the head bleed way more than they should. Kelly's cut didn't even warrant stitches, but for a time, we were convinced her brains would leak out.)

If you just can't stand to have your toddler padding around barefoot, a good compromise are those knit slippers with the sueded leather bottoms that you can find in any department store, children's shoe store or kids' clothing catalog. It's best to buy them to fit right this minute rather than buy large for your little honey to grow into because they are most effective when they are a bit of a struggle to put on. They need to be snug to keep the rubber on the road, so to speak. Since they don't cost much, and are almost always cheaper than shoes, you can afford to replace them as needed. Better still, ask your Girlfriends with bigger children to save theirs for you since these things last longer than foam cups. The knitted part does pill and will most certainly be faded from several washings, but the original owners grow out of them so quickly, it seems a shame to just throw them in the trash. Keep in mind, they were never that attractive to start with, so why get fussy about their appearance as hand-me-downs? Besides, they are not intended for public display, and are therefore no reflection on your personal sense of toddler style.

Of course, older toddlers with full and busy lives outside the home will certainly need to wear shoes. I'm not going to step on your fashion prerogatives here and tell you what to buy, but I have a couple of words you should keep in mind: *Velcro* and *nonskid*. I have spent so many years bending over to tie shoelaces that I have vertigo. (I've recently noticed that I grunt every time I drop to shoe level, which makes me sound even older and more out of shape than I already feel.) If you like a shoe, I suggest that you always ask whether it comes with Velcro closures. The other lesson I learned the hard way was: Never send a little girl off to play with pretty little Mary Janes on her dainty feet. The soles of those party-type shoes are slick and slip right off the ladder on a playground slide. I also learned that just because catalogs show teeny people standing upright in hip little clogs doesn't mean they can do so in real life. If you ask me, the best shoes are those that can be thrown in the washing machine, don't cost over $25 and answer you when you clap your hands like those talking key chains, since I never can put together a matching pair when I need one.

Party Dresses

I really do try to stay gender neutral when I write about kids, no matter how sincerely I believe that boys and girls are born with certain inherent differences, but the subject of fancy dresses for little girls was compelling enough in my own life to make me think it deserves a mention here. Any mother of a little girl knows how frustrating it is to put a dress on an infant; it either scrunches up beneath her in her infant seat or stroller or, when she's older, forms a tent that the baby gets stuck in when she learns to crawl.

When my daughters learned to walk, I didn't just see girls who had mastered a critical developmental skill, I saw two mannequins just waiting to be put in party dresses. I couldn't wait to finally froufrou them up in all the dresses I had received from baby showers and first birthday parties and had stashed in the back of the closet until this magical moment. I felt that if the Duchess of York could dress her little darlings in matching smocked pique dresses with bows in the back every single day (or at least so it appeared from the photos in the *Enquirer*), then I should be able get it together for my girls at least once or twice a month.

It turned out that my girls just weren't the froufrou kind, and they let me know it as soon as they mastered the word "NO." My elder daughter, in particular, loathed all clothing that itched or was restraining in any way, which most party dresses do with their little slips and peter pan collars. I also discovered something even more important: If you put a toddler girl in a dress any time but summer, she needs tights to keep her legs warm, and, as I mentioned earlier, tights are nearly impossible for anyone under the age of four to pull down in time to get to the potty. You might as well wrap the poor little thing in a straitjacket and then force-feed her fluids. Even if she doesn't get tripped up by tights, a little girl in a frock always has a fifty-fifty chance of sitting on the hem or the pretty bow sash when she uses the potty. In spite of their restrictions, dresses do look adorable on toddlers and you should adorn yours in them when relatives come to visit, or better still, for very brief photo sessions. The rest of the time, outfit her for real life.

Toddlers as Miniature Adults

My third child was born wearing a stern expression, and he has been a pretty serious chap ever since. There is nothing he hates more than people laughing loudly, unless it's people laughing loudly *at him*. And we all know there are few things more inclined to make people guffaw than a toddler in full superhero regalia including cape and mask. That's when I learned that my children's fashion expression reached beyond the safety of our own home. It turns out, toddlers actually have a very different agenda for their clothes, and, particularly with younger toddlers, that involves everything from comfort and function to whether they stand out in a crowd or blend in.

Indulge me while I hammer this nail one more time, but too often our children are the outward manifestations of our hopes and dreams. It is beyond tempting to involve them in expressing who we think we are or who we aspire to be. If this phenomenon didn't go any further than fashion, it would probably be nothing more than a harmless annoyance to our toddlers, but it spreads into school performance, athletic performance, and even body image. For this reason, I humbly suggest that we occasionally curb our desire to costume our children as if they were tiny adults who were far cooler and richer (judging by the price of their outfits) than we are. One of the biggest lessons we parents must learn is *our children are not us*. Much as we would love to, we cannot correct our shortcomings or re-create our triumphs through our kids. I guess all I'm trying to say is, when you find that you and your toddler go out somewhere together, and he looks like he came in a limo and you look like you came by Greyhound, you might want to turn your mirror around to reflect yourself occasionally. It's rarely a good idea to try to hide behind your eminently presentable toddler when you look like something the cat dragged in.

Clothes Companions

Combine a toddler's newfound need to have a say in his personal style and his need for the comfort and reassurance of the familiar and, *voilà*, you have that trying toddler behavior of picking one article of clothing and wearing it every single day. This item can be anything from a favorite pair of pants with big cargo pockets to a T-shirt that used to belong to an idolized big brother. My older son's choice was a black Batman cape. Yes, for several months of my life I was fortunate enough to be able to call the Caped Crusader my personal companion. He went to the grocery store in character, he slept dressed for crime fighting and he even wore it over his naked body when he escaped from his bath and went tearing down the hall. Despite the appeal of being little Batman's personal companion, I was constantly trying to lose that cape. Sure, people thought we made an adorable sight, but I really preferred them to see my son in his darling little shorts and miniature polo shirt tucked in with a preppie web belt.

Not only was the cape slightly embarrassing to me, the mother, but it was a tremendous responsibility not to lose or damage it in any way. Any mother of a toddler knows there's hell to pay when a favorite article of clothing has been left somewhere or inadvertently thrown into the washing machine. Occasionally I would get him to compromise with the cape by letting me carry it for him, the thought being that he would have it in close proximity without actually donning it. I can still picture myself digging for my wallet in the huge rucksack I call a purse and pulling out a rolled up Batman cape to lay on the checkout counter like a magician about to begin her act.

I wasn't the only mom running through her errands with a cartoon character in tow. One of my Girlfriends' daughters was like Oz's Dorothy with a pair of ruby-colored sparkle shoes that she even insisted on wearing beneath the blankets. Another's little darling kept his Superman pajamas on all day, even if they had to be layered under the more "presentable" clothing that his mom had chosen for him to wear, and still another's daughter never left the castle without full Belle regalia.

The good news about this clothing fetish is that it passes. The bad news is there is usually nothing you can do to hurry it along. Once again,

I suggest invoking another of the parents' mantras, "Our toddler's occasional bizarreness is not a reflection of our parenting. All toddlers are bizarre." Perhaps it will give you the peace of mind needed to endure this fashion crisis till it resolves itself. In the meantime, you can continue to suggest your little darling try a different shirt or pants, but when that suggestion falls on deaf ears, just let it ride. Whatever you do, don't make it a battle of wills because the price you must pay to win makes everybody miserable.

Clothes Fetishes

My firstborn child, a darling little boy who is now prepubescent (I could just die!) would wear anything I put on him. Even as a toddler and preschooler, when most kids develop an opinion about their sartorial statement, he couldn't have cared less. Then along came my first daughter and the spell was broken. She hated elastic, she hated ruffles that might rub against her face or arms, and she hated any article of clothing that had seams that weren't bound and finished with the care and attention of a French couturier. She also hated anything blue, but loved anything orange (oh, joy!), but that was a lesser problem. If she could have dressed herself every day, she would have worn a pair of slip-on sandals, cotton knit shorts and a T-shirt that she had outgrown months ago. Judging from my quick flip through the family photo albums, she must have dressed herself far more often than I remembered.

My Girlfriend Shelly's little girl, Chelsea, was sock phobic. She could not tolerate socks that were creased inside her shoes or that had thick seams across the toes. Poor Shelly would spend hours going from store to store, comparing the placement and stitching or each toe seam and heel insert. But that wasn't enough; she had to apply Chelsea's socks with surgical precision. The whole family could be in the car speeding to drop-offs, and Shelly would look in the rearview mirror to see Chelsea quietly removing her shoes and socks (and often her panties, too, but that's another story) in the backseat.

This clothing hypersensitivity is not limited to socks. Other kids have a deep-seated need to have their belts and dress sashes tied so tightly that they can barely take a deep breath. Still others can't abide shirts or blouses tucked into pants. There are as many fashion fetishes as there are toddlers, and the fun lies in watching it manifest itself and trying not to let it push every one of your buttons.

Who Needs Hats?

The issue of whether to put a hat on your baby's head presents itself in infancy. As a resident of balmy southern California, I didn't grow up in a hat culture—the only climatic effects we fear in my neighborhood, at least that a hat could help prevent, is premature wrinkling. My New York mother-in-law, however, hated to see a little bald head exposed anywhere out-of-doors. From her parenting perspective, no well-cared-for infant was considered fully dressed without a nice warm hat pulled down over his ears. As I mentioned in *The Girlfriends' Guide to Pregnancy*, she and I compromised nicely here; her grandbabies wore hats whenever Grandma was visiting or we were visiting her. The rest of the year, they went bareheaded.

The hat issue can be even more confusing in the toddler years. You might think that, except for the rare Arctic expedition or Midwestern blizzard, a toddler's head is reasonably well protected by her hair and by having outgrown the general fragility of infancy. If that's so, then why are all the stores showing children's spring clothes with matching hats? Is this a throwback to some fashion designer's secret desire to be Judy Garland in *Easter Parade* or is it a sensible reminder that, while spring is here, there is still a chill in the air and no good mother would send her little bunny out without a boater?

Actually, I think we're back to the toddlers in adult clothing issue again. For those suckers among us who can't look at our toddler without seeing a blank canvas on which to create a fashion statement, the hat is literally the crowning glory. Hats do look adorable on kids, but, aside from the odd cowboy hat or baseball cap, I don't know too many hats that a toddler will actually *keep* on his or her head for more than five seconds.

Once again, comfort is usually the determinative force in toddler style. If a little girl isn't driven to distraction by the stiff straw around the brim of her spring bonnet, she will nearly choke from the elastic string running under her fat little chin to keep the bonnet in place or feel claustrophobic with the knit ski-type hats we send along in winter. We all have those miserable Easter photos of ourselves as little kids, and how happy do we really look in those getups? Bottom line here is, if your child and you both like hats, knock yourself out; if it's freezing, make a hat a prerequisite to outdoor play. Otherwise, I don't care how thin and flyaway your little girl's hair still is, she should not be forced to hide it under a hat.

How to Dress Them for the Day

The mother of an infant delights in changing its clothes several times a day. By the time your infant is a toddler, the bloom is off that particular rose. Toddler moms would like to dress the child once for the day and only change articles as needed after accidents. This is fine in theory, though not in practice. Think about it: Every morning you must evaluate the weather (both actual and probable) and your child's activities for the entire day while keeping in mind that you haven't had a chance to do laundry in a week, so the wardrobe pickings are slim, and then outfit your little adventurer for the day. This is particularly tough when the kid goes to day care or preschool, where you won't be able to adjust the wardrobe if there's been an unexpected change in barometric pressure. I still actually march outside in my pajamas most mornings to look up in the sky for some divine sign about the weather before deciding whether my kids need jackets, sweaters, or just a long-sleeved shirt. Raincoats are still beyond my skills as a weathermother; I never send them along when they are needed, and I always send them when it's dry as kindling and my kids are certain to leave them on the playground or jammed into their cubbies until the next monsoon.

Since none of us can really hold ourselves to prognosticating standards any higher than those of our local TV weatherman, we are bound to call it wrong a high percentage of the time. The most common mistake made in my crowd is when we think the warm morning sun will burn brightly all day, we dress our kids for it, only to look out the window two hours later to see that the wind is howling, the sun is hiding and our child is probably hypothermic by now. Worse, he is shivering and getting blue lips to a noticeable degree, and everyone in the preschool or day care is passing judgments on the kind of mother who would send her child out into the world so unprotected. Well, I may be slow, but I'm not stupid, and I've learned this lesson:

Never send your child out of your care without a wrap.

I don't care if it's as hot as Hades when you dress her, she still might go into air-conditioning or get a chill and need a sweater. Really, is it that hard to throw a thin sweatshirt into his backpack or tie it around his waist? If nothing else, he can use it to wipe his hands and nose on or use as a pillow at rest time.

The other tried-and-true rule to help your toddler dress for success is this:

Layers.

It's true for you and it's true for toddlers, too. Give everyone the opportunity to peel or add clothing on as the need arises. Just make sure that the layering is simple and doesn't interfere with a novice using the potty. Stick to an undershirt or light T-shirt on top with a shirt over it and a sweater packed and ready to go, but leave the bottom half simple and single-layered. It's hard enough to get those pants down when they're in a hurry, and it's unspeakably unfair for a toddler to think he's home free, only to discover that he's peeing all over the pajama bottoms you left on him. But even that kind of clothing disaster can be remedied if sometime at the beginning of the session you have sent a shoebox or a big Ziploc bag to preschool or day care with a complete change of clothes, right down to shoes, socks and mittens (for those of you with Arctic winters).

Check for Fit

Certain articles of toddler clothing are only worn occasionally, but when you need them you really *need* them. These are such things as rain boots, winter coats and party shoes. You can go for weeks or months never taking them out of the closet or even looking at them, then comes El Niño or your nephew's bar mitzvah, and you're digging them out of the back of the closet. Problem is, they may not fit anymore and you are already running so late that a quick shopping spree isn't an option. In fact, brushing your little one's hair is looking pretty iffy. The only sensible reaction to this kind of crisis, at least for the mommies, is to groan and try to find a way to blame the daddies.

Knowing this scenario as intimately as I do, my advice is to pull those puppies out of the closet for a quick fitting session at least once every couple of months. Since my toddlers hated being dressed and undressed, I usually subjected them to this irritating little chore right after a nice warm bath before they got their jammies on. I also tried never to get more than one article of clothing fitted in an evening because a full wardrobe check was sure to leave both of us in tears. Once I knew the wardrobe status, I could calmly pick up a new pair of shoes or a new winter coat when it was convenient, or, better still, when I saw them on sale. By the way, while you have the clothes out in good lighting, make sure that they are clean and aren't missing buttons. The basic toddler button rule is: Once popped, a button is gone for life. You will never find it, and even if you do, you will lose it well before you find your needle and thread.

Every once in a while a toddler is invited to serve as a ring bearer or flower girl or to participate in some other formal occasion. This is almost always a thrilling compliment, not to mention a hysterically funny video opportunity, and it generally starts with a shopping spree. My advice here is simple, since excess is generally not only acceptable but encouraged: Get the garment hemmed the minute you buy it. If the store won't do it for you for a reasonable price (or, even better, for free), go right home and stitch it up yourself because I guarantee that, otherwise, you will forget about it until moments before the event.

Secondhand Roses

There are not enough good words for me to say about the value of hand-me-downs for all kids, but especially for toddlers. How many toddlers do you know who actually wear out their clothes before they outgrow them? Sure, those T-shirts may be good and faded from several presoaks and bleachings and the pants may be a shade lighter on the stress points like the knees, but they can still help you fill in that substantial part of your toddler wardrobe that comes under the heading: "Stuff to cover their bodies while they wage their assault on the universe." Half the time, an outfit you bought or received as a gift was too big for your baby to wear at the time, and by the time it occurred to you to put it on her in toddlerhood, she'd outgrown it.

While pants, dresses and T-shirts are all pass-along candidates, the choice items are those that cost a lot and are rarely worn. In this category are winter coats, party dresses and those adorable little toddler suits with matching jacket and short pants. If you have a good Mommy/Girlfriend network in place, you might be able to make it all the way to your daughter's Sweet Sixteen on inherited clothing. Children are not like Princess Diana (may she rest in peace) in that they usually don't care or notice whether their Yom Kippur outfit was seen last year on little Tommy Burton.

I think that shoes also have terrific hand-me-down potential. I was recently cleaning out my four-year-old's closet and I found the adorable leopard print boots that my oldest son inherited from Sonia's son ten years ago. Granted, leopard boots aren't a fashion staple that are worn daily, but still, they *had* survived five kids' toddling and still looked worthy of another pass-down. Aside from those every day shoes like sneakers or your basic Stride-Rites, rain boots, dress up shoes and those shoes you buy on impulse are all good things to get on the rebound.

A lot of Girlfriends have questioned whether shoes that have been broken in by one toddler should then be passed on to the still-developing feet of another. I'm no podiatrist, but my answer is an unqualified "Yes!" The notion that a foot is formed by a shoe that fits and is comfortable is a little too *Flower Drum Song* for me. Yes, I suppose if you bound your daughter's growing feet in tight bandages twenty-four hours a day, they would be affected, but wearing a pair of previously owned patent leather party shoes for a couple of hours is a different matter altogether. Toddler feet are growing in accordance with a plan far wiser than Baby Nike; Mother Nature (with the help of your and your mate's genes) has genetically determined whether they are going to have hammer toes or fallen arches. Toddler feet are not like bonsai plants and manipulated by the size of their container. If you are concerned that your little one's mastery of the art of walking will be inhibited by strange shoes, let me remind you that walking is best learned with no shoes at all.

Naturally, as with all things toddler, there is a small catch concerning hand-me-downs. Some toddlers are very rigid about what belongs to whom. They often don't want to share *their* things and think it would be a better universe altogether if everyone kept their things strictly segregated. I myself have one of those kids. He has mentally cataloged every single thing he owns, and he plans to keep his stuff forever, thank you very much. After raising two children who wouldn't recognize their own sweaters if you showed them the name tag stitched inside, it's really interesting to have my third child so conscientious about his belongings that he can find a missing sweatshirt in the dark on a three-acre school play yard. If you are the parent of such a child, it's a good idea not to try to "sell" a sweater to you toddler by saying, "Look, honey, this is Dougie's old sweater and he gave it to you!" To toddlers like my third, this is tantamount to saying, "All sense of order and accountability in this universe have been suspended, and no one knows what belongs to whom." For these anal types, Dougie's stuff is always Dougie's stuff and he should take it with him to the grave. On the other hand, if your child is oblivious to these subtle imbalances in the cosmos, and if he knows and loves Dougie, you could have trouble getting him to take the darn sweater off!

Dressing for Success

It's one thing to get a grip on what toddlers want to wear and why; it's a whole different ball of wax dealing with getting the clothes on and off them in a timely fashion. Once again, the demon "I do myseff" rears its ugly head, and parents across America bite their nails to the quick trying to endure this developmental challenge. In a perfect world, children and their loving parents would have nothing but time and patience on their hands—nowhere to go, no timecards to be punched and immeasurable delight in the slow incremental growth of a toddler's motor skills. The world is not perfect; now get over it.

Instead, we parents are faced with two possible dilemmas: Either our toddler is an eager self-starter who would rather rage and incur the penalties than let her parents dress her; or he (like a couple of my own) is absolutely content to let his parents do all the heavy lifting and couldn't care less about mastering the basic skills of attiring himself. For those of us who parent Pu Yi, Last Emperor, our task consists of selecting appropriate togs, getting the child to sit up straight so that the clothes will go on and to plead with him push his own darn foot into his sneakers. There the little emperor sits or leans, watching TV or telling a very long story about what happened yesterday when Kyle put a snail on the lunch table. This ordeal usually takes so long that we moms leave the house in black leggings, long T-shirts and our hair up in those plastic clips. All the while, we are worried that we are raising a child who, as a teenager, will still be incapable of handling his basic grooming.

Worse, however, at least in the short run, is parenting a toddler who has some rudimentary knowledge about dressing herself, is committed to assuming all grooming responsibilities and who would rather spend the entire morning fumbling with the tie on her sundress than accept parental help. (I had a couple of those types, too.) You have to encourage a child who is so obviously devoted to learning independence and self-sufficiency; after all, she has taken on a very difficult developmental chore. Right? But more often than not, accommodating a toddler's need to master the skill of dressing can drive her hovering parents to distraction, consume every minute planned for breakfast and encroach on that precious time devoted to such luxuries as checking the morning headlines and commuting. There are few things more sure to drive a parent to distraction than watching her toddler take off and put on the same little shirt *inside out* and not be able to intervene. Sooner or later, you either have a breakdown or you decided that inside out isn't all that bad, anyway.

Herein lies the crux on the eternal conflict between parents and toddlers:

Toddlers don't wear watches and their parents do.

Yes, it may sound like I have a very keen grasp of the obvious, but this is a much more existential dilemma than it appears on first glimpse. Not only do toddlers not make commitments based on being places at certain times, the very essence of time is all weird and inconsistent for them. Think of those Dali paintings with the clocks melting and distorting; that's how I perceive toddler time. Sometimes a minute can speed by so quickly that the toddler hasn't noticed, as in when you say, "You can play with Daddy's electric toothbrush for one more minute, then you have to put it away." Other times a minute expands to feel more like a lifetime, as when you say, "Honey, I'm just going to talk on the phone one more minute, and then I will get you a sandwich." If you accept this premise of toddler time, then you will see that most of our techniques for hurrying them along, especially in those critical morning minutes, are doomed to failure.

Rarely does it move things along to explain why we all need to move more quickly to ensure that we all get to work, preschool or the baby-sitter sometime before *Blue's Clues* is over. As we Girlfriends have mentioned before, long explanations sound to toddlers like that honk-honking that all adults do in the *Peanuts* cartoons. For most toddlers, getting dressed is not a means to an end—it is the end in itself. If they do it for themselves, then the experience is rich with zipper experiments, putting shoes on the wrong feet and exploring the entire contents of the sock drawer. If, on the other hand, you still do most of the dressing, then this can be a delicious time when your toddler has your complete and undivided attention. Either way, you aren't relaxing over the morning paper, getting started on your day's caffeine quota or deciding whether Kathie Lee is getting too thin.

Lots of Girlfriends with toddlers of their own have asked me how I was able to accommodate my children's needs to "do theirseff" and yet get four little ones to school by 8:15 and me to work by nine. And now I will share the Golden Girlfriends' wisdom with all of you:

1. Eliminate choices where dressing is concerned. If you feel that offering just one outfit with a like it or lump it attitude is too restrictive and a tad cranky, then give the child a choice between two items. You can present a blue shirt and blue pants or a green shirt and beige shorts for your son (or daughter, too!), and you can offer one pair of leggings and a nearly matching shirt and one wash-and-wear dress for your little girl.

Never, ever, let them take this opportunity to rummage through their drawers and closets to see if they like anything better. Of course, you shouldn't be unsympathetic in your options: If you know that little Jackie is on a black Rugrats T-shirt kick, then, by all means, offer it as one of the choices. This is not the time to teach fashion; it is time to demonstrate that you trust your toddler's ability to make decisions (limited though they may be) and to streamline the dressing process so that you, like a good marathon runner, can improve your time to under three hours.

2. Lay the clothing options out the night before. In the relatively peaceful hour before your toddler goes to sleep for at least part of the night, ask her if she has any ideas about what she would like to wear tomorrow. If she needs to inventory her entire closet, take this opportunity to lie on her bedroom floor and do some basic yoga stretches or clean out the dustbunnies that have accumulated under her bed or crib. When you have been lying on the floor so long that you are moments from falling into a coma-like sleep, announce to your little "shopper" that you are going to count to twenty and all choices must be made by then. As ineffective as traditional time measurements may be to toddlers is how meaningful the act of counting out loud can be. Besides, they are usually as interested in learning their numbers as they are in fashion, so you can often make a smooth segue between the two activities. If your little one fails to comply with this simple request to stop all closet activities and get ready for bed, it's time to leave this chapter and review Chapter Seven, "Sleepytime," again.

3. Give your toddler a specific dressing job. You know as well as I do that few, if any, toddlers are able to complete all their morning rituals without parental assistance. In fact, a lot of the morning conflict arises when we explain with noticeable exasperation that, in spite of his elaborate looping of his shoelaces, our toddler is not yet able to tie his own shoes. Rather than devote unnecessary time and tension to debating dressing skills with someone who sincerely believes he can do anything, if left to his own devices for a reasonable time, assign the sure successes to your miniature human and keep the rest for yourself. For example, in the very early stages of toddlerhood, my Girlfriend Tina completely dressed her children, but she put them in charge of collecting the dirty jammies and used towels and taking them to the laundry room. Later, as their motor skills developed, she let them move on to putting on pants, socks and shirts. Shoes were one of the last delegated tasks because every mother knows it takes a rocket scientist to distinguish a left from a right. I still squirm when I think of the times I sent one toddler or another to school with his shoes on the wrong feet and no one corrected the error till I noticed it in pickup. (For those of you who still believe that there is some magic to a proper shoe fitting and a rule against second-hand shoes, just wait till you find that you not only have your toddler's shoes on the wrong feet for several hours, but that he has stashed his breakfast Cheerios in there, too.)

4. Feel free to call the whole thing off. If you have overslept, are in a bad mood or there's a public transportation strike, you have the right, as a parent, to announce that all dressing rituals are off for the day and that Mommy or Daddy is going to get Junior dressed as quickly as possible. Chances are pretty good that you will get at least some pouting out of this scenario, and maybe even a tantrum, but don't be a wuss. The threat of toddler disapproval should never be so terrifying that it prevents a reasonable parent from doing what she needs to do. If you do, indeed, encounter a tantrum, don't rise to the occasion. Your task is to put clothes on the child, not to knock yourself out trying to apologize or make it up to him in some way. You may find yourself in positions that resemble a cowboy trying to rope a calf, but as long as you keep words to a minimum and are careful not to hurt your child in anyway, go for it. The toddler lesson here is: "Life is not one long visit to Club Med." Sometimes circumstances put unusual demands on all of us, and as a card-carrrying member of this family, they have to suck it up with the rest of us. Trust me; they'll recover by snacktime.

5. Weekends are free-dress day. Assuming that you and your mate work Monday through Friday and that those are the misery mornings, Saturday and Sunday can give everyone a much-needed break. Leaving aside the innumerable birthday parties that toddlers attend on weekends and all church and temple visits, there should be no need for your little one to hurry or adhere to a dress code. This can be the perfect time for a toddler to discover the intricacies of buttons, buckles and zippers, and it's no skin off your nose. Mothers around the world are spending their weekends grocery shopping or getting their roots touched up accompanied by little people in nightgowns with ballet tights and slippers underneath. No one should even look twice at you, but if they do, just reassure yourself that you are nurturing your child's individuality and take a moment to mentally photograph this self-expression—you will treasure this memory for the rest of your life.

chapter nine

Toddlers and Babies

No woman can walk down the street or attend a family holiday with her toddler in tow and not be asked, "So, when are you gonna have another one?" I don't know what reproductive magistrate decreed that no woman should experience more than three years, four tops, between episiotomies, but it seems have acquired the authority of common law. Not only will blood relatives boldly delve into the bedroom issues of you and your mate; complete strangers will pontificate about what your sexual intentions should be, whether invited or not.

I guess for some people original conversation does not come easily; how else do you explain all those people who lamely ask very tall folks, "Hey, how's the weather up there?" Not wanting to be caught without a thing to say, people will pick the most obvious clues and spout off on them. You already know that fact from pregnancy: How many times were you asked, "Are you going to have a baby?" when your stomach was so large it entered a room a full ten seconds before the rest of you.

Does Every Child Really Need a Brother or Sister?

Right after your friends, family and complete strangers ask when you plan to have another child, the majority of them will carry on by telling you how every child needs a sibling to share his life with. Naturally, this is presented with tremendous conviction, but in truth, most people think this because *they* had brothers or sisters. You know how that logic works: What is right for me is right for the universe! If you feel like needling the busybody a bit, try asking how often he has seen those essential, can't-live-without-them siblings in the last year. It's actually depressing how many of them say, "Well, we don't really get along anymore" or "She just lives so far away (over thirty miles) that it's hard to make the time." Even the ones who tell you that they can't imagine getting through childhood without a brother or sister to lean on are not so much making a case for siblings as admitting to their own limited imagination. Spend some time talking to "only children" and you may be amazed to hear very few mentions of being lonely or spoiled, the two doomsday attributes prejudicially applied to single kids.

As I've told you about seventy-five times, I am the very proud mother of four kids. I am also the big sister of one absolutely precious brother (who still pretends to let me boss him around). Does that mean I think that everyone should have more than one child? Absolutely not! Several of the most fabulous families I know feature two parents and one child, or one parent and one child. One of the most spectacular ten-year-olds I know is the solitary offspring of my Girlfriend Ann and her cutie-pie husband, Tom. Their daughter, Mandy, makes friends in two seconds, is empathetic to other's feelings and has such close communication with her parents that questionable behavior gets nipped in the bud long before it reaches the disciplinary stage. There is no question that Mandy has extended her family as she has seen fit, including cousins and friends to fill in any societal gaps.

"Sure," you say, "but what was she like as a toddler?" Pretty much like the rest of them. The only differences were, Ann was slightly calmer than the rest of us with multiples, and she and Tom could travel from California to New Jersey without sustaining permanent brain damage during the airplane ride. Perhaps Mandy was just one of those babies who are just born sweet, eager to please and confident. Then again, maybe not spending the greater part of her childhood resenting and being annoyed by a little brother or sister did her a world of good.

There is no rule that says: Once a gestator, always a gestator. Most of the mothers of toddlers I know are still so distracted by potty, sleep and discipline issues that they don't have a minute to think about sex, let alone think about sex with pregnancy as its goal. And, if they have achieved that glorious plateau where there isn't a diaper, Pull-Up or baby bottle in the house, they are deeply tempted to sit back and enjoy the respite. If that's your inclination, then by all means follow it. The decision to jump back into new mommyhood is a big one, and you owe it at least as much consideration as you'd devote to buying a new puppy.

If So, When?

With all that said, you and I both know that most couples do end up with more than one child. Perhaps it was part of an preplanned reproductive scheme, or perhaps (as in my case) it was determined by a certain husband's fortieth birthday bash when a certain wife drank a little too much champagne and couldn't remember if her diaphragm was inserted or collecting lint under the bed. Either way, all you have to do is go to any mall in the country to see that most women dragging toddlers around are also waddling in the advanced stages of pregnancy or pushing an infant in a stroller.

Where I come from, we used to call siblings who were born within a year of each other (like my mother and uncle) "Irish twins." I don't think it was a slur on my ancestors' intelligence so much as their fecundity. Whatever the case, please know that I am a McCarty born and bred, and I can diss my own group, so please don't take offense or remind me of my political incorrectness. In my case, up to a year after my first baby was born, I was still pretending to be asleep when my husband started cuddling me. Sure, I missed our former sex life, but not as much as I missed my former sleep life. That's often the pregnancy pattern for a lot of couples: You finally feel rested enough and competent enough in your mothering to reenter the world of dining out, wearing clothing with zippers rather than elastic or drawstrings, and BINGO, there's another successful docking between the space shuttle and the lunar module.

Longing for a Baby

One reason given almost universally by mothers of toddlers who decide to get pregnant again is "I miss having a baby in the house." To nonparents, this may sound ludicrous because most two- or three-year-olds look like nothing more than upright babies. To a mommy, however, there can be a real sense of loss when the infant she held against her breast is replaced by a little toddler who refuses to be held against anything. As hard as new motherhood seemed at the time, our maternal memories can be quite selective. Sure, staying up all night to nurse while sitting on a hemorrhoid pillow might have seemed like agony at the time, but having a two-and-a-half-year-old hit you in the face while your mother-in-law is looking on makes a couple of hemorrhoids seem like a day at the beach. Besides, when children are infants, there is no doubt that they adore their mommies with all their heart and soul. A cranky toddler, however, can make a mom feel like she's Jodie Foster and she's baby-sitting Hannibal Lecter.

Just to show how primal so many of our mothering instincts are, hundreds of women, my closest Girlfriends among them, have explained the need for a second pregnancy based simply on the need to smell that baby smell again. You may not want to face facts, but the truth is, toddlers don't smell as delicious as babies. You can use the same soaps, shampoos, creams and powders as you used when she was a newborn, but she just doesn't smell like a newborn anymore.

One of Each

There seems to be some elemental yearning for symmetry in mankind, and one place it really plays out is in family planning. Ask a couple pregnant with their first baby whether they prefer a boy or a girl, and the party line goes something like: "We don't care what it is, as long as it's healthy." They might give you the same answer when you ask them during their second or third pregnancies, but believe the Girlfriends: Most of them have a particular gender in mind. Since statistics show that most couples have two kids (no fair counting that one-third of a child that everyone throws in to look like they're being mathematically accurate), many couples find something very attractive about having "one of each." So, if the firstborn is a boy, one of the incentives given for getting pregnant again is to try for a girl, on the assumption that one of each gives couples a chance to experience the full parenting spectrum. Of course, nature and DNA being completely resistant to our human whims, odds are fifty/fifty that the couple will get the variety they seek. That leads to third and fourth babies, as well as all sorts of exotic sexual positions, douches and scientific interventions, but this chapter isn't really about any of that, so let's move on.

Those parents of little girls hoping for boys and vice versa are right about one thing: There really is a difference between boys and girls. It may not be the behavior difference that stereotypes suggest, like boys prefer sports and girls prefer frilly dresses, but the parenting experience in significantly different. We, the parents, put different dreams and expectations on boys than we do on girls. If Dad played football as a kid (or worse, as a college student), he can't help but buy his little man a tiny Nerf football to put in the crib. If Mom was a dancer or gymnast, she is counting the days until her little angel can walk well enough to belly up to the barre. Then, of course, there are some of the inevitable differences in parenting boys and girls, no matter how athletic the daughter may be or how artistic the son is: You will never go shopping for a training bra with a son and you will never have to demonstrate how to wear a jock strap to a daughter. Yes, there is a lot of fun to be had in having both a little boy and a little girl, but kids' uniqueness is based on so much more than gender that it's kind of silly to keep rolling the reproductive dice simply to keep the teams even.

It Takes Twoooo, Bay-bee-ee-ee, It Takes Two

A decision as momentous as whether to have another baby should ideally involve both parents. As you can well imagine, it's as rare as Halley's Comet for two people to wake up one morning and turn to each other with the epiphany, "Honey, I think it's time to get pregnant again!" Much more frequently, Mommy will feel particularly rested and on top of her game and prepared to face gestation again, while Daddy feels like there are already so many toys, swings, highchairs and push cars in the house, not to mention pizza crusts hidden in the sofa and boogers behind the crib, that he's one cuckoo who's ready to fly right over this nest and keep going until he hits Hawaii. Or Dad will feel like his dynasty is just beginning with one perfect offspring, and it's time to go forth and multiply, while Mom is glorying in finally fitting into her favorite jeans again for the first time in three years and she's not going to let anybody mess with her body again.

Clearly, it's time for a heart-to-heart here. Getting pregnant reminds me of jumping off a high dive; at some point, you just have to hold your nose, close your eyes and jump and pray that you don't bellyflop. If I had it to do all over again, I suppose I would have been much more understanding and respectful of my beloved husband's concerns about so many babies in so little time. It's not that he didn't try to explain how he felt. One time he gave me the famous pie analogy: "Vicki, you're like a pie. Everybody gets an equal piece of you and your attentions in the beginning, but with each new baby, the other kids' slices stay the same size and mine gets smaller and smaller." After over a decade into this parenthood gig, I must admit that he had a very good point. I would only add that the one person who seems to get no slice of the Vicki Pie at all is Vicki, but as that was my choice, it's boring to go on and on about it.

At the risk of making even more gender assumptions, I think it's fair to say that, for many men, having more babies means having less money, less sex and more responsibility, not always the most attractive prospects to guys who still hope they are going to be rock stars or millionaires by the time they are forty. I realize that there are just as many men (well, almost) who find that there is no finer destiny than spending the foreseeable future coaching Little League, videotaping dance recitals and driving a car that has Goldfish crackers jammed in all the air-conditioning vents. I'm just saying that it is rare for both members of this reproductive unit to share these feelings simultaneously.

Often, those gung-ho family guys are partnered with women who have returned to careers that they love (or at least tolerate for the income), sleep for at least four straight hours a night and even take a yoga class one night a week while Daddy bonds with Junior. Even more gratifying, they have shepherded a fragile, needy baby no bigger than a loaf of bread through colic, diaper rash and its first inoculations at no small cost to their own psyches, and they have survived. With toddlerhood came a schedule, a child who could hang out with Dad or a sitter for at least an hour or two, smaller breasts (okay, so everything isn't perfect), and a sense that motherhood wasn't nearly as scary as it seemed a year ago. And still there are twists and turns aplenty, what with thumb sucking, tantrums and the ubiquitous "NO!" around every bend, not to mention worries about pre-school readiness and that alarming little eye tic that appeared out of no-where. What rational human being would want to get back on Mr. Toad's Wild Ride when she's already busy trying to keep her stomach contents down on Colossus?

Some moms, like my Girlfriends Beth and Amy, just sigh and throw their hands up in the air when I join the ranks of knuckleheads who pry into their family planning. They both work at demanding full-time jobs outside the home, and I think they both suspect that it would be a second baby, no matter how beloved, that would upset the applecart. The work-force seems to take a blow to the ribs with the birth of second babies. Moms are barely able to manage work, home, mothering and occasional rest with one child. Second children mean more work, more mothering and far less rest. Not only that, child care for mothers with outside jobs can become so expensive that it's often more economical for Mom to stay home and take care of her own kids full time.

Your Second Pregnancy

If you are, indeed, a member of the statistical majority, you will get pregnant again while you are already raising a young child, regardless of whether it was unintentional or as well planned as the Invasion of Nor-mandy. Whether you get pregnant for a second, third or thirteenth time, the Girlfriends think it's only fair to warn you that this pregnancy will have little in common with your first one.

I've talked about this before in previous books, but since even *I* don't remember everything I said in them, I'm certainly not going to quiz you on your reading comprehension and retention of facts. (We moms are in the business of the retention of water; anything more is gravy.)

One of the first things you will notice with your second pregnancy (aside from how quickly you begin showing) is that you're no longer treated like a precious vessel. Remember how, during your first pregnancy, people treated you as if you were made of glass and and had the stamina of a butterfly? Sorry, that is not on the program for this go-round. One reason is that you've already taken your friends and family through gestation, and it just isn't as compelling for anyone (but you) the second time around. The most compelling reason, however, is that your firstborn could not care less about your delicate condition and is not about to cut you any slack in parenting *him*. I can still sheepishly recall how I used to beg the baggers at the grocery store to put my bags (which couldn't have weighed more than fifteen pounds) in my car for me because "I'm pregnant and shouldn't lift anything." Yet, with all subsequent pregnancies, I lifted thirty pound toddlers like they were nothing. Toward the end of the pregnancies, I did what mothers through the millennia have always done; I carried the toddler by perching him on my shelflike belly.

Naps—forget about them! If you are so blessed that your toddler is still taking an afternoon nap (encourage her to do so until adolescence), you will be so frazzled and busy considering such things as preschool choices, where the new baby will sleep after it moves out of your room, and who will care for your firstborn while you are in the hospital delivering, that sleep will elude you most of the day. Come nighttime you will be so tired that you fall asleep while you are still brushing your teeth, but don't settle in for the night because you have a toddler who is coming into your room several nights a week complaining of thirst, tummyache or monsters.

As I mentioned earlier, you will probably look pregnant about fifteen minutes after taking the home pregnancy test, but don't let that freak you out. Your abdomen may have surrendered prematurely, but chances are all things ultimately even out. Pregnant women who are chasing toddlers generally don't have much discretionary time for spontaneous visits to the ice-cream parlor or for lingering over a four-course dinner. They also do a lot of running as they struggle to keep their precious firstborns from dashing into oncoming traffic or upsetting a twelve-foot-high grocery store display of toilet tissue.

If you ignore everything I've said so far, please listen up now: You need just as much rest, nutrition and TLC with your second pregnancy as you needed with your first. Sure, people aren't falling all over each other in their rush to fan you and peel your grapes, but you're a big girl, and it's up to you to nurture yourself and your unborn child. It can be easy to put your toddler's health and happiness ahead of that of the little belly passenger; after all, your universe already revolves around the child you have known and loved for the last year or two or three. Believe your Girlfriends when we tell you that you will, indeed, love this second child with the same blind devotion and rapture as you feel for the first. It's your job as this baby's mother to accept people's offers to baby-sit while you nap, to let your mom watch your toddler while you and your mate reexperience the miracle of seeing your baby's first ultrasound and to suggest a game of Candyland to your toddler when you are too tired to keep chasing her up the slide. During a nonhormonal moment, take the time to fill your mate in on the realities of gestating and parenting simultaneously. If he's is anything like mine, he, and everyone else who has the sensitivity to ask, will truly believe that you are "doing just fine" if that's the only side of your parenting experience you share with him.

Do us all a favor, and don't take that Superwoman myth too seriously: Even the Woman of Steel could use a little help with her toddler while kneeling at the porcelain bowl with raging morning sickness. Yes, mothers have been parenting while pregnant for eons, but if we start comparing ourselves to our pioneer foremothers, we are going to look like a bunch of slackers. Remember, their idea of good mothering was trying not to die in childbirth and to get the kids bathed once a week for church. Things change.

Can You Ever Love Another One as Much?

Here it is, the $60,000 question: How can you ever find space in your heart to love another child when you've already given the whole darn organ (as well as your brain) to the child you have? First of all, you know the new baby can't possibly be as cute and lovable, since perfection was achieved with the first one. Second, you *know* the child you have, from her cowlicks to her toenails, but the baby on the way is a complete stranger. Not only aren't you sure that you can love it enough; you're actually a little suspicious of it. Will it fit into this wonderful little family you've already created? Will it promise to be suitably humble around its big brother or sister? Will it understand that certain family rituals are already in place and that it would be unfair to change your firstborn's precious rhythms to accommodate an interloper?

We Girlfriends are going to tell you exactly what mothers have been telling their children for centuries: Mommies' hearts (and several other body parts) stretch with every baby so that there is always enough love to go around. And (at least until puberty or a bad marriage), mommies love all their children equally, even if the love affair is different with each one.

Actually, the differences in your love affairs is one of the most surprising and stunning things about having more than one child. When you have only one child specimen around to compare to, you can't help but think that he or she is THE type of baby you and your mate make, almost more like a clone than totally original DNA. In fact, when I ask moms who are pregnant with their second babies what gender they prefer, at least as many are as infatuated by the one-boy-one-girl pattern as they are convinced that they want another of whatever they already have. As one Girlfriend put it, "Since Tory is a girl and I am so crazy about her, I really can't imagine adding any testosterone (besides Dad's) to this lovely family." Nearly every mother is convinced that the gender that God gave her the first time is the superior gender, and any other gender will have to prove itself by providing a new set of shopping opportunities or satisfying her mate that the family name will, indeed, be carried on. (And believe me, that male desire to carry on the name is astonishingly compelling.)

"He Wants a Baby Brother"

I know you would never dream of actually consulting your toddler to see if he or she is in the market for a sibling (or at least I would hope not), but many parents have told me they are planning to try for another pregnancy because their firstborn has expressed the desire for a baby of his own. That's a charming notion, indeed, but one completely devoid of any good sense to back it up, at least to my way of thinking. Since when did families become a democracy? And even if they are, who decided that people who still poop in their own pants should get a vote? Heck, even with all your wisdom and experience, you can't even begin to imagine what life would be like with a new baby; why on earth would you trust the instincts of your toddler?

Don't fall for this one, Girlfriend. You are not denying your child an inalienable right to siblinghood if you choose not to reproduce again now or ever. You and I both know that he will ask you to take the new baby back to where it came from the moment he realizes that the infant is a full-fledged family member, entitled to all the love and indulgences of the rest. Don't get me wrong; brothers and sisters are terrific, but it's not a good idea to let a toddler think asking for a sibling is tantamount to asking for a kitten. I know we can be weak-minded when it seems there is something our cherished children want that we can actually give them, but the line must be drawn at reproduction: Any new baby who comes along is yours, *not your toddler's,* for the rest of your life.

When to Tell the Toddler About the Baby on the Way

Learning you are pregnant, even if it's for the fourth time, is always thrilling. If you couldn't wait to start spreadin' the news with your first baby, you will probably start sending smoke signals the minute you see that little blue line on your home pregnancy test. There are two differences that we've noticed between the announcements of first- and second-time moms:

1. First-time moms usually don't tell anyone about the pregnancy until they have shared the magical news with their beloved spouse. Women who find out they are pregnant a second time share the sacred information with everyone from the parking lot attendant to the receptionist who answers the phone at their mates' place of work.

2. Mothers of toddlers who get pregnant again worry endlessly about whether, when and how to tell the firstborn that the team is expanding. My Girlfriend Barbara was so intent on not wrecking her precious little girl's heretofore charmed life that she wouldn't allow anyone, friends, family and particularly herself, to speak of the impending birth of a second child unless they were whispering, standing in the backyard and speaking French. By the way, all her efforts proved fruitless because her older daughter loathed her baby brother for at least a year or two. Who knows, maybe she hated him because her parent's behavior suggested that she had a vote in the matter.

The policy in my house has been to wait until I'm undeniably distorted with pregnancy before I start any meaningful talks about the new baby with my toddler. One terrific reason for this is simply that it buys you time. Why try to explain about a new brother or sister to a nineteen-month-old when you will be so much better understood a few months later by an almost-two-and-a-half-year-old. Keep in mind the language limitations that go with the early toddler territory. Another reason I wait is the "When Is It Going to Be Christmas?" reason. Time moves agonizingly slow for children who are looking forward to something. My kids hated anything but immediate gratification so much that they would throw themselves onto the floor in agony if told that they couldn't see their playmate until tomorrow, or even this afternoon. We mothers who are on the StairMaster of life are certain that forty weeks will never be enough time to prepare for a second child while devoting our lives to our first.

Toddlers, however, with no appreciation for the art of anticipation and preparation, really couldn't care less about anything that isn't happening imminently.

Perhaps your toddler won't be quite so self-obsessed as mine were, and she might actually ask you why you haven't had a lap in months. Then my advice is different; by all means, tell her you're having a baby. This might also be a good time to explain briefly and succinctly that the baby is growing in your tummy, but that as soon as the baby is born (don't go into details here), her beloved lap will come back (probably even more comfy and padded than before).

If she asks how the baby got into your tummy (and even if she doesn't ask, since many assume it got there because you ate it), tell her any one of a number of enchanting reasons. If you start in on the seed and the sperm thing, I promise you your Girlfriend status will be called into question. Children never tire of hearing about how loved they are, so this is your opportunity to say something like "When a Mommy and a Daddy love each other so very much and want to share that love with a baby, God (Krishna, Vishnu, Mother Nature, Home Shopping) lets a baby grow in the mommy's tummy." Then spend some time telling the story of when God (*et. al.*) put her, your firstborn, in your tummy and how the angels sang and the animal kingdom celebrated (like in *The Lion King*).

I think it's best to save all discussion of mommy leaving to have the baby in a hospital until the very end of your pregnancy. Why mix a lovely Simba-like story with descriptions of abandonment and doctors? As delivery day approaches, and assuming your toddler could give a tinker's damn, let her help you prepare for your brief absence. If she is going to stay with friends or relatives when you go into the hospital, get her a little suitcase or duffel like what you're taking with you and help each other pack your favorite things. Ask her if she wants to draw a picture or send a book or photo with you to show the new baby as soon as he's born, and reassure her that she can come see her sib the next day or that you will be home with him or her before Grandma has run out of ice-cream money.

On the subject of virtual mothering, toddler style: When I was pregnant with my third child and had two dubious toddlers hanging on my legs, I bought one of those dolls that looks eerily like a newborn, right down to its protruding belly button. Both my son and my daughter played with it, but I don't think they truly associated it with the baby that I was bringing home. Put it this way: I hope they didn't because they used to put their "baby" to sleep by holding it by the feet and swinging it in circles. Perhaps later, when you are actually caring for a living, breathing baby, your child will like a baby of its own to mimic you. My experience, however, is that they want to put "powdy" on the real McCoy, not some lifeless, unattractive plastic doll.

The Hospital Stay

To my way of thinking, mothers who are delivering their second babies don't stay in the hospital or birthing center long enough to recover and get their wits about them. Some of this blame can be laid at the feet of insurance companies and HMOs that would love to avoid paying for one extra hour of medical attention whenever possible. The real culprits, however, are the moms themselves. I know because I was guilty of this myself: I was so worried about my toddler at home when I gave birth to my second child that I practically stood up and headed for the car before the placenta had come out. It wasn't that I feared Number One wasn't being cared for in a proper and loving manner; it's just that I couldn't bear the suspense of discovering how he would accept his new little sister.

In hindsight, rushing home was not necessarily the best idea. For one thing, my toddler had absolutely no tolerance for me lying in bed and taking it easy until my stitches dissolved or at least until my first postpartum bowel movement. Getting the nursing business under control was also harder with a toddler around because he either cried when I nursed the new baby or tried to sit in my lap while I held the infant in my arms. Talk about interfering with your letdown reflex!

I found that I did most of my most delicious bonding with my new daughter in the middle of the night, when her inquisitive big brother was sound asleep. I would encourage her to nurse to her heart's content, and when she wasn't nursing I purposely kept her awake so that she could play with me. That was all well and good for the first two or three weeks, but by the end of a month, I was so sleep-deprived that I was begging complete strangers to shoot me between the eyes and put me out of my misery. If there is any moral here, it is this:

> Don't expend all of your energy in the first few months trying to keep harmony in the family: The kids are certain to try to maim each other at various times over the next sixteen years; and you will have collapsed by then. Besides, if you crumble now, who will be around to break it up when they are big enough to slam doors and call each other horrible names?

Bringing the New Baby Home

When you do bring the little interloper home, there are some suggestions we Girlfriends have for making the introduction as smooth as possible. First of all, keep in mind that almost all toddlers are enthusiastic and thrilled with the prospect of meeting a new baby, especially one that belongs to him. All that stuff you have heard about sibling rivalry and toddler resentment comes later in the game, so relax and have fun with this initial integration. Remember, by this time your toddler is a master at reading your feelings and moods, so approach the trip home as the happy, calm encounter it should be.

One of the best suggestions made to me about bringing a new baby home to a mommy-hungry toddler came from my Girlfriend (who also happens to be a pediatrician) Laura: Have Daddy carry the infant into the house so that Mommy has both arms free for all the hugging that needs to take place. If the first message you give to a waiting and uncertain toddler is, "Watch out, honey, you're going to hurt the baby!" you're not exactly getting this relationship off on the right foot. Some of my Girlfriends have stacked the deck even more in their favor by walking in with a present for the waiting toddler, but I think that's unnecessary; besides, who wants to stop off at Toys "R" Us on the way home from the hospital?

If your firstborn is eager to see the new addition immediately, go for it. I happen to think that newborns are quite accommodating and will put up with being inspected from head to toe by a big brother or sister. Then again, if your toddler would rather do just about anything other than devote time and attention to a silly little baby, I see no reason to force the issue. Keep in mind that the two of them have the next two decades to discover each other. Don't let the fact that you're curious and your husband has the video camera running push you into making a big deal out of something your toddler clearly isn't ready to address.

I can't leave the subject of bringing the new baby home without mentioning a phenomenon that my Girlfriends and I all experienced: In a matter of seconds, right before your very eyes, your precious firstborn transforms from being a baby to resembling something akin to Baby Huey. No matter how recently you had your first baby, you will have forgotten how minuscule a newborn really is. It's truly breathtaking to compare a "real" baby with an "occasional" baby to see how much your firstborn has grown. Not only does the elder child look bigger, he looks germier and far more menacing than ever before. It's staggering how quickly the light of your life transforms into a potential infant-breaker. You love them just the same; it's just that an element of caution has been added to the equation.

Visitors and Toys

In case Mommy's Alzheimer's has hit you harder than we thought, let us remind you that with new babies come lots of visitors. Consider them the Magi, if you will; they hear the news of a precious new birth, and they come from miles around to witness the miracle for themselves. Also, like the Magi, they bring gifts. This gesture, while very much appreciated by mothers and new babies (if they could comprehend it), can lead to some very sad and unattractive behavior in toddlers. "Hey, wait a second," their toddler minds object, "Not only is this baby going to hog everybody's attention, but he's gonna get presents, too? This is where I have to put my foot (and perhaps the rest of my body) down!"

It's really your job as the mother of two to set the tone for the newborn visits. If your visitor is a mommy herself, she will probably be innately sensitive to the toddler's feelings. She may spend the first fifteen minutes of her visit with the older child, going into his room, to inspect his most recent fingerpainting. Afterward, she might even ask if the toddler would like to show her "his" new baby. Don't count on this sensitivity from all guests, however. Even grandmas, who are as doting over the toddler as they are over the new baby, have been known to rush into a house calling "Where's Nana's little darling?" and be referring to the new baby. If your hands are full with nursing, wiping and weeping (don't forget that postpartum stage), then put your mate or some other trustworthy person in charge of the toddler. Better still, perhaps, would be for you to play with the toddler while besotted Granny sniffs and cuddles her newest progeny. Never underestimate the value of Mom's undivided attention to a toddler with a new baby in the house. The newborn can be holding an audience of fifty people, but if you are not one of them, your toddler will feel he got the better end of the deal.

Several Girlfriends recommended that I keep a well-hidden bag of cheap toddler toys on hand so that I could give a gift to my sensitive first-born to open while his father and I received the countless gifts that come hand-in-hand with visitors. (All the stuff that comes in the mail or UPS should be opened in the middle of the night, in your bathroom, behind a locked door, just to avoid stirring sibling rivalry to a full tempest.) I know that life is not always fair and all gifts are not evenly distributed in the real world, but we're talking survival here. If your episiotomy hurts as much as mine did and if you're as tired as I was, the last thing you need on your plate is the job of teaching that justice is not always achieved in this dimension.

Don't think that I am cavalierly suggesting that you spend several discretionary dollars you don't have, either. The goodies you keep in the toddler gift stash should be such things as lollipops, bubbles, keychains (don't ask me why; they just love them) and cheap games like Barrel of Monkeys to keep them busy while you try to get one moment of adoration for the new baby in before the visit is over.

The Inevitable Confrontation

I can't recall a Girlfriend who didn't call me up a day or two after she presented her new baby to her toddler who didn't announce with obvious pride and immeasurable relief, "Henry just *loves* his little sister. I don't know why I was so frantic with worry about sibling rivalry." Perhaps this is intended as a subtle dig at me because I maintain that a toddler who doesn't resent a new baby is either severely repressed or not really paying attention.

Who in his right three-year-old mind would welcome a newborn to come share his parents' adoration, wake him during the night, and get him in trouble when he tries to draw dots on its face with Magic Markers? It might be a different story if Mom and Dad were bringing home a groovy four-year-old because that would be someone he could play tag with, someone to teach him more bathroom talk and someone to help him look for that hidden toddler goodies bag. But no, they've brought in someone who does no fun tricks, who sleeps in the toddler's recently surrendered crib and who might even nurse on those breasts that the toddler believed were his exclusive birthright (in this instance, tell him to get in line behind good old dad).

Once again, I tip my hat to Mother Nature because she gives you a little healing time before your toddler has the epiphany that this little novelty, this baby thing, is actually here for good. This is a crucial time because toddlers, living pretty much in the moment as they do, don't immediately understand that the baby won't disappear just as suddenly as he appeared. This is when all my Girlfriends who called me to gloat about the fraternal bonding going on in their houses call back to tell me that Cain is going after Abel in a big way. Through their weeping I hear the universal worry: The kids will hate each other for the rest of their lives. The truth is: They will, but they will simultaneously love each other more than any other living creature. Hey, I never promised the relationship wouldn't be complex; only that it would be normal and work out with just a little common sense on your part.

Toddler Coping Behavior

Just because your toddler isn't pinching or hitting your infant doesn't mean that she is adjusted to the family expansion. Lots of darling, sensitive toddlers live to make their parents happy and proud of them. These kids are smart enough to know that hitting the new baby with a whiffle ball upside the head doesn't go very far in the parent-pleasing department. So, instead of acting unloving to the baby, they internalize their anxiety. I'm no Freud, but I am a semiconscious human being, and I do notice when my previously potty-trained three-year-old needs diapers again or when my toddler takes the pacifier out of the baby's mouth and pops it in hers. Psychologists call a lot of this behavior **Regression**. It's when kids who were happy with new, grown-up behaviors start to yearn for their cribs, bottles, diapers and mommy like they did as babies. The Girlfriends' best advice when this happens to you is threefold:

1. Stay calm and matter-of-fact. If you drop your dentures when your toddler enters a room in a diaper and a baby tee, and nothing else, you not only humiliate the toddler, but add drama to something that is completely normal. Trust me, I know how embarrassing it can be to have guests for dinner, call for your toddler to come say hello to everyone, and have him crawl into the room on his hands and knees and carrying a baby bottle.

2. Let them do it. This backward climb down the evolutionary ladder is usually short-lived. Toddlers ultimately realize that it's more fun to run than crawl, that diapers feel all icky and clammy and baby bottles, well, they're still kind of nice, but a juice box does quite nicely. I remember watching one of my children, one who, by the way, never sucked its (no gender giveaways here!) thumb, take up that very habit when the newest baby came home. I knew he/she wasn't getting any great soothing satisfaction from it, but it was overt baby behavior, and that was satisfying enough.

Give your toddler some time to be ambivalent about leaving babyhood; with any luck whatsoever, she will realize that toddlers have a lot more fun and privileges than babies. In the meantime, you can help keep the odds in your favor by noticing all good "big kid" behavior and praising it enthusiastically.

3. Don't think this is your fault. A toddler's desire to be a baby again does not mean that you have failed in your attempts to show equal love and attention to both children. All other mothers worth their salt (meaning Girlfriends) will understand exactly what's going on, and they might even help you get a giggle or two out of it. Ask your friends how many of them not only let their toddlers take a taste of their breast milk, but even gave Daddy a squirt when he was dying of curiosity.

Another way that toddlers-trying-to-be-good will express their anxiety and jealousy about the new baby is by acquiring all sorts of irritating **tics and habits**. Just like anxious adults, they may start picking their noses endlessly, chewing off their fingernails or twisting their hair around a finger. You'll recognize this behavior as your typical self-soothing stuff. They do it because it makes them feel calmer and distracted. The way I see it, if more of us felt free to indulge in self-soothing, the less of a Prozac Nation we might be. At least two of my kids (please don't hold me to specifics at my stage of brain damage) used to grind their teeth any time they were near their newest sibling. They would smile and say "Nice baby," but their jaws were so clenched that I was constantly worried that they would lose that last bit of self-control and just bop the baby. I have home videos of my firstborn "playing" with his baby sister when he thought no one was looking: The baby is sitting in a reclining infant seat, and her brother is taking her pacifier out of her mouth and shoving it back in every two seconds. Her stunned look and his determined one pretty much summed up their early relationship.

Please don't take this source of comfort and relief away from your toddler just because it embarrasses you or gets on your nerves. If the behavior is something a little more antisocial (like holding one's genitals), you might calmly explain how that particular indulgence is best saved for the privacy of home, but if you think your toddler is the only nose picker on your block, you have another think coming. Remember, your child is not you. Your child's behavior is not yours. Just because your child holds his penis in times of crisis does not mean the community thinks you do the same (although it's not really a bad idea). If your toddler doesn't give up the habit within about six months, you might try a rewards system in which he gets something for keeping his finger out of his nose, but since most of this behavior is unconscious it can be difficult to isolate. If I were you, I would wait for preschool and kindergarten to come along and let the reliable influence of peer pressure take care of it for you. There's nothing like a snotty little four-year-old to point out any questionable behavior in another kid.

Will There Ever Be Enough of You to Go Around?

Moms who are running a day late and a night's sleep short while parenting one child wonder how they can ever find enough time in the day to give that much attention to a second child. The glib answer would be that a mommy's time is like her heart; that it expands exponentially to accommodate each baby. That, however, is not the truthful answer. No matter how great your love, how true your intentions, there are still only twenty-four hours in a day, and they will be increasingly difficult to allocate.

Let's start with a fundamental truth that my Girlfriends and I wish someone had been honest enough to share with us, to save us immeasurable guilt and frustration:

YOU WILL NEVER HAVE THE SAME INTENSE, WONDROUS AND EXCLUSIVE RELATIONSHIP THAT YOU HAD WITH YOUR FIRST BABY WITH ANY OTHER CHILD.

Hold your horses, I'm not saying you won't love the subsequent babies with the same devotion, that you won't delight as much in their presence or that they will in any way be second-class babies. As a matter of fact, there is endless anecdotal wisdom that says that second babies are a lot more fun and far less neurotic than firstborns. Since the world has never revolved around them, they have far fewer episodes of behaving like Louis the Sun King. A grandmother once told me that life would be far simpler if children were like pancakes; you should always throw the first one away because it takes one pancake to get the griddle, the melted butter and the batter just right.

There are several reasons why your mothering experience will be different with all children who are not your first. One of the most obvious is the fact that the shock of motherhood has dimmed. You already know it's not going to kill you and you aren't going to kill the baby. Confidence is a huge difference. Remember when you brought your first baby home from the hospital and you were terrified that its head would fall right off its wobbly neck, that you had to stand at attention next to its bassinet to make sure it kept breathing and that your husband was covered in germs just waiting to be transmitted to the helpless newborn? Those days are over, if not because your fears have been allayed, then because you are just too tired to give a damn.

Fatigue plays a big role in your second stab at motherhood. Remember, all the things you did for your first baby (assuming you had a helpful mate and a respectable maternity leave), such as sterilizing the bottles, making your own baby food and keeping your baby book up to date, were done in the relatively relaxed fashion of a person unconcerned with keeping a toddler safe and sound. Who has time to make their own crib mobile of photos of the immediate family when they are sharing a house with someone who is learning to open the front door, swing a Nerf baseball bat and insists on poo pooing on the floor beside the cute little potty you bought her? You won't mean to be less persnickety in parenting your second; you just won't have the energy and undivided focus you had with the first. Once again, let us reassure you that this is not a bad thing. In fact, the white-hot glow of a mother's focus on her first child is often almost too much for any human being to bear. Sometimes God created siblings just to diffuse the intensity of the spotlight on the first one.

Logistics present another challenge to a mother of more than one. Few things make a mother more sweaty and skittish than trying to navigate the course between her parked car and the grocery story while carrying an infant seat and holding a toddler's hand. Leaving the house to run errands or even doing a little socializing required planning and patience when there was just baby in tow, but now that the first baby has wheels of his own, so to speak, and your arms are full of a ten-pound being who couldn't find his own feet if he needed them, going anywhere is worse than unnecessary root canal work. Not only do you have the full toddler travel paraphernalia—backpack with boxed juice, blankie, two beloved naked G.I. Joes and an extra Pull-Up—your new little bundle's contribution of car seat/baby seat, spit-up cloth (which you wear constantly like a scarf or poncho, anyway), gigantic diaper bag with fifteen changes of clothes, diapers and baby Motrin for those early-onset fevers. Then, of course, there is usually some sort of stroller or buggy to cart these little people and their endless stuff around. You have to ask yourself: Is there anyplace in this world important enough to go to that you would willingly turn into a human pack mule?

That leads to the second rather common phenomenon of subsequent babies: They seem to go fewer places than their older sibling did. Those of us moms of three, four or five *little* kids have a deep, dark secret that I (because I have little or no pretense or pride left after all this parenting) am going to share with you. Feel free to judge or condemn us, but remember, we were once enthusiastic and motivated, too, before life knocked some sense into us. Anyway, here's the confession:

If we had access to a baby-sitter, nanny or nearby granny, we did not take the third child out of the house for the first year of its life.

Okay, so confession brings out the drama in me and I exaggerate. Naturally, these little darlin's got to go to the pediatrician, were permanent passengers in the older kids' carpool and might have spent some time at family reunions, but they were frequently excluded from malls, swap meets, sporting events and parties for anyone too old for pin the tail on the donkey. By the third or fourth child it occurs to us moms that infants have very different expectations from life than toddlers and elementary schoolers do: They like to eat in peace. They like to nap in places that allow them to lie reasonably flat. They love to be held and cuddled. And they really appreciate not getting scared out of their wits. Toddlers and preschoolers, however, are beginning to embrace a world where no one naps and spectacles like circuses and Harlem Globetrotter games are thrilling rather than terrifying. Trying to slow a toddler or two (or three, for some of us lunatics) in his great life adventure to give your infant a chance to nurse in a calm, relaxed fashion is like trying to put a collar on a bee. The toddlers hate it and you feel overcome with guilt and failure. The only one who doesn't seem to be suffering is the infant, since babies are incredibly resilient little people.

Still, mothers of more than one child traditionally go to bed at night counting parenting failures instead of sheep. We think of the three chubby books that we intended to read to our toddler, but instead handed to him for solitary study when the baby started crying. We think of the hours we didn't spend cuddling with the newborn in our bed while we nursed her to sleep and let her just stay on the nipple. We think of the times we put a wide-awake-and-eager-to-smile infant alone in his crib so that we could help the big constipated brother try to make poo poo in the potty. We love them all so much and we want to give them rich and enchanting childhoods, but we see evidence every day that we aren't up to the job and it's killing us.

Do the Girlfriends have a answer for this dilemma? Sorry, no. We are still grappling with it, and we continue to do so even when the kids are talking about taking driver's ed and wearing shoes that look like they belong to Shaquille O'Neal. I guess that's the message: It doesn't ever really go away, this fear that there's not enough of us to go around, so we might as well take a tip from your average twelve-step programs:

"God grant us the serenity to accept the things we cannot change.**"**

In all my years of butting into other people's family business, I have yet to meet a child who says, in essence, "You know what, Mom, you have devoted most of your day to my needs and you deserve a break. Here's a buck; go get yourself a burger." No child ever thinks that he is getting enough attention, at least until he is old enough to get in trouble and would like to avoid mom's watchful eyes. If you are going to hold your breath waiting for some statement of appreciation from your kids, be prepared to wait until they become parents themselves, and then realize what a champ you were.

Go Ahead: Live Dangerously!

If the yearning to procreate is still making your ovaries ache, even knowing what you know now, our advice is: GO FOR IT! It will be hard, it will be confusing, but there will come a day when you see your two children kiss or the older one will protectively take the younger by the hand and your heart will break with a delicious pain. No matter how bumpy sibling rivalry can be, chances are your kids will share a closer relationship with their brothers and sisters than any other till marriage.

Don't expect your family to integrate as smoothly as the Brady Bunch did. In fact, that's one of the functions of brothers and sisters; to be the anvil on which they forge their personalities. Birth order, gender differences, blended families are all the spices that make the family stew more tangy. Your job, in its essential form, is to show up and love to your heart's capacity. The rest you'll make up as you go along.

"School Days, School Days"

Preschool is a critical period in a toddler's life. We all know that as parents; that's why 50 percent of us fret and agonize over it and the rest of us do our best to downplay or even ignore it. I confess that I subjected my own resilient darlings to much of my own preschool insanity, while my Girlfriend Sonia couldn't bear the pressure and expectations, so she kept her little son and daughter home with her until it was time for that coy new first step for "real school" called pre-kindergarten.

What the Girlfriends would like you to know going in is that all children not only survive preschool, they get to have a graduation ceremony when it's all over. Yes, even the biters and paint splatterers, even the little girl who wet her pants every day during storytime, even the ones who howled for a full hour every morning after their parents dropped them off. They all learn what they need to know, and it's Next Stop, Kindergarten.

The stunning thing is, the child who graduates nursery school bears little or no resemblance to the toddler you have known and loved for the past three years. Preschool is like a chrysalis factory: In creep little baby caterpillars, and after a year or two, the sky is filled with butterflies. You must sense this already, or else the prospect of preschool wouldn't feel so scary and significant that it keeps you up at night. Beneath our feelings of excitement and anticipation lurk the fear of losing control over everything that touches our babies and the sadness that they are growing away from us in very literal ways.

Relax, Girlfriend. You know there isn't any law forcing you to put your child in preschool. If you want to keep her tucked in the downy feathers under your wing for another year or two, that's your prerogative. But let's be real. You have already noticed how much fun and stimulation your toddler gets when she's with kids her own age. Besides, preschools seem bottomless in their supply of activities designed to keep toddlers interested and occupied. We all know how much you love your child, but we're with you if you'd like to have some time every day (or even three days a week) to pursue adult activities, like, say, earning money or taking care of a new baby. Besides, there is some important learning to be done— such as cooperating in a group of people and discovering she can function without a parent in tow—in that time that can help make kindergarten or pre-K less foreign to your little one when she gets there.

Ancient History

There used to be a very funny, very New Yorky image of two professional, upwardly mobile parents priming their anxious toddler on how to ace a preschool entrance exam. The joke was based on the belief that this was the first critical step in the toddler's journey toward the ivy-covered walls of academia, a professional career and ultimate success in everything he did. Now that I've been through the preschool experience four times myself, I can state without hesitation that nearly every American parent I've met recently is as intense as this cartoon couple where their toddler's preschool is concerned.

In the olden days, where a toddler went to preschool (or *nursery school* as it was unenlightening called in some circles) was usually determined by such considerations as geography (walking distance from home was always a plus), sponsorship (as in, sending your toddler to your church or synagogue's own preschool) and cleanliness (of the preschool, the other students *and* the teachers). Now, in addition to the old considerations, parents are choosing preschools based on such philosophies as "pre-academic," "developmental instruction" and "artistically motivated."

The current wisdom seems to suggest that we parents should take a cold, hard look at our precious toddlers and, based on whether they can hold a crayon, count to ten or recite the opening monologue from *Sleeping Beauty*, predict their future talents and academic performance. Is she a budding musician? Is he a Hemingway-to-be? Would your family like him to grow up to be a doctor? If you study your own pre-preschooler and can discern little more than that she wants to cook baby dolls in her pretend microwave and he wants a future in anything having to do with mud, don't be too alarmed. That's really all you should be seeing at this point. If you read your toddler's future *too* clearly, you just might be looking into the wrong crystal ball.

When I traveled this terrain with my oldest, the most experimental any of the Girlfriends were getting with preschools was good old Montessori. I confess, having to learn the appropriate Montessori lingo, like calling all toddler activities "work" (no matter how much they looked like play to me) took me a few weeks, but I liked the gentle ways of the teachers and the way they encouraged very young children to respect each other's space, all of which was very important to a mother terrified that some other child would sneeze on or bite her precious toddler.

Ivy League Wishes and Graduate School Dreams

By the time I addressed the preschool crisis for the third time, I had clearly been infected by the "Good Preschool/Good College" strain of bacteria. No longer was I content to go to a charming little school with the neighborhood kids that was half a mile from my house. You might wonder just how thickheaded I could be not to have learned anything by my first two preschool experiences, but, I promise, there was some rationale for my succumbing this late in the game. Because I also had children aged four and six, I was beginning to look beyond the preschool horizon to the big time: ELEMENTARY SCHOOL. Would my kids go to public or private school? Did their preschool have anything to do with how they'd do in whichever school system we selected? Did I intend to stay in this school district forever, or would we move to our dream house in another town? Would they be smarter and on some secret "academic track" if they attended a preschool and elementary school that was known to push the three R's? All of the sudden, preschool wasn't an encapsulated experience for those twilight years between babyhood and childhood; it was all part of an enormous plan for the next fourteen years, eighteen if the gods of educational excellence were with us. My head still aches just thinking about it.

The "Studio 54" Attitude

You'd think that preschool directors and teachers, who should know much more about this than you and I, would calm us parents down and remind us that the purpose of preschool is simply to *prepare* to learn in a social and structured fashion, NOTHING MORE. But no; they seem to have recognized our madness and decided to capitalize on it because now there isn't a preschool in any major metropolitan area that will answer your first inquiry with the words "Bring Junior in! We'd love to meet him! Of course there will be a space for him here in September." Forget about it! Just trying to get an application to any old preschool can be met with more attitude than the maître d' at Le Cirque. If you should be naive enough to ask if there will be openings in the next session, you may be reminded that there are always more applicants than openings, or the person might just laugh at you and hang up.

Well, Girlfriend, I know that *I* didn't let anyone even suggest that my toddler wasn't smart enough or good enough for their school, and I bet you wouldn't, either. I just pulled out my Rolodex and started dialing every friend of a friend I could think of who might have some pull for me. I spent hours over applications, careful to mention that my husband and I consider it not only a duty but a profound privilege to give all our extra time and money to our children's school; that my little applicant was not only smart, but very well behaved; and that he told me he wanted to be a surgeon to the poor when he graduated from medical school at a

Doogie Howser kind of age. Oh, yes, and had I mentioned about the time and money stuff?

When the Dust Has Settled

My youngest did, indeed, just graduate from preschool this summer, so I have done that drill four full times now, and this is what I learned: First, I needed to calm down. Second, there really are differences between preschools. And, third, rarely is a child's fate determined by his or her success in preschool. I learned that preschool is symbolic and significant in so many ways, and that it's my job as the mom to keep the experience from becoming heavy or restrictive. The bottom line is that preschool is a chance for toddlers to try out being independent human beings with a big safety net spread below them. They can fly like eagles on the swings, or they can curl up in a beanbag chair and go to sleep. Most of all, they should feel terrific about themselves and proud they're able to go into the world and meet people and learn things that even Mommy doesn't know.

Qualifications for Preschool

Most preschools stipulate the age range of their students and whether they must know how to use the potty with minimal assistance or not. Other than that, the only other qualification that a toddler needs is his parent's belief that he would have a good time there (even if not for the first week or two, but more about separation in a bit). So, that said, you'd think that we parents would relax, but many of us just can't leave well enough alone. My Girlfriends and I knocked ourselves out teaching our kids their colors, numbers, the ABC song and, of course, long division. (Just KIDDING!) I remember a friend of a Girlfriend who bragged in play-group that her little girl was so smart that preschools were practically recruiting her, as evidenced by the fact that she was already bilingual. Well, call me a party pooper if you like, but I'd heard her daughter speak her mother's English and her housekeeper's Spanish, and it was a largely unintelligible blend that did a disservice to both languages. Then again, that friend of a Girlfriend used to drag her little girl around on auditions for TV commercials and kiddie modeling jobs because she thought she'd given birth to the next Brooke Shields, so she was always a sandwich short of a picnic, if you ask me.

When it comes to preschool readiness, a child's willingness to submit to a gently structured atmosphere, follow directions and say goodbye to his mommy or daddy for a few hours a day is actually more important than knowledge of academic facts. A successful preschooler is one who is willing to sing when the class is singing, work on puzzles or paint without relying entirely on an adult to do all the heavy lifting and who is ready to learn to wait for his turn, share the crayons and share the teacher's attention with several other little chatterboxes. They won't participate equally well in all things at all times, but they'll get the drift of how they're expected to work in a social setting.

If the Girlfriends and I ran the universe, a happy and curious toddler with reasonable self-confidence would automatically get into any preschool his parents selected for him. As you may have noticed, especially if you live in an area where applying to preschool is more involved than submitting to a tax audit, we Girlfriends don't yet run the universe. We have filled out more applications asking for paragraphs describing a typical day in our toddler's life (we never failed to mention his mornings devoted to feeding the homeless and his independent reading in the afternoons), what our aspirations were for our two-and-a-half-year-old (omitted all references to our deepest wish being that she was potty trained by the time she was four), how much education we, her parents, had (we felt compelled to justify our lives to these strangers with comments like "Although her father didn't finish his undergraduate degree, he went on to invent the cellular phone and has changed technological communication as the world knows it").

Letters of recommendation are also requested by some paper-loving preschools, and these really crack me up. What does one write about a person who has only been walking for two years and who rarely even does that without his finger up his nose? Sure, you can mention that adorable time he turned on the computer and "wrote" a note to Nana and actually printed it out. Or you can say how very much he loves other children and they love him. It gets risky, however, if you delve too deeply into a description of his great intelligence, because, unless he's Mozart and already playing concertos, you end up sounding a little deluded. What ultimately happens, in my experience, is that the best letters of recommendation focus more about the toddler's family than on the toddler, on the theory that the apple never falls far from the tree. In other words, Mom and Dad are nice, they love their toddler to pieces and the whole family is a good addition to any school.

The Inquisition

Most terrifying of all aspects of application to popular and competitive preschools is the dread interview with the child. While it's common practice for most preschools to want to meet the family sometime before admitting the child, those Studio 54 type schools actually insist on having a little one-on-one time with your toddler. I can pretty much assure you that these interviews or "assessments" are much more benign than your nightmares make them out to be. In my travels across the preschool countryside, searching for just the right place to launch my children's academic careers, I've sat just outside the door of many an interview. Never once have I heard a teacher ask my child to spell anything, add anything or name the presidents of the United States.

More typically, the teacher has set out a project or a game for the your innocent little applicant, and he or she just plays unobtrusively alongside your child. They notice all sorts of things, I'm sure, from whether they pick up a paintbrush by the handle or the bristle or whether they attempt to eat the wooden puzzle pieces, but what they seem to be most interested in is whether your child is able to listen and converse in a composed fashion (at least most of the time) and whether she interacts with someone other than the mother or father. After all, what good is it to put a child in preschool if she doesn't yet recognize that there is a program going on?

Teachers are humans, too, and they seem to be attracted to the very same things that other humans find attractive. For example, a child who looks them in the eye, who occasionally looks interested and "present" and who smiles or laughs can't help but seem "happy." Even though they don't say it, some preschool teachers or admissions directors are sometimes more impressed with children who are articulate and outgoing than with those who are shy and reticent on the theory that the little entertainers are going to find school an easier place to be than someone who isn't yet as socially skilled.

Since we all have good days and bad days, don't collapse in disappointment if your toddler's preschool interview falls short of your expectations. One of my children actually wet their pants during the assessment! I felt like moving to another city. Actually, he/she was coming down with a bug and had a temperature of 103 degrees by the time we got home. After one very bad day of alternately feeling miserable for my child and disappointed for me that the interview had tanked, I had a divine realization: *I could call the preschool director back, tell her about the illness and ask for another interview.* I thought I was the first person to think of such a brilliant solution to this caliber of disaster, but they rescheduled me so quickly that it became evident that mothers all over the city were giving their toddlers as many chances as they needed to feel comfortable with the interview. My Girlfriend Jill, another mother of four, felt that anything from bad biorhythms to scarlet fever were all reasons for rescheduling, and the schools were always completely understanding.

Yanked from the Arms of Love (a.k.a. Separation Anxiety)

It might happen as soon as the interview: You will be asked to step outside while your toddler does his thing alone with the teacher. Lots of kids just follow the teacher into the room full of toys and crafts and miniature kitchens, never noticing that they have left Mommy standing in the dust. Others, however, hold as tight as orangutans to their parent. Each preschool has its own ideas about whether a parent is allowed to stay during that initial visit, but almost all preschools insist that some reasonable time after the session has started, all parents and nannies and grandmas are expelled. This is not always good news to a preschooler.

Walking out the door of a preschool while your toddler is screaming out to you "Mommy, help! Mommy, help!" and crying so hard his nose is running into his mouth is far more painful and difficult for a mother than climbing the stairs to her own gallows. Four fall seasons of my life have been spent sitting in tears outside a preschool while I knew my toddler was suffering at the hands of strangers. "It's your own selfishness!" I would accuse myself. "You don't need to ship off your own three-year-old to be cared for by people who can't possibly love him as much as you do! What's so important in your life that you can't just devote your mornings to re-creating a preschool environment in your own home? That way Junior could even come to preschool in his pajamas and he'll never catch head lice from any strangers!"

Preschools are hip to this separation problem nowadays, and most of them have a nice, gentle transitional period during which the parents and toddlers get used to spending time apart. One school in my neighborhood is very structured in its approach: The first week of school, toddlers and parents all play together in the school room; the second week the parents sit on tiny chairs along the walls of the room while the toddlers play amongst themselves; and the third week the parents all sit in a room next door to the preschool room. The kids know they're there, but they are not encouraged to go looking for them. At this point a teacher's aide or another preschool teacher discreetly pops between the two rooms, giving both toddler and parents up-to-the-minute reports on how the other is doing. After that, the general rule is "Go ahead and cry, Little One, because we know you'll stop as soon as your mother is out of hearing range." Those preschool teachers are pretty wise; most kids do stop crying at that very moment and proceed to have a wonderful day.

Still, even the most enthusiastic preschooler loves to feel his mommy's presence every once in a while. Perhaps, after the separation anxiety has been overcome, you can volunteer to be an escort on field trips or teach a special art project. If work or other children make carving that kind of time out of your schedule nearly impossible, send a basket of muffins or some other treat for your child to share with his classmates. Most teachers are wonderful about making a big deal out of the child who's responsible for "snack," letting them pass out the goodies and making sure that all the kids say "thank you." Best of all, my experience has been that little kids actually prefer the flavor of grocery store baked goods to those you've labored over yourself. See, there is a Goddess!

What to Look for in a Preschool

Go ahead and play Ivy League preschool if you want. There isn't really anything bad about it as long as you don't let on to your toddler that his entire future is being planned as precisely as the building of a space station. If you can take the emotional wear and tear, that's up to you, but don't share your concern or anxiety with a perfectly naive little toddler.

But just because a school is hard to get into or the most selective joint in town doesn't automatically earn it the Girlfriends' Guide seal of Pre-school Approval. It's still your responsibility to spend some time at the school, looking around, eavesdropping on other classes (and other parents whenever possible) and getting to know the teachers. Don't be passive about this part. The "Studio 54" schools may suggest in some subtle way that any question asking will be done by them, thank you very much, but be bold and politely ask about everything from how often the bulletin boards are changed to how often they clean up the paintbrushes. You might be interested to know if the teachers closely supervise the children when they eat lunch, perhaps making rules like no pudding cups until the sandwich or pasta noodles are eaten. I was always particularly interested in whether there were several times during the day that the teacher en-couraged the entire class to use the bathroom, since my kids, when left to their own devices, were quite apt to find fingerpainting too fabulous to interrupt for a potty break.

The Teachers

Everyone who has been to school in his life knows that the individual teacher is the contact point for where the rubber meets the road. The school could be a tepee in a park, but if the teacher is magical, the school is magical. Conversely, the school can be state of the art, with maybe even a couple of computers thrown in for good measure, and a dull, uninspiring teacher makes the whole setting inconsequential. That's why you owe it to your toddler to get to know as many of the teachers at a prospective preschool as you can. Remember, your toddler may spend two years at that school, so you'll want to be reasonably assured that any teachers she gets for any class will be good. Many states have laws about the teacher to student ratio for children under five or so. It's commonly dictated that one teacher per four or up to six kids provides sufficient supervision. Find out your prospective preschool's ratio and decide if it's enough individual attention for your kid. Keep in mind, this ratio doesn't just apply when the kids are all seated quietly at lunch; it also applies when they are outside running in different directions, climbing on the jungle gym, racing the tricycles and digging in the sand.

Once you have found your magical teachers, make sure that they are given enough backup staff to allow them to work their magic. If the teachers are so bogged down cutting up apples for snack or answering phones or cleaning spilled juice off the floors, your child is being robbed of her gifts. This doesn't mean you need to find a school with tuition high enough to rival the local college fees, just so that they can afford a janitor and receptionist; lots of schools require that the parents themselves pitch in one or two days a month to lighten the teacher's load. Just think, every two months you get to spy on your child from inside the room instead of from behind the bushes along the play yard fence.

This leads to another Girlfriend-to-Girlfriend suggestion: Do spy on your child and his teacher from time to time. Pop into the class with a "forgotten" sweater or to offer some flowers from your garden. Park yourself unobtrusively where you can see the playground action. Offer to stay and read a story every once in a while. Face it, none of us can relax unless we know that our child is having fun, staying safe, being interacted with and getting hugged as often as all the other kids, and you can't know that stuff without a little espionage.

I have teacher Girlfriends who tell me that they have often adored a particular child even though they hated the parents. Perhaps the child was a wounded bird in some way, or perhaps he just overcame the misfortune of his genetics. I, however, still work on the premise, "Love me, love my child." In other words, I want my children's teachers to like me in hopes that they will keep an especially soft place in their hearts for my kids. I want them to tell me things, too, like if the school is being sold or if some of the other parents are moving or getting a divorce. Somehow, I feel that anything that remotely affects the air my children breathe is my business.

Another reason I am always polite and friendly with teachers is because they have an incredibly hard and crucial job, and, at least to my mind, they don't get paid nearly enough. I have learned so much about my children from their teachers that I can never thank them enough for the value of their insights and their well-informed advice. Trust me, Girlfriend, the child you have in your home, the one you have known since his first minute on Earth, the one who shares your DNA, *is a completely different person when he's at school*. When the teacher calls you to discuss your child's bad language, don't be boring and say something inane like, "He never, ever uses bad words at home." Just believe her and ask what she thinks you should do. If she's been working as a preschool teacher for any time at all, she is bound to have far greater wisdom than those of us who are parenting toddlers for the first time.

The Curriculum

Even though we're talking toddlers here, not kids preparing for their SATs, curriculum is very important in a preschool. As nearly every parent knows after the recent revelations by doctors and scientists, the first three years of a child's life are the most critical learning years. That may sound like an awfully big responsibility for us parents, but it's really not news to most preschool professionals. They know that certain fine and gross motor skills are developing, they know that this is the time of language fluency, they know that judgment and self-control are developing and they are keenly aware that with every single day, toddlers notice more and more about the world around them.

The Girlfriends suggest that you ask the preschool what study areas or themes they intend to offer throughout the year. They may divide the year into seasonal events like studying leaves in the autumn and snow in the winter, or they may divide the year up between dinosaurs, sea life, farm animals and jungles. It doesn't so much matter what they pick as long as they have a fully developed plan to keep your child interested and motivated to learn.

In addition to the concepts of study areas, every good preschool has a schedule or a ritual to their days. For example, in my youngest daughter's preschool, the mornings began with the kids sitting on the carpet, learning to count the date on the calendar, taking roll by pulling a card with their name printed on it off a sticky board, describing the weather and then feeding the goldfish. If a child were to skip ahead to the goldfish feeding before the roll call was complete, two or three other kids were certain to screech in painful protest. You know how much toddlers love rituals and repetition, and preschool is no exception.

One more note about ritual and repetition, while I have your ear. I have a dear Girlfriend, Donna, who felt that preschool was just one of many fun ways to spend a toddler's day. Therefore, when her daughter, Minnie, took a long time getting ready in the morning or said she didn't want to go to school, Donna felt no qualms about keeping her home for the day. On one hand, that makes total sense: After all, what's Minnie going to miss by skipping a day of "Farmer in the Dell" and making stained-glass windows out of wax paper and flower petals? On the other hand, now that it's been several years since Minnie went to preschool, I think that there actually might have been some value to Donna making her attend a little more regularly. It occurs to me that the security and safety that children find in the predictable might have been undermined by Minnie never really knowing what was a school day and what wasn't, since the decision seemed so arbitrary. All I'm suggesting is, if you have committed your child to an appropriate program, whether it's five mornings a week or three afternoons a week, it's a good idea to stick with the program whenever possible to show some consistency to your toddler. Believe me, they learn their schedules very quickly.

Safety

Take a good leisurely stroll through the school and the play area. Is paint peeling from anything? Is there a lot of dust on high places (remember, I am the mother of a former asthmatic)? Are the swings equipped with safety belts or wraparound seats? Does the slide empty the child out onto soft sand or rubber mats? Do the little ones have to climb stairs to get to their classroom? Is the bathroom clean and suitably equipped for tiny folk, especially when many of them are ambivalent about the potty anyway? How does the place smell? I once rejected a preschool when my nose detected that the enchanting little sandbox on the playground had long ago been discovered by the church cat and claimed as his litter box. Your nose will also alert you to any mildew problems (like carpets that never dried properly) or plumbing insufficiencies.

Nowadays, with experience on my side, after my playground stroll and sniff test, the very next thing I would inspect would be the "let's pretend" area. I used to love to see a huge basket filled with dresses, boas, funny hats and shoes. Now it's all I can do not to want to douse a pile like that with kerosene and throw a match at it. You see, I am a head lice survivor. Not just once, but three times I have had to strip my children's beds and store their pillows in garbage bags in dark closets for two weeks, three times I've had to shampoo four little heads (five, including my own) with foul-smelling delousing chemicals, and three times I have sat on the lawn with the sun shining on four little heads while I searched for nits. I don't want to seem hysterical here, and your toddler will probably have his or her own run-in with anything from head lice to pinkeye to chicken pox within a year of joining the academic world and still live a full and wonderful life. It's just that you don't need to invite the bugs in *and* offer them a place to live.

Speaking of germs, you should inquire as to the preschool's procedure for reporting any exposure to infection or bugs or any minor injuries your toddler might have suffered while you were away. Many states have laws that require the schools to tell you if such communicable afflictions as chicken pox or pinkeye have popped up in the student population. This doesn't mean you have to take your child out of school and run for the wide open spaces, but rather to be heads up if any funny symptoms show up in him. And, Girlfriend, no matter how embarrassing it is to you, you must do the right thing by the other parents and contact the school if your child has unwittingly infected the population. Don't worry, no one will think you're a slacker as a parent, but they will be grateful to be able to warn the other parents.

Even if your toddler is potty trained (or if you are pretending to that effect), it is a good idea for you to ask who's in charge in the event of an "accident." They are bound to happen, and you will want to know that there is someone kind, understanding and oblivious to foreign poops who will help your darling out. The last thing you want to do is arrive for pickup to discover that your child has been wearing soiled panties for more than fifteen minutes. People have committed murder for less egregious crimes.

You'll also want to know who's in charge of first aid, since some preschoolers get hurt (with varying severity) several times a week. Ask him or her to enact the scenario of what he or she would do if your child fell on the playground and split his forehead (God forbid). Thank heavens, most injuries just require a wash with soap and water and some extra special loving from the teacher. As far as injuries to the preschoolers that might have involved tears, but didn't require a trip to the emergency room or a call to mom, I've always liked the schools that sent a "boo-boo report" home with the little one. First of all, my toddlers usually appreciated a chance to cry again for Mommy, and second, it took some of the shock out of finding a goose egg on one of their heads while shampooing that evening.

Make New Friends

I was always more nervous than my toddlers on the first day of pre-school. Not only did I wonder, as I looked around at the sea of strange little faces, whether my little angel would make any friends, I wondered whether I would hit if off with anybody. All of us parents there for those first few days were just bubbling with enthusiasm for all the fun and wonder of preschool, hoping that maybe our enthusiasm would wear off on our child. We were also checking out potential playdates for our darlings and potential coffee dates for ourselves. As I've mentioned before, I have made several lifelong friends among the parents of my children's friends, so be open to that possibility.

While you're searching for future friends, you're bound to notice a couple of people you know right away you don't want to share a school with, let alone play with. There will be the little boy who hits his mother in the face and she doesn't stop him. There will be the little girl who couldn't even get through the first week of preschool without biting another child. And there will be another toddler who snuggles into the teacher's lap during every story, so that there is never any room in that lap for anyone else. You will hate them all.

The Girlfriends and I warn you not to get too locked into this position because it will probably change by winter break. The cuddler may climb out of the teacher's lap long enough to forge a powerful friendship with your kid. You may start talking to the mother of the biter one day when you're both early for pickup and discover that they just moved to town and that the little chomper is all stressed out. Not only might you feel a little more tolerant, you may actually become quite fond of her after she gets a grip on herself. Who knows, maybe their family moved into a house with a wading pool and swing set, and you'll be invited over whenever you want?

Eventually, you will be the same sentimental sucker we all are about toddlers and you will have a soft spot in your heart for all of the little people who went from caterpillar to butterfly with your own angel dear. As they all march in a line to a boom box playing "Pomp and Circumstance," you will weep as you think back to the babies they were when they started school and realize that they are no longer babies of any kind: They are tall and stretched out, they are competent and agile, they have ideas and dreams, they think the world is their oyster and they want to eat it all. THEY ARE FOUR YEARS OLD and they are flying! It's your job to let go, Mom. Trust your Girlfriends; they'll be just fine.

Top Ten Things
We'll Miss Most About Toddlers

10. The swish-swish sound their diapers make when they walk.

9. The way their tummies peek out from under their shirts and over their shorts.

8. The way they say the word *remember*.

7. How juicy their kisses are.

6. How they can turn back into babies when they're tired.

5. How you can tell their temperature by holding their hands.

4. The way they truly believe the magic of the universe.

3. The way they pretend to talk on the phone.

2. How their hair looks when they wake up in the morning.

1. How they hold your face between their hands and say "I wub you."

More Than a Mommy

*I*t occurred to me halfway through this book that I hadn't spent as much time talking about you and your life as I had in the previous Girlfriends' Guides. There were no chapters on sex positions, your figure or, most important, your psyche like there were in the other Guides. After much soul-searching, the explanation I've come up with is this: Pregnancy is all about you. Sure, there is a baby in there, but you don't really know him yet and you still cling to the belief that your life will return to its non-maternal state as soon as he is born. Even during the first year of motherhood, when there is a real live baby who's stolen your heart, you have vivid recollections of your former life and secretly believe that you can reclaim the parts you miss the most. But by the time you have a toddler, you realize that not only is your life not about you right now, it's not going to be about you for the foreseeable future. As far as you can see, this job is only getting bigger and more complex, and, if you add another baby to the equation, you are certain that there is no going back to non-maternity.

As your Girlfriend, I feel it's my duty to encourage you to take this bull by the horns and define motherhood in your own image. Yes, it's harder to nurture your sex life, your professional aspirations and your spiritual growth when you have kids hanging all over you, but it can be done if you want it badly enough. (That, by the way, is the most critical issue.) You probably won't find yourself on too many month-long retreats or any grand tours of Europe any time soon, but if those things are essential to your happiness, it's your responsibility to find a way to have them.

This chapter is intended to remind you of some of the blows you, the mother of a toddler, might sustain. Keep in mind that they hit all of us in one way or another, and we're still standing. Not only that, we are actually finding a few moments to remind ourselves that we are more than "Anthony's mother."

The Blow to Your Marriage

Traditionally, it is marriage (or a reasonable facsimile) that leads to parenthood. Coincidentally, it is often parenthood, however, that deals the harshest blows to a marriage. As wonderful and marriage-affirming as creating a child with someone you love can be, that same miracle adds a complexity to marriage that makes juggling chain saws look simple. I know that surveys and polls indicate that money problems are the source of most divorces, but if that is true, I maintain that child rearing is the source of the most passionate battles. Sure, people may decide to part ways because one is overspending and the other is underearning, but it takes an energetic discussion about the pros and cons of circumcision, spanking or tap-dancing lessons for boys to get most couples into their full sparring equipment. Even when we're not "discussing" our plans for raising children, we're dealing with sex lives stunted by toddlers sleeping in our beds or are so preoccupied by potty-training setbacks and baby-bottle attachments that we can't even remember whether we have taken our birth control pill in days, let alone get into a seductive frame of mind.

If you ascribe to the Girlfriends' Guides' theory of postpartum recovery, you can expect the first year of motherhood to be one quick rollercoaster ride; slowly up, up, up to hemorrhoids, then crashing down into cracked nipples, then whipped around by complete lack of REM sleep, jolted by the end of maternity leave, then another crawl upward with inconsistent dieting, screaming to a close with a FIRST BIRTHDAY PARTY! In other words, it can take about a year before you really feel you have your head above ground and can participate in some of the previous pleasures of adulthood, like staying out a little late, talking about current events or even dragging out the old stash from Victoria's Secret. I don't have to tell you how eagerly your mate has been waiting for this day—it's as clear as the whine in his voice.

You'd think that our dear friend Mother Nature would cooperate here by designing children between the ages of one and four to be calm, predictable, accountable and accommodating—rather like tiny Boy Scouts. So what was she thinking when she took this lovely recipe for rediscovered romance and threw a toddler into it? Heaven only knows. All I can tell you is that just when you think you might have a clue as to how to combine motherhood and wifehood, the motherhood ante gets inched up a notch. Parents of toddlers are in the unique situation of having tasted the forbidden fruit and then being told they were on a fructose-free diet. Not only that, but they are simultaneously given responsibility for the care and feeding of a charming little human. The combination can conspire to make it necessary for most couples to make an effort to redefine their relationship within the context of being mommies and daddies. The Girlfriends aren't going to hype you and suggest that we have these competing identities handled. We will, however, share our best insights with you, tell you where we tripped up and make a couple of suggestions here and there.

The Blow to Your Health

It is absolutely critical that you take measures to ensure that you are as healthy and fit as you can be under these extreme circumstances. Enough with the starvation diets supplemented by caffeine and adrenaline.

It's true, most of us live on fumes as new moms, but after several months of that kind of neglect we are guaranteed to get, sick, cranky, tired and something else . . . if only I could remember what it was . . . oh, yeah, forgetful. Many of you have been nursing for several months; that in itself can suck every nutrient out of your core. Even while our inner voices are suggesting a bit more protein and fiber, we are alternately forgetting to eat, snacking on whatever we can eat while driving a car or finishing every untouched meal our toddlers reject. (It's amazing how quickly you can put on the pounds eating just three Tater Tots, half a plate of buttered pasta and applesauce.)

Part of maintaining your vitality is ensuring that your are healthy and awake. If every activity not devoted to the care and maintenance of your child and your work threatens to send you to bed with exhaustion, or worse, just to the sofa with total lack of enthusiasm, you not only miss a significant part of life, but you begin to look like a big party pooper. I'm not telling you this to make it you feel guilty and overwhelmed over the fact that your idea of a perfect New Year's Eve is to watch Dick Clark on TV and go to bed at nine, since I have felt that way for several years now. As a matter of fact, ever since we got one of those satellite dishes installed, my husband and I have taken advantage of the three-hour time difference between California and New York and poured our champagne when the ball dropped in Times Square. I don't think I have to tell you that I find raising kids challenging, interesting, and deeply fulfilling, but the Girlfriends and I suspect that a life focused entirely on the concerns of one small person can leave us standing like a choir of Peggy Lees, wondering, "Is that all there is?" Trust us, your mate has probably been wondering the same thing.

As I've said a thousand times before, there is no use in burning yourself out too early in this mothering race because there is no identifiable finish line. Just keep up a healthy jog, stop to rest occasionally, and then join the race again. I cannot speak for the universe, but I can tell you what I've noticed here in my little corner of it: The mothers are the heartbeat of the family. Your child and your mate will take their cues from you about everything from whether they are well and happy to whether they should wear a sweater outside. Perhaps this sounds old-fashioned or sexist to some people. I don't mean to offend; just to throw my humble little observation into the pot, and I observe that, when the mother is down for the count, the whole house gets anxious and out of sorts. If I get sick, for example, my husband immediately claims the same virus for himself for fear of being left the only capable adult left to run the home.

You must take time now and then to have fun without a child. Heck, you must take time to have a good cry without a child, or even visit the bathroom without a child. You know this, but if you're like most of us, you are sitting around waiting for someone to tell you when. Here's the news: That's not going to happen, *ever*. Every mother I know is longing for a "doctor's note" to give her official permission to take it easy, but those are hard to come by till you really get sick, and then it's not any fun. The trick is to become your own doctor. Why not? You're already practicing medicine on your mate and kids!

The Blow to Your Sense of Perspective

The Girlfriends are unanimous in their refusal to allow competitive mothers into our tight circle. We've seen it everywhere since the minute we were pregnant: women who were certain they were gestating better than the rest of us, women who nursed longer than we did, women whose babies were better sleepers, walkers and talkers than ours. This is a ridiculous contest and can only be played if you are so self-deluded that you actually think you have a handle on the ball of Crisco that is motherhood or if you are so uncertain and frightened about your ability to be someone's mother that you let anyone inspire your self-doubt. We Girlfriends believe that motherhood is an altered reality to which we are never fully adjusted, and we rely on each other for reassurance that we are doing the job as well as anyone can under the circumstances.

I'm going to play the odds here and assume that you or your mate comes from a home with divorced parents. That may or may not be significant to psychiatrists for their own reasons, but for this Guide I bring it up only to suggest that those of us who did not have traditionally stable and happy family lives might be a tad misguided about what family life is really supposed to look like. I think that I, personally, watched way too much TV and took Carol Brady and Mike Brady too literally: all those kids, and still plenty of time to solve each one's problems, have a romantic love life, all while wearing perfectly coordinated clothing. I don't recall any episodes about Carol beating herself up with the conflict over not being able to get to Greg's baseball playoffs seventy miles away, get Jan's braces tightened, get her own roots touched up, buy groceries because Alice has quit without notice, all while wondering if she should have quit her job after all. And to top it off, she wants to discuss her concerns with a compassionate adult, but Mike is too busy at the office to take her calls. Boy, oh boy, I wonder what they'd be saying around the dinner table after a day like that!

Trust me, it is excruciatingly difficult for us failing Carols to refrain from turning to the nearest person (our Mikes) and laying a healthy serving of the blame on him. Even in those relatively rare relationships where the child rearing is shared equally (as I've truly yet to see in a marriage where the child is over a year old), it is entirely normal and expected that the fear of doing something wrong and "ruining" your toddler can send you searching for someone to lift this incredible burden. When you turn to your cherished mate and see him standing there, shrugging his shoulders in confusion, too, you might want to hit him upside the head with the baby potty you have in your hand.

This, too, goes both ways. Since daddies love their toddlers as intensely and devotedly as mommies do, they can be just as inclined to go postal as we are. My husband could not even go to the pediatrician with me for our kids' vaccinations because he would want to blame *me* for the needles! And on the nights I stood outside of a crying toddler's room waiting for him to learn to put himself back to sleep, my pained partner looked at me as if I were a certifiable child abuser. Do you think I took his ambivalence and fear into account and overlooked his momentary lack of support? NO WAY! I filled in every ten-minute gap between reassuring visits to my crying toddler's cribside hissing at my husband that none of us would be in this trouble if he hadn't gotten me pregnant in the first place!

Don't Be a Martyr

Does this scenario sound familiar around your house: It's Sunday morning, and you and your co-parent are planning to have a "family day." No preschool or baby-sitters to get in the way of that precious bonding time between parents and child; just a day devoted to the little darling you both are so crazy about. How about the zoo? Great idea! Junior will love the zoo! Well, Junior and Mom fight for nearly an hour over whether he can wear a girls' T-shirt that his cousin left at the house during her last visit. Crying has tuckered him out, so Junior falls asleep during the car ride to the zoo. Dad and Mom don't talk too much in the car because Mom's feeling fragile from the cross-dressing encounter and Dad doesn't want to invite a fight. At the zoo all Junior can concentrate on are the Slurpees they sell in animal sports bottles; he wouldn't notice a sleeping lion at forty paces even if there weren't such potent distractions. Mom looks at Dad with a "Do Something" expression, and Dad begins to concentrate on the list of endangered species on the back of the zoo map. Doesn't that sound fun?

Here's the Girlfriends' theory: For the most part, toddlers are too little and unsophisticated to bear responsibility for his parents having a good time. We really should take another look at this "quality time" concept that is such the rage. In case you haven't noticed, toddlers are not all that hard to amuse as long as you're willing to fully participate. Remember, so much of the world is brand-new to them; that's why toilet paper rolls and stackable Tupperware have so much appeal. They don't need elaborate trips or outings if those trips and outings aren't going to be fun for Mom and Dad, too. The only real exception to this rule is birthday parties. Toddlers may love birthday parties more than their parents, and it's the parents' job to accompany them (at least 50 percent of the time; then "lose" the other invitations) out of the love in their hearts.

At the risk of getting too analytical here, I want to discuss one of the most common reasons we parents have for combing the Sunday paper for the announcement that a circus has come to town: We are too tired or overwhelmed to want to be the ringmaster ourselves. If that rings true

261

for you, then join the club. But if that's the case, then be honest enough about it that you don't try to overcompensate by making the activity more burdensome and planning intensive than the Invasion of Normandy. The world is a circus to toddlers, so try to think of something like walks on the boardwalk or around the local reservoir that allow you and your mate to get some fresh air and exercise and for your toddler to stare at the other kids and to look for snails in the dirt. I have spent years trying to "create" stimulating family activities, and I have the scars to show for it. It's just not worth it to work the whole little family into a lather of unmet expectations when you can have just as much fun together wrapping crescent roll dough around weenies to make pigs in a blanket.

Allow for Changes (In You *and* Him)

I have no doubts that a single parent can raise fabulous children and have a great life. But, since most of us still get into the "family way" with someone else whom we'd really like to keep around, I want to spend a minute talking about adjusting to the new mommy and daddy that you and your mate are becoming. The two of you probably don't know it yet, but you both have a lot of getting to know each other ahead of you. I don't care how many years you spent together before you had a baby, but now that you are settled into your new life as parents, it's time to reintroduce yourselves. Nothing more momentous happens to people than becoming parents, so it's only logical to think that some growth and change may have occurred. Sure, it's great to get your sex life back, but don't neglect the chats, the times that you both share how you feel about being officially grown-up. Not only will you regain a precious intimacy, but you'll find tremendous relief in sharing your own cluelessness with someone who loves and trusts you anyway.

So many parental couples are secretly terrified that change means disaster for the relationship, but that doesn't have to be the case. My husband and I have been together for sixteen years, and over that time we have, as he puts it, "revised the marriage contract" so many times that the original plan is a distant memory. We've learned over the years that the only agreement we can consistently keep through all these life changes is the agreement to keep talking and to compromise. Well, that *and* no extramarital affairs or poor personal hygiene. I don't want to jinx myself, but (knock wood), we continue to love each other and stay committed to our family as long as we mutually set the goals and general rules. You may want to change from pursuing your career to being a stay-at-home mom, or vice versa. He may feel the need to step up his efforts at work so that you can afford to buy a house for these kids you're having. You may rediscover your church and he may feel drawn to golf on Sundays. It can all work if you stay light on your feet.

You will have already noticed that a prescription as simple as "keep talking" is much more easily said than done when there is a toddler in the house. These little cuties have an uncanny ability to thrust themselves and their needs into the center of any family gathering, and it's almost biologically impossible for us moms to ignore them when they do. Our advice is to schedule regular time away from the little darling so that the two of you grown-ups can speak in full sentences and give your full attention to each other. It's amazing to me how intuitive toddlers can be: They can sense how serious an adult conversation is even if they don't understand the words being used, and they insinuate themselves as energetically as the situation demands. For example, if you two are lightly discussing whether to accept a dinner invitation for next week, your child may simply smear his Pudding Cup contents on the kitchen cabinets. If you're loudly "discussing" who's in charge of picking up the dry cleaning (since there are no clean shirts in the house), expect to find your toddler on top of the refrigerator and ready to jump.

It Really Gets Better

You might find this difficult to believe right now, but raising older children is, in many ways, easier than raising toddlers. The Girlfriends and I have noticed that the stakes seem to get higher as the kids grow up, what with school grades, drugs and unprotected sex, but the physical chores are far lighter. I actually have a couple of Girlfriends who spend at least one day each weekend golfing or taking a class! They can just yell through the house, "Come on, we're going to school" and all the children miraculously show up at the car with shoes tied and backpacks in place! They can even take the whole family out to eat without one spill or injury. What do they have that we don't? Older children. Sure, they live in morbid fear of the day one of their offspring is given a driver's license, but they haven't thought about head lice in a decade.

You may be reading this chapter and saying to yourself, "Sure, Vicki can get on her high horse and talk about nurturing her inner self, but in this house, we could all go up in flames at any minute. If I want to do so much as read a paper, I have to do it while I'm doing the dishes at two A.M." Look, if it were easy, no one would need a book like this! I'm not telling you these things to add still more pressure, but simply to remind you that there is life after motherhood (even, occasionally, *during*). If you find yourself completely unable to carve out any time or attention for yourself right now because you have the Roadrunner for a child, don't give up hope; I promise there is a light at the end of the tunnel. All of that changeling behavior actually crystalizes into a real live child with almost all survival abilities mastered. It's a thing of beauty. Keep the faith, and get back to me by your toddler's fourth birthday. The birds will sing a joyous chorus, even the Roadrunners. Beep-beep!

I n d e x